YOU DON'T SAY

Navigating Nonverbal
Communication Between the Sexes

YOU DON'T SAY

Navigating Nonverbal Communication Between the Sexes

AUDREY NELSON, PH.D.

with Susan K. Golant, M.A.

PRENTICE HALL

Published by The Berkley Publishing Group
A member of Penguin Group (USA) Inc.
375 Hudson Street
New York, New York 10014

Prentice Hall Press edition: March 2004

Library of Congress Cataloging-in-Publication Data

Nelson, Audrey, 1948–
You don't say: navigating nonverbal communication
between the sexes / Audrey Nelson, with Susan K. Golant.
        p.   cm.
Includes bibliographical references.
ISBN 0-7352-0347-4
1. Interpersonal communication—Sex differences.
2. Nonverbal communication—Sex differences.
3. Sex role.   I. Golant, Susan K.   II. Title.

HM1166.N45 2004
302.2'22—dc22

                                        2003068933

Printed in the United States of America

10   9   8   7   6   5   4   3   2   1

To Alexandra and Armand

ACKNOWLEDGMENTS

Thirty years ago, as an undergraduate changing her major for the third time, a good friend said to me, "I know a good fit for you— communications!" Rick Mullins was right, and three communications degrees later, I am still crazy about the field. Thanks, Rick! And thank you for directing me to a course of study that led me to my mentor and sponsor, Dr. Larry Samovar of San Diego State University. He not only opened doors, but he also gave me the encouragement to continue on to earn my Ph.D. after years of student poverty and peanut butter and jelly sandwiches. "What is three more years?" he asked me.

I owe a great deal of gratitude for the generosity of thousands of individuals who have attended my seminars over the years, and who opened their lives to me. They have also been my teachers. I am equally indebted to my professional colleagues and personal friends who sustained me in various ways throughout the writing of this book. Dr. Sonja K. Foss helped me formulate some of the ideas in the book, and our shared passion for working with women during the past three decades continues today. Dr. Linda Manning graciously read chapters, giving me more in-depth insight into how nonverbal communication operates between the sexes.

I am professionally grateful for the support and guidance of my agent Ken Atchity and the expert editing and cheerleading Michelle Howry at Perigee/Prentice Hall Press provided.

The members of my chosen family of friends cheered me on and offered champagne, every step of the way! This family includes Christine Brautigam, Dr. Claire Brown, Cheryl Bolinger, Peggy Clute, and Ginny Landes. Thanks, gal pals!

I had the supreme privilege of working with a veteran writer and author, Susan Golant. She and I must have shared a past life. Susan has the gift of taking ideas and transforming them onto paper.

To my mother, Renee Houston, thank you for planting the seeds by insisting that education is the ticket to liberation and the only way a woman could get a fair shake in this world.

And most important, I would like to acknowledge my personal gender laboratory here at home, my daughter, Alexandra, and my son, Armand. They provided me with countless anecdotes from their own experiences of how the sexes are socialized and treated differently. I have used their stories in my seminars, and in *You Don't Say,* to illustrate that boys and girls are different and are reminded of this as they learn from a very early age what it means to be a boy and a girl.

Geoffrey Wade Simpson—thank you for the reminder that the differences between women and men are good! Forgive me for all the

Acknowledgments

hard times I gave you during the writing of this book. You continually help me grow, and I can always count on you to offer the male perspective.

—Audrey Nelson, Ph.D.
Boulder, Colorado

I am grateful to Audrey Nelson for having found me and drawn me into this book. I've learned quite a bit about the mysterious divide that forever separates men from women and have had great fun in the process! Audrey's flexibility and openness to the process made the writing of *You Don't Say* a pleasure from start to finish. I am also indebted to Michelle Howry for her enthusiasm for and commitment to this project and to my agent Bob Tabian for watching over my interests. Finally, I am forever grateful to my husband, Dr. Mitch Golant, whose enduring love and support make everything possible.

—Susan K. Golant, M.A.
Los Angeles, California

CONTENTS

It's the Elephant
in the Middle of the Room

Man is a multi-sensorial being. Occasionally he verbalizes . . . and we must seriously examine the implications of the fact that man does not communicate by word alone.

—RAY BIRDWHISTELL, PH.D.

In Praise of the Unsaid

You've been in a meeting with your boss, and you know he was displeased even—though he never said so. Was it his lack of eye contact? The grimace that briefly flitted across his face? The smile that seemed stiff and forced? Some of the above? All of the above? Perhaps you could add more to this list. Never mind. Join the crowd. We have all been engaged in interactions in which we felt much more was going on than was said.

Indirect as they may be, our nonverbal cues have more impact than our verbal messages; they are weightier in terms of the meaning of a message. In fact, researchers have estimated that nonverbal messages carry more than four times the weight of verbal messages. That may explain why you can experience a good deal of malaise if you miss nonverbal cues. Think back to the many times you have said, "I feel like a bomb hit me, but I can't tell you why," or, "It's not what they said . . ."

Of course not. It's what they *don't* say that means a lot. The nonverbal channel is a useful avenue for subtly manipulating people, and the manipulation does not even have to be consciously perceived. Because nonverbal communication is often oblique and off the record, it has implications for hurtful behavior. We are only semiconscious of much of the hidden, nonverbal meaning in our interactions. Like the elephant in the middle of the room, it's an enormous factor that many of us fail to take into account, often to our detriment.

> *Nonverbal messages carry more than four times the weight of verbal messages.*

Did you know that:

- There are 100,000 words in the English language.

- Five thousand of those words have double meanings.

- The average individual commands a vocabulary of from 30,000 to 60,000 words.

Sounds pretty impressive, doesn't it? But actually all of our verbal abilities amount to a small hill of peanuts when compared to our nonverbal vocabulary.

- Social scientists have estimated we humans use an astonishing 750,000 nonverbal signals in our interactions.

These cues consist of all human communication that transcends spoken or written words: body movement, posture, position, personal space and territory, facial expressions, gestures, vocal characteristics (such as pitch, tone, pace, inflection, quality), pauses (filled and unfilled), and even artifacts like jewelry and clothing.

Nonverbal communication is the process of one person stimulating meaning in the minds of others without benefit of actual words. As communication expert Julia T. Wood defines it, "Nonverbal communication . . . includes not only visual cues (gestures, appearances) but also vocal features (inflection, volume, pitch) and environmental factors (use of space, position) that affect meaning. . . . Like language, nonverbal communication is learned through interaction with others." Most of the ways men and women communicate with one another on a date, at home, or in the workplace has nothing at all to do with the power of their words. But because nonverbal cues are sent and received at a low level of awareness, we overlook and underestimate their power and importance.

In fact, despite our penchant for conversation, the realm of the nonverbal is far more telling during interactions:

- Nonverbal communication is a truer, more accurate indicator of our feelings and emotions—our internal states.

- Nonverbal behavior is relatively free of deception and distortion. It's hard to lie about our true intent because our nonverbals give us away.

- We make many personal and work-related decisions based on nonverbal cues. A first impression based on nonverbal cues will often determine if a deal will go forward.

- Nonverbal cues actually regulate our verbal interactions. Behaviors such as turn-taking, how we orient ourselves toward a person when speaking, a stony expression, or talking louder or over someone else all exert control over the flow of conversation. These covert behaviors determine who gets the floor, who doesn't, and who is going to talk the most.

- Nonverbal signals provide additional clues to clarify the intent of our verbal messages. A smile can be reassuring even if the news is bad.

- First impressions are predominantly based on nonverbal data. During the initial thirty seconds of an interaction, we draw an average of six to eight conclusions about a person before a single word is uttered. We only have one chance; there are no dress rehearsals for first impressions.

In this current era of pagers, voicemail, email, e-commerce, hectic schedules, and juggling family with work, we've all felt the need for "face time." That's because the face is the richest source of data among people. Even young children develop the capacity to discern discrepancies between verbal and nonverbal messages. In fact, when our words don't match our facial expression, others will intuitively go with the latter. Our nonverbals cancel out whatever else we might be saying.

Still, nonverbal messages are pretty slippery. We send and receive them at a low level of awareness. Linguists like Deborah Tannen have looked at how our spoken language patterns impact our personal and workplace relationships, but no one has taken a sharp look at nonverbal behavioral patterns that can hinder gender communication. In *You Don't Say,* I aim to bring to awareness these hidden behaviors. I will be looking most especially at the nonverbal communication that passes between men and women—those subliminal cues that can cause confusion and dissension in the family and at work and ultimately interfere with our success and our sense of well-being.

A Caveat or Two

Despite our beliefs (and several very familiar book titles) to the contrary, there is no such thing as "body language." If a person folds his arms, it doesn't necessarily mean he hates you. He could be cold. He could have indigestion from lunch. He could just assume this position out of habit. (Even for Freud, a cigar was sometimes just a cigar!) The truth is there is no dictionary of nonverbal meaning—it just doesn't exist.

Even though our nonverbal messages are weightier, we can't ignore the words that accompany them. Don't imagine yourself an armchair psychologist and believe that you can properly identify nonverbals without putting them in the entire context of a vast array of other information—what is being said, where and around whom the communication is taking place, the power differentials in the relationships, and so on. Indeed, we must look at *all* of the circumstances surrounding an interaction to avoid the confusions and mixed messages that can undermine relationships.

In addition, there are many individual differences in communication. We know that not all males are he-men and not all women are ladylike. We also know that communication characteristics can't be categorized by gender alone. Some individuals exhibit a variety of behaviors that do not fit the prescribed sex role norms—a male psychologist who is an excellent listener, for instance, or a female architect who is tied to the bottom line. When I ask these individuals why they think they've adopted behaviors from the other gender, they come up with a variety of explanations: he is the only boy in a family of all sisters, she is the second daughter of a father who wanted a son, they work in male-female-dominated industry, and so on.

No matter what the reason, if you identify yourself as one of these more androgynous individuals, you still must bear in mind that most of the others with whom you'll be interacting behave in a sexually prescribed fashion, however subtly these behaviors are embodied. It behooves you to understand their nonverbal cues.

Everyday Nonverbals

Our nonverbal behavior varies predictably according to our gender. In any society, males and females each have their own set of prescribed (and proscribed) behaviors. In our culture, the dissimilarities in male and female nonverbal communication styles are vast. During the 1960s, pioneering anthropologist Ray Birdwhistell proposed that humans evolved certain nonverbal characteristics to emphasize gender. These characteristics are cultural inventions. In studying peoples of seven disparate societies, he found that men and women distinguished typically female nonverbal behavior from that which is typically male. They also were able to identify feminine males and masculine females.

However, what is perceived as acceptable feminine or masculine behavior in one culture is not necessarily seen as such in another. For instance, Western European men cross their legs when they sit down, and they even carry purses. But I can't recall the last time I saw an American guy carry a purse. And how many men do you know who regularly cross their legs, particularly at the ankles? The same can be said for feminine behavior. In China, women's voices take on a finer, thinner quality. Females are also apt to cast down their eyes as they interact with men. No such deferential behavior exists among American women, however, who are quick to make eye contact. Chinese women are often taken aback by what they perceive as these boldly aggressive American women.

Rather than being a natural consequence of biology, some of our nonverbal behavior has been culturally shaped to point out our sex differences. In our society, women can toss their hair with impunity, but men would be laughed at if they did so. On the other hand, men can appear stoic and stony faced, but women would be cajoled to "Cheer up!" or "Gimme a smile!" should they wear a more serious expression.

Birdwhistell's work is a critical underpinning to *You Don't Say*. He has made it clear that human nonverbal communication patterns can be described and codified. Once we decipher these hidden nonverbal codes, we can better understand what others are *really* trying to convey as well as alter our own counterproductive behavior.

Nonverbal rules and norms are quite different among loved ones than they are in work or social life. We are allowed to step into our partner's personal space in ways that would be considered invasions in other contexts. We feel less inhibited about touching a loved one and do so more freely. We will also look at nonverbal "gender signaling," the cues men and women send to indicate sexual interest and attraction. What I call the "intimate moment"—looking into your lover's eyes lovingly, holding hands, kissing—is almost entirely defined nonverbally. The truth is, we can become better friends, parents, and spouses by recognizing and becoming more responsive to our loved ones' familiar patterns of nonverbal behavior.

In the work environment, the difficulties and misunderstandings generated by innate and enculturated sex differences in nonverbal communication not only reduce productivity but also lower morale. Clear communication between genders is crucial at the office. Historically, women have been the ones to bridge the communication gap because they came late to the workplace and felt the onus was on them to fit into an already established masculine work culture. But today there are nearly as many women working as men. With a 52 percent divorce rate, the latest statistics from the U.S. Department of Labor show that women comprise 46 percent of the workforce. About 60 percent of all women over the age of sixteen work. It's the rare employee who doesn't interface with someone of the opposite sex on the job.

Organizations all have their eye on the bottom line, and much attention is paid to training an efficient workforce. Many corporations now commonly provide diversity and cross-cultural training. Speakers of foreign languages are helped to be more proficient in English. But how many organizations train their members to be fluent in gender differences? Not many, to be sure. And fewer still, if any, pay attention to nonverbal gender communication—the most important element of all.

What You Will Learn

I have been in the field of gender communication as a researcher, speaker, and consultant for twenty-five years, talking to roughly 2,000 people a month. Crisscrossing the country hundreds of times over, I've been privy to America's dirty laundry. I have heard every story, every scenario, every possible episode of miscommunication between men and women at home, in the workplace, and out in the world. In the process, I've found that the realm of nonverbal communication is filled with booby traps and minefields for both genders. And it is exactly this rough, uncharted terrain that we will be exploring in *You Don't Say*.

This book is about day-to-day, face-to-face nonverbal communication and listening (or lack thereof) among men and women. I will debunk the myth of the all-important verbal arena and underscore the importance of nonverbal cues in communication. You will learn how to analyze your own counterproductive nonverbal behaviors, and become aware of how people interpret what you're really conveying. Other key points will include:

- How little boys and girls acquire their distinct nonverbal repertoires.

- How to analyze your own nonverbal behaviors and recognize how people interpret what you're really conveying.

- How to decipher male and female nonverbal cues at home and at work.

- What happens when these nonverbal styles clash.

- How to alter, accommodate, or modify nonverbals to be a more successful communicator with the opposite sex.

- How to become skilled in impression management, so you can learn to control judgments others make of you.

- How to resuscitate your communication by getting off autopilot.

You will come to understand the politics of nonverbal communication. And you will discover how your face, eyes, smile, touch, need for personal space, posture and positioning, gestures, voice, listening and conversational skills (or lack thereof), and attire all contribute to or detract from your relationships and quality of life. Along the way, I will provide advice as to how to best present yourself, and in a closing chapter, I will suggest what I call "gender-flexing" as a way to deal with the inequities your nonverbal communication style can provoke.

My Promise

What if I told you that by altering a few simple nonverbal behaviors, others would take you more seriously? You would do it in a hot minute, wouldn't you? You just need to learn what to change. I believe our nonverbal dilemmas are primarily an educational problem. By reeducating yourself, you can identify and use nonverbals to your advantage as an integral part of your interactions with members of the opposite sex.

In *You Don't Say*, I take a prescriptive, how-to approach that will help you become more effective in your communication. I will explain how your own nonverbal behavior can undermine your credibility with others as well as how dominant nonverbals can cue you to take a more narrowly defined, dependent, and acquiescent role than you might want to. The gender gap will never disappear, but *You Don't Say* goes a long way toward furthering the never-ending efforts of men and women to understand each other.

CHAPTER ONE

A Barcode on Her Forehead

*Those of us who keep our eyes open can read volumes into what
we see going on around us.*

—EDWARD HALL, THE SILENT LANGUAGE

One day a man walked up to me after one of my gender communication seminars and, with furrowed brow, launched into a typical diatribe: "Why are women so hard to understand?" he wanted to know.

I smiled briefly. Ah, the age-old "What do women want?" question. But before I could respond, he continued with some vehemence, "You know, I wish my wife and my teenage daughter came equipped with barcodes on their foreheads so I could tell what's really going on, and what they're really trying to tell me."

What a remarkable image; for a moment I was struck uncharacteristically speechless. And yet, based on my years of research, training, and corporate consulting in gender communication, it certainly rang true. In essence, this man was saying to me, *I feel awkward and need guidance. Please tell me how I should treat women, and espe-*

cially the most important women in my life. The fact of the matter is we're on the coattails of a major social transition, and men and women are still learning how to live and work together. Men are not the enemy. Most want to do the right thing, but they just don't know what that is.

That's where a barcode would come in handy. Many men are confused. Their communication style is more direct, and therefore they may send fewer contradictory cues than women. Indeed, the latter are quite a bit more complicated and sophisticated in their communication patterns than men, who often have difficulty decoding what turn out to be mixed messages.

Take the case of Karen, the thirty-two-year-old director of advertising at a midsized apparel company. I observed her and her team when I consulted at one of its monthly staff meetings. When it was Karen's turn to speak, the vice president of her division turned to her and asked, "How are you doing?"

"Not all that well," she replied gravely. "It took six months for me to finally get my raise—the one that was retroactive to January 1. I couldn't believe how much bureaucratic garbage I had to go through." As she shared the gory details, the rest of the staff nodded supportively.

"That's awful," one of her colleagues said.

"What a pain," chimed in another.

Even the vice president was taken aback. "They should never have put you through all that," he said, shaking his head.

Then, just as Karen was about to finish her tale of woe, she flashed a quick smile. As if on cue, the men in the room shifted uncomfortably in their chairs. They looked perplexed. What did that smile mean? Was Karen really as upset as she said she was? Could they take her complaints seriously? Would the vice president feel compelled to follow up on her grievance, now that she seemed to discount it so handily? The notion of a "female message barcode" might have appealed to many of the men in the room at that moment.

If you want to know what people think or feel, you don't look at their kneecaps, you look at their faces—and Karen's face contradicted her words. Indeed, that seemingly innocuous smile undermined her compelling verbal expressions of frustration and distress. No wonder her male colleagues seemed puzzled; Karen had shot herself in the foot with her female nonverbal style. Unfortunately, women often subvert their own credibility by these kinds of conflicting messages. And Karen's obvious lack of consciousness about what she had just done would most likely come back to haunt her later in her career.

What could Karen have done differently? As in any learning situation, awareness comes first. Karen needed to become conscious of her habitual, inappropriate smiling before she could change her behavior. Once alert to her unconscious reflexes, she could then monitor herself to check whether her words matched her appearance. All she had to do was better manage her facial expression so she looked serious at the conclusion of her complaint. It's as simple as that.

Of course this kind of behavior doesn't limit itself to the boardroom. Imagine that Karen visits her doctor about abdominal pain she has experienced since he started her on a new medication. Although she expresses her concern—and, in a sense, challenges her physician's authority with her complaint—she ends this interaction, too, with a girlish giggle. The doctor, following human nature, pays more attention to Karen's nonverbal cues than to her words. If he were unaware of the function of that giggle among women, he could patronize Karen or even ignore her complaint altogether, possibly leading to an uncomfortable if not dangerous situation for her.

Vive La Différence

From head to toe, men and women in our Western culture have entirely different repertoires of nonverbal cues. In fact, many nonverbals are absolutely taboo from one gender to the other. Someone near and dear must die before a man will cry and hug another man. Besides funerals and sports triumphs, there are few other occasions when males will touch each other in our culture, though in Europe you're more apt to observe men kissing or hugging openly on the street. You'll also never see men giggling or rushing at you with an excited, "Guess what I just did!" Few women, on the other hand, would ever dare undertake the aggressive, in-your-face stare-down. They'd also rarely point a finger in an accusatory fashion or shake a fist at another person, male or female. It's just not done.

The differences between genders mean that each sex has its own private, tacit code. And unless we understand the code of the opposite sex, it makes it difficult to communicate fully with our family, friends, and colleagues. This can be all the more important at work, given that more women are in the workplace now than ever, and many are still struggling to push past rigid stereotypes into senior positions. The kinds of miscommunication gaffes that Karen so unwittingly committed can easily impede career progress. And in families, the misreading of nonverbal cues can lead to conflict and even divorce. Once we become aware of the differences in nonverbal communication between men and women, we can take steps to properly decode the messages this unspoken information conveys.

Haven't Things Changed?

Often people assume that with three decades of the women's movement behind us, women have arrived. Haven't we given enough attention to this gender problem at home and at work? Aren't we beating a dead horse?

I'm here to tell you that with years of consciousness-raising, coupled with my work as a consultant and trainer in gender issues in corporate America, I can attest to the fact that old attitudes are pretty firmly entrenched. In fact, my audiences, large and small, still ask me the same few questions:

- How did men and women acquire their communication styles? Aren't we just born that way? Did we learn it? Is it nature or nurture?

- Which communication style is better, male or female?

- Is gender really that important in defining the way people interact with each other?

- Can men and women learn to change and adapt their styles? Haven't we been this way forever? How do you expect us to change?

- Are there individual differences as well as gender differences?

- Who acts as though they're responsible for effective gender communication, women or men?

- Haven't things changed in gender relationships?

This last question is most telling.

Tom, an executive at a factory location of Lucent Technologies, recently said to me, "When I began here as an engineer thirty years ago, there wasn't a single woman in my department. Now a woman heads it. Women are everywhere. Things have changed!"

I have to admit that he has a point. Twenty years ago, it was easier to identify inequities between men and women because there were far fewer females in the workplace, especially in senior positions. And it is true that women comprise 46 percent of the workforce, and according to the most recent Census Bureau statistics, 7.1 million women (as compared to 9.4 million men) are in full-time executive, managerial, or administrative positions, up 29 percent from 1993. Women seem to be everywhere. Moreover, we all know how we're *supposed* to behave now. Overtly, it seems as if we've altered our actions to meet the new requirements of corporate America, which often has zero tolerance toward any communication inequities such as ignoring women, hoarding power and information, or excluding them from the good-old-boy networks.

Women comprise 46 percent of the workforce.

But Tom mistakenly equates the larger number of women holding jobs with equitable treatment. Just because there are more professional and working women doesn't yet mean that they have arrived, or that attitudes toward them have changed. Men still dominate senior executive and CEO positions, and they still make more money than women, even for the same jobs. When the General Accounting Office of Congress recently conducted a study of ten industries, it found that not only did most female managers earn less compared to their male counterparts, but also the gap was even wider than it had been five years earlier. In other words, not only are women making little progress in this area, they are actually losing ground. New York Representative

Carolyn Maloney lamented this thickening of the glass ceiling, saying, "I don't find one line of good news in the report. Yet I think people believe women are doing better."

For me the crucial question is this: *Even though there are more women in management, have internal attitudes changed?* The myth is that they have—and many well-meaning people just like Tom buy into it. But from my experience consulting with as well as training large corporate groups, I find that, in fact, we have not changed all that much.

Although outwardly we all know how to behave, internally certain mind-sets still prevail at work as well as at home. Attitudes drive behavior, and attitudes are not all that plastic or flexible. In spite of everything, they're tough to change. Holdovers can be found in a whole host of nonverbal subtleties, such as men making eye contact with everyone in the room but the women, men allowing other men in a group to have more turns talking than women, men interrupting women in mid-sentence, men stonewalling when they feel under attack, or men rolling their eyes when a woman becomes excited about an idea.

These are what I call **"micro-behaviors,"** and we give and receive thousands of such millisecond signals daily. They consist of a fleeting nonverbal loss of control. Primarily micro-behaviors are executed in the face (a wife asks, "How did your day go?" and her husband grimaces but then quickly recovers with an, "Oh fine, fine," so as not to engage her in his work life), but they can also occur in the rest of the body (your shoulders droop momentarily when you receive bad news). These micro-behaviors are quite revealing; they serve as "leakage" into what people are really thinking or feeling. But because they're so quick, you must be an astute (or an informed) observer to catch them. They occur with great regularity every day in myriad situations, and eventually all of these small, subtle, but common actions add up to keeping the status quo just where it is.

What Men and Women Think of Each Other

In research I recently conducted with men and women across the United States, I asked just four simple questions:

- What do you feel is the greatest strength in women's communication?

- What do you feel is the greatest strength in men's communication?

- What do you feel is the biggest weakness in women's communication?

- What do you feel is the biggest weakness in men's communication?

The responses to these questions revealed my respondents' self-perception as well as their awareness of how their gender communicates with the opposite sex. One of my striking findings was that there was no debate. Men and women had significantly shared views of their own and the opposite sex's weaknesses and strengths in communication—and these are weaknesses and strengths that seem to have been written about since time immemorial in women's magazines and the like.

Here's what men say about their own weaknesses in communication:

- "Men fail to read nonverbal communications, and we don't show emotion."

- "The biggest problem is men don't express ourselves clearly, and we try to solve women's problems."

- "Men cannot stay focused solely on what the other person is saying."

- "Men hold things in."

- "Men seem to come from the self aspect in communicating. We can be overbearing and loud at times."

- "Men don't listen, and we don't even make the effort to pretend we're listening."

Yes, they actually come right out and say it. Men clearly perceive women to have the edge in the interpersonal area. Men say to me, "That's their job! It's not man's work. They should be good at it!" I also believe men perceive that this "division of labor" is an accepted norm. Men admit that they are poor readers of nonverbal cues; they are "out to lunch" when it comes to that sensitivity.

WHEN I ASK women what they feel is the biggest weakness in men's communication, 75 percent of their responses indicate men's poor listening skills. Here's a sampling:

- "Men assume they know what you are going to say before you finish. They interrupt your conversation."

- "When men listen to what others say, they do not actually hear and absorb the right information."

- "Men are unable to really empathize with another person's feelings; they're too focused on trying to fix the problem."

- "Men don't look at you when you speak."

- "Men zero in on only one aspect—the verbal."

On the positive side, the majority of women's comments indicated they believe men are direct, speak with confidence, and get to the point. According to the women I surveyed, men's strongest areas include forcefulness and control.

What did the men I surveyed think about women's skills?

- "Women are good at the observation of subtle nuances."

- "Women have a clear perception of the total picture of communication."

- "Women are usually more thoughtful and sensitive to other people's communication."

- "My wife can read my mind."

- "Women are concerned about the impact of the message on the person who is receiving it."

WHEN I ASKED women about their strengths, they most frequently reported listening, empathy, and the ability to express emotions.

- "Women relate to the information by putting themselves in the situation."

- "Listening, compassion, and empathy."

- "The ability to read between the lines."

- "We know how to express ourselves."

- "We put the human element into conversation—caring, compassion, interest in the other person."

- "Women generally communicate with all of their senses: hearing, seeing, feeling, and speaking. As a result, they are better at picking up details and listening empathically."

Moreover, in critiquing their own communication style, women admitted to being overly emotional and indirect:

- "We read more into what was actually said."

- "We think with our hearts, not with our heads."

- "Too much empathy is provided."

Surveys such as these help us identify where the problematic miscommunication occurs, and where we can focus our efforts. Clearly, male listening is still one of the big issues; both men and women identified it as the number one problem. My research revealed that men and women hold the same perception. They are in agreement about what causes the disconnection. So what do we do about it? The answers will be found in the pages of this book, and our understanding begins with identifying the communication paradoxes that plague both genders.

The Female Paradox: Social Skills and Acquiescence

My survey reinforces what others have made clear: females are more responsive to nonverbal cues than males. In fact, not only are women more responsive, but they read these stimuli with greater accuracy. They know that they "know things," but they may not even understand that they do or why. The following is a common interaction between a man and a woman as they discuss the upcoming sale of their home:

MARCIA: I don't think that couple is going to buy our house.

GLEN: Why not? I didn't hear them say anything . . .

MARCIA: (shaking her head): Nope, it wasn't in what they said. There was a lot going on between them.

GLEN: What are you talking about? I was in that room with you. I didn't hear them say they weren't interested.

Even though Marcia was unable to articulate why she had this understanding, it's clear that she was picking up on the potential buyers' facial micro-behaviors—cues to which Glen seemed oblivious. Indeed, since he didn't see these subtle signals, he denied their validity—along with the accuracy of Marcia's insights.

Females are better than males in decoding nonverbal behaviors. Their advantage is most pronounced with facial cues. I believe this in large part results from women maintaining face-to-face interactions more than men do. As they preserve eye contact, they study the face more and consequently glean more information. Women have a history of scrutinizing the face and paying more attention.

Robert Rosenthal, a psychologist at Harvard University, conducted the single most important study to analyze sex differences in the decoding of nonverbal behaviors. He developed a test called the PONS (Profile of Nonverbal Sensitivity) to ascertain people's ability to read nonverbal cues. The PONS consists of a series of video clips of young women expressing a range of emotions including maternal love, gratitude, the seeking of forgiveness, seductiveness, jealous rage, and hatred. In each clip, the words are muffled. In addition, at least one of the nonverbal avenues is obliterated; in some, only the facial expression is evident, in others, only the body movements and gestures. In testing boys and girls from third grade through college with the PONS, Rosenthal and his team found that in 77 percent of the studies, females were superior to males in accurately judging messages communicated by facial expressions, body movement, and voice quality. Other research studies have confirmed that women are superior in the interpretation of facial expressions cross-culturally—it's a universal attribute.

Not only are women adept at receiving nonverbal cues, but also they're quite proficient at sending them. They are better "expressers" than men, and they are less concerned with monitoring how they act. Here, however, is where they can run into a particularly nasty double bind. Consider Carole in a Monday morning staff meeting. She is enthusiastic, passionate, and absolutely convinced that her plan is the best one; the group should adopt it. She presents her view in an animated fashion. Her eyebrows are lifted, she's smiling, her voice is filled with excitement, and she gestures with gusto.

This may not seem like a bad thing to her, but Carole's zeal puts her at risk with the men in the room, who may interpret her freer expression as lacking in control, overly demonstrative, and a sure sign of her instability. Indeed, women are often thought of as emotionally volatile. Paradoxically, rather than helping them, their extraordinary nonverbal expressive skills have served to perpetuate such stereotypes; they even become the source of social stigma. For instance, upon witnessing Carole's behavior, the men in the staff meeting might become patronizing. One might mutter, "Oh my god, does she have PMS?" Another may tap her on the shoulder and say, "Calm down, Carole. Why are you so excited?"

Carole is good at expressing herself. You can clearly see that she believes in her plan wholeheartedly. But, as a result of her male colleagues' responses, she suddenly feels diminished. Moreover, she loses credibility in their eyes, and this makes her angry. "God, men can get excited about their ideas," she complains to me out of earshot of her male colleagues, "but just because they don't convey them the way I do, does that mean mine aren't legitimate?"

Unfortunately, a woman's lack of nonverbal control coupled with highly expressive behavior can lead to the erosion of her authority among men. Most males aren't allowed the kind of open expression in which Carole freely engages, and they may find her enthusiasm threatening because it's alien to them. In a man's world, the minute you get into the emotional arena, it means you're losing control. Control is related to power—the greater your control, the more power you have. Consequently, as soon as a woman becomes animated, a man might think, "I don't see you or your power as credible." The implication: That's not how things are done.

It's obvious that Carole could have monitored her own behavior and tried to tone down a little bit. Hers was a context-bound situation, and this may be an appropriate approach. However, some women feel this kind of adjustment interferes with their integrity— they can't be who they really are. For those women I recommend a strategy I call **"pre-cuing."** If they're feeling intense about something, they might say, "This has been on my mind for a week, and I feel strongly about it." With such an announcement, men are less apt to infer that it's "her time of the month" or that she's let her emotions get the better of her. However, it's also important to bear in mind that male negative reactions to female enthusiasm operate on a subtle basis to maintain asymmetrical relationships. Men have more power than women in the workplace. They (but not women) will dictate what the social norms and rules should be.

Women are the champions in the interpersonal arena, but not when it comes to power. That's just not in their sex role description. If anything, they're cast in a supporting role to men. Little girls learn that women are indirect, process oriented, other directed, and interdependent. Little boys, of course, learn those same lessons about girls, and as adults believe that women should be empathetic, supportive, nurturing, amiable, relational, and willing to share power and information.

Indeed, although women may be masters of sending and receiving nonverbals, they can still undermine themselves by placating and showing deference. They may express themselves assertively, but then, to make themselves seem less powerful and to better fit within their feminine role (that is, to soften the blow), they may counterbalance direct, authoritative verbal statements with contradictory, acquiescent nonverbal cues—the squeaky little girl voice, the inappropriate giggle, or the gratuitous smile. Unfortunately, this further erodes credibility. A man might think, "She says she's upset, but she's smiling. I don't get it." And, like Karen who grinned after complaining bitterly about the trouble she had in securing her raise, these women will most likely wonder, "Why doesn't anyone take me seriously?"

Compensatory strategies like unwarranted smiling or giggling can be confusing to men—ergo the need for a "female barcode." Unfortunately, this very behavior is what causes men to accuse women of being manipulative. Men are more congruent in their verbal and nonverbal styles (that is, their nonverbals will more closely match their verbal expression) whereas women are less so.

Here's the age-old dilemma: Would women rather have power or be interpersonally competent? What do people value in the office? They value power—the male way. Because men have dominated the workplace, Tom Peters and Kenneth Blanchard have jumped on the bandwagon to legitimize the social and interpersonal competencies that women bring to the table. Peters and Blanchard have gone so far as to say that feminine traits are valuable for managers. That's all well and good, but there is still a debate about the legitimacy of these skills. A post–September 11 article in the *Harvard Business Review,* for instance, argued for the importance of compassion in the office, especially after a disaster or other trauma. Why would such an article be necessary if the business world readily accepted a more "female" approach?

Still, I believe that these two options—power and interpersonal competence—don't have to be mutually exclusive. Women can learn to present themselves in a more powerful and convincing way to men while maintaining their superior nonverbal abilities. In this book I will show them how. And for their part, men can learn from women how to enhance their interpersonal communication skills—how to connect and bond.

The Male Paradox: Social Inattentiveness and Power

Men are the champions of power, which has been described as the ability to manage or direct one's environment. Men are socialized to be in control, to have and exercise authority. Genetically, they are physically larger and more aggressive. In fact, both women and men overwhelmingly believe that men should be the more dominant gender. Today males (and white males, at that) still hold the majority of "power" positions (CEOs, company or board presidents) at Fortune 500 companies. A man must "earn his stripes" by fiercely competing and constantly proving himself. Masculinity is far more entrenched in our society than femininity. A girl can engage in cross-gender behavior—she can become a tomboy without many repercussions—but a boy perceived as a sissy is taunted and rejected.

Moreover, men's nonverbal behaviors command attention and exude power. Men know how to direct and control their nonverbals. If they are unrestrained (that is, too expressive), not only do they give away their power, but they may also be denigrated. Here's how one man framed the problem during a corporate training session: "When I got my bonus and raise, I wanted to run home and jump up and down and squeal, 'Guess what just happened to me!' just like my girlfriend did when she got promoted. But I couldn't. Men just can't be animated or show excitement or joy the way women can."

Men symbolize their authority through nonverbal cues. Whereas a woman is expected to be and act small, a man's man should be large—the taller the better—and loud. He takes up lots of space, interrupts during conversations, makes expansive gestures, initiates touch, commands a bigger office, and pilots a more powerful car. At the same time, he exerts control over his facial expressions (called "masking") and tone of voice, using little or no inflection (this is analogous to a masked facial expression) and a lower pitch associated with authority. Everything nonverbal about a man must communicate control and power.

But here's the male dilemma. Although men know how to present themselves in an authoritative way, they are challenged in the face-to-face interpersonal arena. Here they are definitely not winners. "They just don't get it" is a phrase women use when referring to men's inability to pick up important interpersonal (especially nonverbal) cues. I hear this constantly in my work; it's women's daily mantra. Here is how Ben, a male participant, conveyed the problem:

> My wife came home after being gone all day Saturday and asked me that loaded question: "Do you notice anything different about me, honey?" I immediately went into a cold sweat! I scanned her from head to toe. What was it? A new dress? Did she color her hair? New jewelry? I looked at her shoes, but I remembered them from last week.

To protect himself, Ben answered with a blanket compliment, "You look great, honey." But Sarah began to press him. "What looks different?" she insisted. He just didn't see it, and when he couldn't tell her, she became deflated and resentful. Sarah had had a makeover at the Lancôme counter at Bloomingdale's, but Ben was unable to discern her new look. It is little wonder that when women congregate among themselves, they complain, "Men just don't get it." Such statements imply that the sexes are the antithesis of one another.

Male social inattentiveness is borne out in research. Harvard psychologist Robert Rosenthal documented that paying attention is just not men's forte. His investigations showed that most men are inferior to women at both reading (decoding) and sending (encoding) non-verbal cues. This, of course, comes as no surprise to many women. Indeed, one female seminar attendee blurted out, "Men are emotionally challenged," as she tried to come to grips with her frustration in dealing with the males in her life. And, as we have seen, women taking my survey have characterized men as unable to "listen or read between the lines," easily distracted, and downright insensitive.

Why do men misinterpret (or miss altogether) nonverbal behaviors more than women do? Perhaps their skill pattern derives from the fact that their attention is not directed preferentially to any one channel but instead is spread diffusely. They may perform an overall scan of a situation, but may not focus on any one thing—especially not the face. They may not recognize that something is to be gained or lost by attending more to some cues than to others, and they have no particular need or motive to read leaky cues. The latter are the real avenues into people's internal states. They seep out despite our attempts to hide them.

Men pay attention differently. It's as if they're distracted by extraneous cues. They don't know how to make sense of them or integrate them so they don't serve them well. Men can wind up at a relative disadvantage only because women are attending actively to leaky cues and other micro-behaviors. Women focus where they should—on the face. They take the whole message in context. Because they can show empathy, they get people to open up more. In short, women walk away from an interaction with more information. Information is power, and this is one area where women have power and men don't.

Men have a twofold problem. Not only do they have more trouble decoding messages they receive from women, but because of their use of masking, they also have a stonier demeanor and are less adept at sending out what they feel.

While women struggle to accommodate interpersonal needs, men don't place the same emphasis or value on the skills required to do so. Many don't admire interpersonal effectiveness as much as they covet power and control. For instance, they may feel no need to read nonverbal cues or lubricate relationships. They may even say, "Let the gals handle that," when referring to social maintenance activities. Women keep the social calendars (some men even jokingly refer to their wives as their social directors) and are assigned to arrange all the parties, gift purchasing, baby showers, and greeting cards for birthdays, deaths, births, and so on. Feminine skills in the interpersonal arena still "don't get no respect" among some men.

Although men are the champions of nonverbal credibility and power, they are poor readers and senders of nonverbal cues. Men are taken seriously; their nonverbals demand it. Women, although superior in the nonverbal realm, complain that they are "not taken seriously." I call this the credibility gap!

The Large and the Small of It

Let's look at the chicken-and-egg of the politics of nonverbal expression. Has women's past power-down status produced her nonverbal behaviors? To a certain extent we may say that their behavior is cued. Women may appropriate gestures of acquiescence and submission because they have been shown gestures of dominance.

Conversely, we all teach people how to treat us. Others pick up messages from how we sit, walk, and hold ourselves. In myriad tiny ways, we communicate how we perceive ourselves, and others, in turn, choose how to interact with us based on our projections of self. If a woman's behavior contributes to the impression that she is easily dominated or compulsively pleasant, this will influence the way she is treated in society—and in turn the way she behaves nonverbally.

The truth of the matter is, all the subtle nonverbal messages enacted every day by both genders maintain the current social fabric; our micro-behaviors support the macro-structure. In fact, the larger political structure needs these numerous minutiae of human interactions to sustain and reinforce it. Nonverbal cues fall somewhere on a continuum of social control that ranges from socialization or cultivation of minds at one extreme to the use of force or violence at the other. As University of California, Los Angeles psychologist Nancy Henley so wisely put it, "The more men and women interact in the way they've been trained to from birth, without considering the meaning of what they do, the more they become dulled to the significance of their actions."

I hope this book will serve as a guide to awaken you from that kind of torpor. Our nonverbal actions are significant. For the last three decades, as women have entered the workforce in droves, they have brought a new interpersonal skill set to the table. Unfortunately, the expertise that they bring, like their ability to send and receive nonverbals more accurately than men, have not been recognized or validated by others, let alone themselves.

Throughout the book, I will be presenting Gender Prescriptions—suggestions to both men and women about how they might pay attention to and adjust their nonverbal behaviors in order to be more effective communicators. However, bear in mind that these suggestions are set within a certain framework:

• There is a time and place for almost every nonverbal communication behavior. And not all behaviors are appropriate for every situation.

• *Vive la différence!* I am *not* suggesting men become women and women become men. Quite the opposite!

• Understanding nonverbal communication is not a "blame game." Both men and women bring unique skills to the table that are appropriate for different contexts. As actress Drew Barrymore once said, "I can't stand people who can't stand one of the sexes. We've only got two. Why would you dislike one of them?" We can borrow from each other. We can learn from each other. We can expand our behavioral repertoires! I call this "gender-flexing."

• The majority of the nonverbal behaviors described in this book are learned. Boys and girls learn and internalize nonverbal characteristics from same-sex role models and through self-socialization. If these behaviors are learned, we can unlearn, modify, and adjust them.

• It is the responsibility of both men and women to increase awareness of their own as well as others' nonverbal behaviors. Traditionally women have engaged in social maintenance. After all, someone had to do it! But today's women want men to contribute in this arena as well.

We can't do anything unless we build relationships with others, and we build those relationships by establishing good interpersonal communication. One of the keys to good communication—and one of the best ways to eliminate the need for barcodes on foreheads—is self-awareness when it comes to reading and sending nonverbal cues. The beginnings of that awareness grow from an understanding of how these behaviors develop in boys and girls in the first place. And that's the subject of our next chapter.

CHAPTER TWO

Girls Will Be Girls, Boys Will Be Boys

*When my daughter was about five, she tended to take much
smaller steps than my son did when he was that age, and I
remember that even when my son was young he'd always look me
in the eye when I yelled at him while my daughter would lower
her eyes at the first sign that I was angry.*

— *JULIUS FAST*, THE BODY LANGUAGE OF SEX, POWER, AND AGGRESSION

D rive by any elementary school playground at recess, and
you'll get a vivid example of the differences in male and female nonverbal behaviors. The boys will be running around,
shoving pals to the ground, playing tag. One little guy may be caught
in the act of ripping a baseball cap off a buddy's head and running
away with it. You might even see some boys scaling the chain-link
fence, pushing the boundaries.

Now observe the girls. Most will be huddled in clusters, seemingly engaged in intense interpersonal interactions. One may stand isolated, crying, and another girl—presumably her best friend—will come up to her to soothe and nurture her. A separate group may be engaged in cooperative games of jump rope, hopscotch, or patty-cake. As you stand there watching this spectacle, it will soon become clear to you that boys and girls live in significantly different worlds.

Where do these nonverbal gender differences come from? Recent research has made it clear that some of them are biological. Male and female brains are wired differently. Hormones also impact behavior. Boys are genetically programmed to be more aggressive than girls; girls are genetically programmed to be more nurturing than boys. Admitting that there are biological sex differences is not a step backward in the battle for equality, it's just accepting reality. There are even some inborn nonverbal gender differences that cannot be ignored: girls acquire language sooner than boys, who tend to be better in spatial-relations ability. We are not the same; we don't want everyone to be the same. This is the *nature* part of the equation.

However, although there has been more emphasis in the last few years on the biology of male-female differences, I believe that how children become men and women stretches beyond simple biology. The *nurture* factors—how children are socialized or learn to be girls and boys in our society—also strongly influence the development and maintenance of male and female nonverbal communication patterns. And if many of the communication behaviors we are examining are learned, they can also be unlearned or otherwise modified once we become aware of them.

In this chapter, we will look at the complex psychosocial factors that underlie every child's socialization. In so doing, we will explore three major themes:

1. How children begin orienting themselves to the world nonverbally from the moment of birth.

2. When and how boys' and girls' nonverbal behaviors begin to differentiate from each other, based on gender.

3. How these differing nonverbal styles eventually impact what we do as adults.

You should know, however, that this area of research—the developmental studies of children's nonverbal behavior—is (no pun intended) in its developmental stage. That is, we don't know a whole lot about it. Research into the emergence of sex differences, too, is still in its beginning phases. Nevertheless, in this chapter, I aim to give you a broad overview of what scientists already do know about how "boys will be boys" and "girls will be girls," especially when it comes to nonverbal behavior. Armed with this information, we can then learn how to modify and control the multitude of micro-behaviors we give and receive each day.

Nonverbal from Birth

Babies enter the world communicating exclusively through nonverbal channels. What choice do they have? They certainly can't be verbal. They can't talk yet! Their orientation and interactions with others—indeed their very survival—depends on their ability to connect to others and convey their emotions without the use of words.

According to Susan Ludington-Hoe, a maternal child health expert at Case Western University, this kind of communication begins at the moment of birth. During the first two hours, a newborn will enjoy a period of alertness that will not recur for at least two months. During those precious minutes, he will look around for his mother and father with a searching, intent expression. "He wants to learn their voices and faces," Ludington-Hoe explains in her book, *How to Have a Smarter Baby*. These nonverbal behaviors constitute the beginnings of bonding.

How is this possible? You may be surprised to learn that a newborn infant sees quite well at birth. He can see clearly within thirteen inches of his face and can identify his mother by the time he's four days old. In fact, research has shown that above all other visual stimuli, babies find faces most interesting of all. I can attest to this from personal experience. When my children were infants and we went out for dinner with our extended family, we used to play a game called Please Pass the Baby. If one of the grandmas asked me to Please Pass the Baby, as if the baby were a salt shaker or pitcher of water (so that everyone could get a squeeze or a kiss), it was quite evident that my child only had eyes for me. The child would lock onto my face and track it while she made the rounds of the ten or twelve relatives seated at the table, even if it meant her squirming in order to maintain visual connection with my face.

Babies also have a preference for eyes. An infant responds positively to his mother's eyes very early. According to some researchers, by the fourth week, infants attempt to visually search for the eyes of the person caring for them. Since babies are helpless, eye contact serves a crucial role in establishing bonding.

Smiling is another nonverbal behavior essential for a child's well-being. "Infants manage the beginnings of a smile within hours of being born, then start grinning in response to other peoples' smiles at about four to six weeks. This survival tactic insures that babies are irresistible to their parents," Carroll E. Izard, a psychology professor at the University of Delaware, explained in an interview for O, The Oprah Magazine.

Smiling plays a vital role in the development of a child's attachment. When a baby smiles at his parents, they respond in kind with their own smiles accompanied by cooing and talking. A smiling baby is a charming baby. Indeed, by the ripe old age of three months, a baby will smile differently for different people, reserving his most radiant countenance for his parents. He'll even laugh out loud and coo when spoken to, much to his parents' delight, thus ensuring their continued interest in him. By the end of the first year, children exhibit smiles as well as other recognizable facial expressions.

We also know that shortly after birth, babies begin learning to interpret various nonverbal signals received from others. By three months of age, infants behave as if they know they are the objects of their mother's voice. They gaze, smile, kick, wave their arms, and/or coo when their mother speaks to them. If a stranger interrupts the interaction, these activities stop.

Not only do babies begin to express nonverbal behaviors from birth onward, but they also begin reading them in others very early on. In Emotional Intelligence, Daniel Goleman describes his observation of a mother and baby in a waiting room. When the mother became distressed and seemed as if she were ready to cry, her child offered his blanket as a means to comfort her. In fact, research indicates that children begin to perceive the meanings behind facial expressions long before they can manage these behaviors themselves. It is also well documented that they are able to recognize and respond to positive and negative facial expressions. Even a very young baby will become distressed and will cry at a photograph of an angry, tense face but will smile at a happy image.

Although infants fixate on a few facial features, particularly the eyes, it is not until between the ages of two and five months that they actually scan the face fully. By the first year, they recognize facial expressions quite well. Babies therefore become adept at reading cues about the moods of those around them, which may explain why they become fussy when emotional conflict rocks the home.

The Growing Repertoire of Nonverbals

It's clear that even infants have a great range of nonverbal behaviors—as they smile, crawl, and laugh their way into our hearts. Additional nonverbal behaviors evolve with the child's development. For example, babies expand their range of nonverbals when they start to walk. Their new mobility allows for posture, position, and spatial relations to develop.

Gestures become part of a child's nonverbal repertoire around one year of age. Pointing is a common response to new events. According to child development psychologist Ng Bouton-Jones, it always involves the child looking at her mother, standing still, and orienting her body and face halfway between her mother and the novel object. When a year-old child waves spontaneously, she is usually signaling imminent interaction, not "Bye-bye."

If you spend any time in line at the grocery store, you'll also see toddlers engage in coy behavior. This typically includes a child smiling, then looking at you and averting her eyes (alternating eye contact), turning her body away, and maybe burying her head in her mother's legs or chest. The nonverbal message here: "I want to interact with you, but it's a pretty complex social skill and you're a stranger. But I still want to engage." This kind of approach-avoidance behavior usually emerges among boys and girls toward the end of the first year and persists throughout the second.

Young children also begin to develop self-adapters—those touching behaviors we all use to soothe and comfort ourselves. You may observe kids twirling or pulling their hair or an ear, sucking their thumb, or rubbing on the satin part of a blanket.

At this age, children have no boundaries. In fact, toddlers have almost no sense of personal space. They climb all over us, and we let them. How often have we witnessed a toddler or preschooler clambering over a booth at a restaurant to see what we're eating. Young children lean up against strangers, and I even once observed a little boy, bored from standing too long in a movie line, doing a head-plant into an unfamiliar man's rear end in front of him. Over time, however, children are exposed to gradually increasing distances for various communication situations. They learn appropriate conversational distances by about age eight.

Generally, youngsters express their emotions with more body parts and in a less subtle fashion than adults; few are the adults who would jump up and down in excitement or stomp a foot in rage and get away with it. With increasing age, we develop finer muscular control. Our cognitive abilities become more complex, and we learn and respond to various social norms and pressures. Because of this, kids gradually increase their ability to simulate facial expressions and emotion. Sudden shifts from one emotional display to another decrease as youngsters get older.

Head nods, eyebrow raising, or some type of smile that indicates, "Yes, I'm listening to you," are nearly absent in young children and even in youngsters up through fifth grade. Children make this type of nonverbal response only when someone else in the interaction pulls it out of them. A parent or teacher might say, for instance, "Nod your head if you're listening to me." Listener responses increase dramatically by early adolescence. In the seventh and eighth grade, children begin to acquire these behaviors and become more refined in acknowledging that they've heard what was said.

The same, however, doesn't hold true for eye contact. Any parent of a teenager will attest to the fact that adolescence represents a low point for eye contact—unless, of course, the teens are locking eyes with their current love interest. Generally, children are less likely than adults to look at the person they're talking to at the beginnings of their utterances—to make sure that person is attentive and plugged in—as well as at the ends of their utterances—signaling, "I'm done and now you can talk." This so-called gatekeeping behavior is fairly sophisticated.

In fact, kids don't fully emulate adult eye contact until they're in their late teens. This is why adults can misinterpret teens and become frustrated with them ("Are you paying attention? Look at me when I'm talking to you!"), especially if the adolescents don't yet have command of these subtle signals. When we impose an adult model unfairly, we misconstrue the lack of eye contact for a lack of respect. I believe this is simply a skill many teens haven't yet fully developed.

Barbie Versus G.I. Joe

Some behaviors are universal. However, over time—and sometimes quite early on—we make distinctions between what we consider to be appropriate male and female nonverbal behavior.

Take, for instance, touch. A parent's touch during infancy may establish the foundation for all other forms of communication the child later develops. Touch is vital to the recognition of symbols and speech. Infants receive more touch than they ever will in their later lives. Research indicates that the frequency and duration of touch among mothers and infants is at its peak when the child is between the ages of fourteen months and two years. Interestingly, however, female infants receive more touch and are encouraged to engage in touch more frequently than males. This suggests that as early as the first year, parents are socializing their children's behavior to conform to the expectation of their eventual adult sex roles.

What is socialization? Children grow up with multiple systems: parent and child, child and siblings, child and peer group, child and school. A child's family system includes what people say and do in relation to her, what she says and does, and how people around her respond. Every family system and society has rules or limits for how we should behave. In our society, for instance, we stop at red lights, wait (more or less) patiently in the checkout line for our turn without ramming the shoppers in front of us with our carts, and refrain from touching people we don't know. We abide by certain socially acceptable rules that we have imposed on ourselves, for our own good and that of others. That's how we create social order.

Some of these rules are spoken and some are understood, but part of a parent's job is to convey them to their children, thereby socializing them. These rules teach youngsters important lessons about the world, and they promote safety. Jennifer must hold your hand while crossing the street. She must not pick up her skirt or hit her sister. She must not poke the cat in the eye or pull the dog's tail. Social psychologists have delineated areas in which families and societies set these sorts of limits and rules. These problems of socialization are shared by all cultures around the world and include rules relating to:

- Eating and excreting

- Aggression

- Dependence and interdependence

- Emotional development and attachment to others

- Achievements

- Competition and cooperation

- Life and death

- Mating and sexuality

- Right and wrong

- Nonverbal behavior

- Sex role development

This last area is of particular interest to us when it comes to nonverbal communication between men and women. Children learn how boys and girls *should* act from the way their parents, siblings, caregivers, and teachers treat them; from their observations of adult behavior; through peer pressure; and from media exposure. And we care very much whether youngsters behave in the prescribed fashion. Every society forms certain expectations for each gender—men go off to fight in wars, women keep the home fires burning; men bring home the bacon, women fry it up.

Of course, these expectations have evolved over the millennia and reflect our particular cultural biases, though some of them certainly have been changing. Marlo Thomas's beloved anthology and tape *Free to Be You and Me,* originally published in the 1970s, directly challenges the childhood acquisition of restricted sex roles with stories and songs like, "Parents Are People" ("Some mommies are doctors, some daddies are chefs . . .") and "Ladies First."

Such forces for change notwithstanding, in our society, traditional masculine attributes include assertiveness, ambition, and independence. Sensitivity to others' feelings, and the ability to express emotions, warmth, and passivity are considered traditionally feminine attributes. The way that coy behavior evolves among boys and girls is an excellent case in point. Girls continue to enact this kind of social peek-a-boo even at the ages of four and five. They'll turn around and hug their mother's leg and either make eye contact and smile or, for safety's sake, ask Mom to pick them up and hold them when encountering an unfamiliar adult.

Boys stop playing coy after about the age of two. They are beginning to learn that they should be strong, tough, and bold and that they should not acquiesce, not even to a stranger. Boys have been socialized out of this behavior because coyness is a traditional feminine attribute, not a masculine one. A five-year-old boy who persists in acting coy might be thought of as "painfully shy," "overly sensitive," or borderline "sissy."

These long-established expectations for behavior still remain, especially in the ways the genders behave toward each other nonverbally. In fact, these so-called sex roles—behavior that's specific to each gender—are so important, they are inculcated consciously and unconsciously even before birth.

The World of Boys and the World of Girls

Children are generally "gender neutral" up to about age three. This is why we see preschool boys holding hands with each other and not hesitating to bring their favorite stuffed animal to school. Although by this age, youngsters begin to identify themselves by sex and accurately apply gender-related labels to themselves, they don't recognize the permanence of their gender until they are between the ages of five and seven. In fact, young children don't perceive sex as a factor of anatomy at all, but rather as a changeable role, like a hairstyle or an outfit.

This point was driven home to me with my own children. My daughter Alexandra took off for school one morning, leaving her younger brother, three-year-old Armand, in charge of their collection of Cabbage Patch kids. I walked into their playroom and found my son sitting in a corner, holding one of their "babies" to his chest, his T-shirt covering its head. Intrigued, I asked, "Armand, what are you doing?"

"I'm feeding Bam Bam," he replied innocently.

"Honey, you're a boy," I gently corrected him. "You can't nurse him."

He immediately burst into tears. "I've got boobies like you do," he cried with some indignation. "Why can't I?"

"Because your boobies don't make milk," I replied.

Armand was devastated by his deficiency. At his age, gender was still an exchangeable entity.

Young boys and girls have a generalized view of women and men in their gender roles. But as they grow older, their interaction with certain individuals leads them to see some people as "significant others." These are the ones who begin shaping the individual meaning of gender for a child. Who are these significant others? A father, mother, grandfather, grandmother, uncle, aunt, or sibling. This is the point at which children start to understand themselves as individuals, separate from others. They begin to grasp that others see and respond to them as individuals—unique people with a particular gender.

Like other behaviors, gender roles are learned through reprimands and rewards and indirectly through observation and imitations. My trying to set the record straight with Armand—"Honey, you're a boy"—is a perfect case in point. Indeed, I remember my mother instructing eight-year-old Alexandra to "sit like a lady" when she found her slouched in a chair with her legs apart on a rare day when she was wearing a dress.

The logic is simple: different reinforcement occurs for behaving either girlishly or boyishly. As children consider the consequences of various behaviors, they learn to act in accordance with that which is associated with rewards. They develop an awareness that the two sexes behave differently, and two gender roles are proper. This becomes the basis for gender identity.

By age six, a girl knows she is a girl and will remain one. It is at this point that a gender identity can solidify. It is also at this point that a child begins to develop a sense of self, with gender at its center. The two notions become strongly entwined. Indeed, once children develop a gender identity, they organize most of their behaviors around it and seek models labeled girl or boy. As they understand their own gender, they tend to behave in a manner consistent with that label. They would say, in effect, "I am a boy, therefore I want to do boy things."

Gender roles are taught by a child's significant others, but they are also reinforced indirectly by myriad stimuli that constantly repeat within society. Take television, for example. By the time a child reaches eighteen, he or she will have spent more time watching TV than engaging in any other activity other than sleep. Interestingly, research has shown that young children, unable to actually follow the plots of situation comedies, may, in fact, learn much about sex roles from simply observing and absorbing actors' nonverbal behaviors. Even highly regarded, politically correct shows such as *Sesame Street* err toward the representation of more dominant male characters; Burt and Ernie, Big Bird, Oscar the Grouch, the Cookie Monster, Kermit, and Grover are all male Muppets.

Advertising also makes an impact on the solidification of sex roles. According to psychologists Clara Mayo, at Boston University, and Nancy Henley, at the University of California, Los Angeles, even when TV ads reflect shifts in our culture by portraying a woman in what was once thought of as a more "masculine" role, like that of a physician, "the models' nonverbal displays reflect traditional femininity in facial expression, hairstyle and makeup, [and] body posture." Think of the pain killer ads with women dressed in a doctor's white coat but with perfectly coiffed hair and full makeup. These messages are not restricted to the airwaves. Psychologist Jean Umiker-Sebeok also found sex role cues in magazine advertisements in which toddler girls are depicted differently from boys. "Clothing, hairstyles, nonverbal behavior and size relationships combine to associate females with smallness, weakness, and subordination," she wrote in a book chapter titled, "The Seven Ages of Women: A View from American Magazine Advertisements."

Lessons Learned

School is also a powerful socializing factor. Female teachers call on boys more often and allow them to interrupt, while girls are encouraged to politely raise their hands. Of course, girls' relatively docile behavior creates a situation in which teachers have to spend more time dealing with the more difficult male students. But it also reinforces a more passive interaction style. In their groundbreaking book, *Failing at Fairness: How America's Schools Cheat Girls*, researchers Myra and David Sadker document how teachers unwittingly impart "subtle gender lessons along with math and spelling." In observing a fifth grade class learning about the presidents of the United States, the Sadkers singled out one boy and one girl for comment, as they describe how these ten-year-olds react to their teacher's questions:

> First the boy waves his hand straight in the air so that the teacher will select him from the surrounding forest of mainly male arms. He waves and pumps for almost three minutes without success. Evidently tiring, he puts his right arm down only to replace it with the left. Wave and pump. Wave and pump. Another two minutes go by. Still no recognition. Down with the left hand, up with the right. He moves to strategy two—sounds: "Ooh, me. C'mon. C'mon. Pleeze. Oooooh!" . . . He gets out of his seat, stands in front of the desk, and waves with sound effects for another thirty seconds.

Eventually, the teacher calls on him. According to the Sadkers, "He has spent more than nine minutes in his effort to get a half-minute in the sun." While this is going on, they observe what happens with the girl:

> She begins the class with her arm held high, her face animated, her body leaning forward. Clearly she has something she wants

to say. She keeps her right hand raised for more than a minute, switches to the left for forty-five seconds. She is not called on. She doesn't make noises or jump out of her seat but it looks as though her arm is getting tired. She reverts to propping the right arm up with the left, a signal she maintains for two more minutes. Still no recognition. The hand comes down.

Having failed in gaining the teacher's attention, the girl then sits quietly, stares out the window, and plays with the hair of the girl in front of her. The Sadkers explain, "Her face is no longer animated. She crosses her arms on the desk and rests her head on them, which is how she spends the final twelve minutes of class time. Her eyes are open but it is impossible to tell if she is listening."

How many of us can identify with these two scenarios? I'll bet plenty. What's even more interesting is that when the Sadkers played back the videos they'd taken of kids in class, most of the teachers were "stunned" to recognize that they gave their male students more attention. But by their actions, the teachers were imparting many important lessons. According to the Sadkers, the message conveyed to both genders was, "Boys should be academically assertive and grab teacher attention; girls should act like ladies and keep quiet." We should not be surprised, therefore, that in the workplace, men interrupt more, get the floor more often, and talk longer than women do. This is how they have been socialized to behave.

Nonverbal Differences Begin to Emerge

With continued reinforcement, nonverbal differences between boys and girls begin to emerge. According to psychologists Barbara Bate and Judy Bowker, girls hear from many sources that they should be restrained and avoid calling attention to themselves. Boys, in contrast, are told early in life to stand tall, act like a man, and show confidence and assertiveness even if their façade contradicts their own feelings. "Young girls generally figure out they will be rewarded for being quiet, clean, passive and polite. Young boys learn that being active outdoors and forceful in defending themselves will win them praise," Bate and Bowker explain. Over time these messages play themselves out in how youngsters behave nonverbally. Girls in our society are missing in action; they don't call attention to themselves and are less bold and active than boys.

Linguist Deborah Tannen also analyzed conversations of children and young adults of both sexes to compare nonverbal cues during conversation. At each of the four age levels she studied (second, sixth, and tenth grade students, and twenty-five-year-old adults), girls and women sat closer to each other, aligned their bodies more directly facing each other, had greater eye contact, and touched more. At these same age levels, boys and men sat at angles to each other, looked more at their surroundings than at each other, and gave the impression of restlessness and diffuse attention. Boys appeared to be less engaged than the girls.

However, Tannen points out, the appearance of detachment does not mean that the chats were disengaged. In fact, the tenth grade boys were involved in disclosing conversations. Tannen concluded that conversational patterns differ between males and females. It's clear that these nonverbal differences can be detected as early as age seven.

During adolescence, male and female sex role identification becomes entrenched. This is the time when girls engage in coy behavior while boys cement the aggressive stare-down. Bulimia and anorexia are excellent if not tragic examples that nonverbally to be female must mean that you should be as petite as possible. On the other hand, the cultural messages would dictate that teenage boys become addicted to bodybuilding or athletic competition in the hope of approaching their own gender ideal.

Adherence to sex role norms is stronger for boys than for girls; boys will be admonished for playing with dolls more than girls will be for playing with trucks. This is partially driven by homophobia. When females cross over and assume masculine behaviors, they may be called tomboys. But in no way do girls experience the degree of rebuke that boys do when boys slip into feminine behaviors. According to Bate and Bowker, there are fewer and less visible attempts to change the climate for young boys than there are to change the climate for young girls.

Moving Toward Adulthood

Being the mother of both a son and a daughter, my own home-based gender lab reminds me on a daily basis of how children are constantly learning the cues and being reinforced on what it means to be a woman or a man in our society. Recently, my son walked in with his tenth-grade school photos. When I looked at them I couldn't help but gasp and blurt out, "Wow, Armand you have such a tough look on your face!"

"Well, what do you want?" he replied. "Should I look cute and smile like the girls?"

Becoming men and women in our world goes way beyond biology. The different nonverbal treatment of girl and boy infants illustrates that socialization begins at birth, shaping us to behave in "appropriate" ways. These sex role messages are so strong, in fact, that gender communication expert Judy Pearson claims, "it may be surprising that children do not develop specific sex role conceptions earlier than they do." The evidence makes it clear that the majority of our nonverbal behaviors are acquired through the socialization process. This is particularly true of gender display. Sex differences in nonverbals are expected.

Children are bombarded with subtle and not so subtle messages on a daily basis of what "maleness" and "femaleness" are, and they begin to act out these messages verbally and nonverbally. We know that boys are more rigid than girls in their sex roles and in exhibiting the appropriate behavior. This strict adherence and lack of flexibility will be part of our discussion in later chapters.

Gender Prescriptions

We have made the argument that we are unaware of much of our nonverbal behavior. It is a challenge to change something that has become so ritualized, routine, and unconscious. If we can better understand the underpinnings and how these roots are established, we can start to change the nonverbal behaviors that work against us. That is the mission of this book: to peel away the layers and identify the undesirable nonverbals we can change. In the coming chapters, you'll learn how.

GENDER RX

- Boys and girls live in very different worlds.

- Some of this difference is attributed to biology, but much is based on how kids are socialized.

- Babies enter the world communicating nonverbally—reading and expressing nonverbal signals.

- Gender is critical to how parents orient themselves toward a new baby. By their interactions and socializing influence, parents begin teaching nonverbal behaviors to their young children from very early on.

- Children also learn gender roles through reprimands, rewards, and observation. By age six, they have clearly defined sex role identities.

- School also has a powerful socializing influence.

- Nonverbal differences begin to emerge among boys and girls; by adolescence, they solidify.

- Adherence to sex role norms is stronger for boys than for girls.

CHAPTER THREE

Let's Face It

Your face, my thane, is as a book where men may read strange matters.

—SHAKESPEARE, MACBETH, ACT I

A friend of mine, a psychologist, told me the following story that really illustrates why the face matters so much when it comes to nonverbal communication. Diane had applied for a great faculty position at a prestigious school in New England. During the American Psychological Association's annual convention, she met with the chair of the department's search committee. "The interviewer told me that I was their top candidate," she later recounted to me. "The job was mine if I still wanted it." Soon after her interview, Diane ran into a colleague at the convention, a professor at a university in Florida. He had been trying to get a better job for several years, and since they were both in the field of personality theory, he frequently vied for the same positions she did.

"Unfortunately for Jim, I always got those jobs over him," Diane admitted. "So when I saw him at the convention, I asked how his job search was going. 'I applied at a university in Boston,' he told me. 'I think I'm quite high on their list and have a good chance of getting it.' Although I knew otherwise, I didn't want to let on that I was after the same position and was likely to land it, which, in fact, I did.

"At the next national convention," Diane continued, "I ran into Jim again and apologized for not telling him what I had known the previous year. 'Oh, you don't have to apologize,' he said. 'I already knew you had applied and that you thought you were going to get it just from the expression on your face.'"

Although Diane believed she had concealed the truth from Jim, her face gave her away! As we'll see more extensively in this chapter, women externalize their emotions. They have been raised to be expressive, as evidenced by common adages such as, "You can read a woman like a book," and "She wears her heart on her sleeve."

> *Human beings are capable of making 250,000 facial expressions without uttering a word.*

Women engage in a greater variety of facial expressions of all sorts than men. They smile, blush, and grimace and look sad, surprised, and perplexed with much greater frequency. And this makes a big difference in how men and women relate to each other.

Why is the face so important? Of course we communicate from the neck down, but the majority of meaning and the richest source of nonverbal data come from the face. Our visage provides the most information about *how* we feel, and our body movements indicate the *intensity* of the emotion. According to anthropologist Ray Birdwhistell, human beings are capable of making 250,000 facial expressions without uttering a word. Other researchers have found that we can more accurately pick up stress messages from others' facial expressions than from what they tell us verbally. We know not to believe "Oh, no, I'm fine. Not to worry . . ." when furrowed brows, sagging cheeks, and downturned lips tell us otherwise.

In this chapter, we will explore the importance of facial expression as well as the strong dichotomy in facial management that exists between women and men, and the miscommunications that can occur when these two very distinct styles clash.

How Do We Acquire Facial Expressions?

Why do we smile but not scowl when we're happy? Why do we turn up our noses but not raise our eyebrows when we feel disgust? Some researchers argue that facial expressions are inborn reactions of the nervous system common to all cultures. In 1872, Charles Darwin suggested that shaking your head to indicate "no" developed from a baby's turning away and refusing the mother's breast when satiated.

German ethnologist Irenaus Eibel-Eibesfeldt agreed with Darwin and offered the example of children born blind who—without deliberate training—nevertheless exhibit the normal repertoire of facial expressions that sighted children do. Paul Ekman, a professor of psychology at University of California, San Francisco, suggested a neurocultural theory of nonverbal expression. Along with his colleague Wallace Friesen, he found that emotions like happiness, anger, fear, surprise, disgust/contempt, interest, and sadness were expressed similarly in all cultures. And work with families shows that family members express the same emotions in the same way. This could be one reason that relatives look alike (this is even true when children are adopted—perhaps because the muscles in the face are exercised in a certain way and so develop correspondingly).

So, our facial expressions are inborn but are subtly influenced by our families and cultures. In addition, we humans are also relatively adept at controlling them. Ekman and Friesen argue that there are four reasons for us to do so:

- *Cultural Rules.* Cultures dictate certain rules for facial expressions. For example, in our society, men are not supposed to show fear in public, and women should not show anger. Rules may vary. For instance, men are allowed to cry at funerals. But even funerals have a pecking order: at the memorial of a male boss who died suddenly, the female secretary should show less grief than the wife or she might suggest something improper about her relationship with him.

- *Personal Rules.* Families may enforce idiosyncratic imperatives: "Never look angry," "Overplay every emotion," or "We're one big happy family."

- *Vocational Requirements.* Actors, doctors, nurses, psychologists, lawyers, and politicians, among others must manage their facial expressions to be successful at their jobs.

- *Need of the Moment.* Moment-to-moment requirements of particular situations that are not connected with your work may necessitate control of facial expressions. Consider, for example, staying cool while lying, or maintaining a poker face when you encounter your lover while you're with your spouse.

In essence, the expressions on our faces result from a blend of nature, nurture, and personal will—a complex mix, indeed.

The Resting Face: Friend or Foe?

Several years ago, I was teaching one of the more difficult communication courses at the University of Colorado in Boulder. For the entire semester, a young man sat in the back row of the classroom with a knitted brow and scowl. His expression conveyed a combination of perplexity, anger, and confusion. In trying to determine what made Mike so unhappy in my course, I went through a host of questions in my head: Does he hate 8 AM classes? Does he understand what I'm saying? Is the material too tough? Could I explain it better? Does he disagree with the course content? Maybe he doesn't like *me*. I was starting to take his negative expression personally.

The other students were receptive and animated; they leaned forward in their seats, their eyebrows were lifted showing interest, they nodded their heads as I made my points, and they smiled or laughed when I cracked a joke. But this fellow never seemed to move off his bad mood, and I didn't know what to do about it. As a good communicator I usually make adjustments, so I tried this with Mike; I framed my message in a different way, I made eye contact, I smiled at him. However, during the course of the semester, nothing that I did made a difference with Mike. I began withdrawing from this young man. In fact, I did adjust by minimizing my eye contact with him, because his off-putting expression started having a profoundly negative influence on my classroom presentation. Eventually, I chose to ignore him because his expression was just too distracting.

At long last, the day of the final exam arrived. When the exam period ended, Mike walked up to the front of the room, handed me his blue book, and proceeded to shake my hand. "Dr. Nelson," he said with surprising enthusiasm, "I just wanted to thank you. I'm a business major, and this is one of the best—if not *the* best—communication course I've ever taken."

You could have knocked me over with a feather! "You're kidding," I couldn't help blurting. I quickly regained my composure and said, "Mike, I need to share with you how you come off nonverbally."

"Oh no, I know what you're going to say," he interrupted. "Friends tell me they see me walking across campus, and they don't want to say hello because I look like I'm mad and grumpy." Then he apologized.

Once Mike started talking, he seemed congenial. His scowl simply evaporated.

I explained to him that he was going to have to take responsibility for his nonverbal behavior: "For your professional health in the business world, you'll need to pay attention to the messages you're sending people."

Our natural affect is the expression our faces take on when we're not trying to express anything. It's what Emory University psychologists Stephen Nowicki Jr. and Marshall Duke call the "resting face." "You're 'in neutral emotionally,'" they explain in their book *Will I Ever Fit In?* The natural affect that we develop is really a composite of who we are—our personal history and experiences over time, including the set of our jaw and the accumulation of wrinkles. If we're often amazed, we lift our eyebrows and consequently develop lines on our foreheads; sadness and depression etch deep furrows around our mouths; crows' feet or "laugh lines," the crinkles at the corners of our eyes, betray a merrier temperament. I once met an unhappy woman whose habit of pursing her lips in disapproval constantly made it seem as if she had just eaten a bitter nut.

You can see the toll that stress takes on one's resting face by simply observing before-and-after photos of our presidents (save perhaps Abraham Lincoln whose battle with depression gave him a dour, careworn aspect no matter what stage he was in his presidency). We can easily read the burden of holding the highest office on our leaders' resting faces.

Our natural affect is also inborn and dependent on physical bone structure and weight. Thinner people with angular features and narrow lips look harder to us (and are often cast as heavies in the movies) whereas those with more rounded cheeks and full lips seem softer, and we call them baby faced. One's resting face can even be drug induced. People taking cortisone or other steroidal medications develop rounded "moon" faces over time, and certainly many celebrities and appearance-conscious women have tightened their resting faces with the help of a plastic surgeon's scalpel. Whatever your natural affect (and you can check it out by studying your own blank expression in the mirror), be aware that it is the countenance others will observe when you're least aware of it. It's also the canvas upon which your other facial expressions will be painted.

In our culture, we expect women to have a more affable resting face. Females are engaged in building relationships, connections, and interdependence. Because they often are "other" oriented, I believe that women generally want to appear facially open and receptive. Many a female will walk around with a subtle smile on her face. Since women seem more approachable, strangers will come up to them and ask, "Do you know where the tuna is?" or "Can you reach that box for me?" in the supermarket. It's rare that someone would approach an unfamiliar man for that kind of help.

The genial expression is so important to how women are perceived; if they don't display an open or friendly natural affect, others may seek to correct them. In fact, this very predicament happened to me. I was at the airport, on my way home from a three-days-in-a-row, six-hours-a-day training session. I was exhausted, and my feet hurt (darn those new heels!). I leaned against the waiting area podium, grimacing in pain. Suddenly a man walked up to me, a complete stranger, and offered, "Hey, you're not smiling."

"I don't feel like smiling," I shot back. "My feet are killing me." He acted as if I had the bubonic plague and hurried away in a huff. I had stepped out of the prescribed sex role. To conform to this stranger's expectations, I should have quickly changed my affect to a happy face—that's the requirement for women.

The Animated Woman

As I've pointed out, developmentally young girls are socialized to become "high expressers." And as they grow into adulthood, women in our culture are far more facially animated and expressive than males.

As journalist Daryn Eller notes in an article in *O, The Oprah Magazine,* "Somewhere in the back of minds we know that expressiveness is beautiful. It is, after all, one of the first things we pull out of our bag of tricks to attract others. . . . It's not Audrey Hepburn's wide eyes that make us never tire of watching her in *Breakfast at Tiffany's.* It's the way she lifts them in wonder and surprise. It's not just Meryl Streep's high cheekbones that rivet us to her face. It's the amusement, intelligence, and vulnerability that play across it." Think of other highly expressive actresses—Halle Berry, Julia Roberts, Nicole Kidman, Renée Zellweger, Winona Ryder, or Julianne Moore. Part of their appeal, attraction, and certainly their success is owed to the transparent emotionality that illuminates their beautiful features.

Female facial expressiveness has even been measured scientifically. Monika Thunberg and Monika Ulfdinberg, psychologists at Uppsala University in Sweden, report that when placed in emotion-evoking situations—such as when they're shown pictures of angry faces or snakes in a laboratory—women actually generate larger facial muscle activity. Their faces move more than men's faces do. Although we don't know why this is true, it may be that females have a more sensitive perceptive ability and therefore react more intensely. That is, because they are better at reading nonverbal cues, they may also be more dynamic in expressing them.

The female animated face acts both for and against women. Because they are so expressive, women often do give themselves away. This can be endearing, but it may not always be an advantageous strategy. Sometimes it might be better to conceal what you feel, like when you're negotiating a contract or buying a car. On the positive side, we often believe that we do know how a woman is feeling. She is more authentic and available because her emotions are more transparent. We are drawn to people who are animated and have expression; their openness increases our comfort level.

Yet we cannot ignore the fact that some women might use their expressive physiognomies to manipulate others. Recent research explores the possibility that charismatic women (but not men) who are highly animated and skilled at nonverbal facial expression may learn to use those skills to mask dominant or aggressive personalities, which are not acceptable in females in this culture. Perceived by others as friendly, these women may appear to be warm and unthreatening when, in fact, they have quite another agenda on their minds.

And, as a final note, we can't ignore the female head tilt. Darwin once said, "Women cock their heads like barnyard chickens." Head tilts are a universal sign of acquiescence that are exhibited cross-culturally and even among other species. When a dog wants to show submission, it tilts its head toward the dominant animal, exposing the vulnerable jugular. Women often employ the head tilt when they're engaged in empathic listening. You couldn't listen to someone benevolently with your nose in the air. On the other hand, the head stretch dominance display (chin/nose up) is a sign of power and control. It says, "I'm in charge." In contrast to "holding your head high," the head tilt conveys empathy but also can communicate submission, thereby undermining credibility.

The Smiley-Face Syndrome

The song lyrics are so true: "When you're smiling, the whole world smiles with you." Dr. Susan C. Vaughan has written, "If you serve up a smile to people they usually bounce it back. Hit them with a snarl and watch them scowl instead." Facial expressions and the moods that accompany them are contagious. As Michael Cunningham, a psychology professor at the University of Louisville, explained in an interview in *O, The Oprah Magazine*, "Facial expressions are nearly as important as physical features in determining attractiveness. When people are smiling, others are drawn to them much more than if they look cold." Indeed, psychiatrist R. D. Laing once explained that when we assume different body positions, we begin to feel the emotions that go along with them. The smile can actually put us into a happier state.

Yes, smiling is wonderful. It brings people together; it makes them happy. It is a marvelous nonverbal expression that we all should cherish. I would never assert that women should stop smiling. But when they overuse the smile or use it inappropriately, it can certainly hurt them. In fact, smiling at the wrong time can get them into trouble.

A friend recently relayed her experiences as a twenty-year-old coed, spending her junior year abroad in the romantic city of Paris. "Coming straight from Durham, North Carolina (a quiet, Southern college town), to Paris (a noisy, European metropolis)," she told me, "I had a lot to learn about appropriate facial expressions. For the first two months of my stay, I was the recipient of innumerable unsolicited advances. Apparently the open, friendly (smiley) facial expression that worked so well on the quad did not work at all in the big city. I soon learned to keep a no-nonsense, flat facial demeanor on while I walked purposefully from the Metro stop to the Sorbonne. As soon as my face stopped looking so 'invitational,' I was freed from unwanted attention. My face began to blend in with the sea of city faces." My friend's troubles stemmed from cultural differences; what passes for an amicable face in one country can be an open invitation in another.

Moreover, people who smile inappropriately or excessively may have problems in our culture. They can be perceived as untrustworthy or insincere—even phony. Former President Jimmy Carter had a reputation for smiling inappropriately; often his grin seemed to act like a punctuation mark after he had delivered some serious news. Consequently, he developed a credibility problem with the American public. People in dominant positions don't need to smile. They already have established power and status through their title or position. Positive and likeable facial expressions can even be counterproductive for them.

Women often get in trouble with smiling too much or inappropriately—what I call the "smiley-face syndrome" or the "painted-on smile." Think of the Cheshire Cat in *Alice in Wonderland*. It smiled all the time. In fact, even when its body disappeared, the smile remained. What we recall about the cat is not its substance but its smile, in much the same way that what we may recall about a woman is the fact that she's smiling rather than her verbal complaints about mistreatment or other injustices.

This sort of perpetual smile may be driven by women's need to ingratiate themselves and appease the men in their lives. They will smile to ensure goodwill, to neutralize a threatening environment, to gain acceptance, to keep the peace, to promote safety and well-being.

Gina, a friend of mine, grew up in a large Italian family. She once shared with me how her mother used the perpetual peacekeeping smile. "The dinner table at our house was where we all came together at the end of the day," she explained. "We would share the day's events, but my father was sometimes unhappy to hear the individual reports from all his children especially when they included a bad test grade, a fight on the playground, or the cost of a uniform for sports.

"One day, my younger sister sat down for dinner with a ring in her nose. This was not merely a stud, but a sizeable ring; it was so large you could probably put a rope through it and lead her around like a cow. We all stared in disbelief. My father's jaw dropped, and then his expression quickly turned into a scowl. He looked at my mother, who sat there with a beatific smile as if it were a beacon sending the signal to keep the peace so we all could digest our dinner with minimal tension and resulting indigestion. This was a signal I had learned to heed. It meant, 'Not here, we will discuss this later.'"

A smile also serves to contradict or soften the verbal message: "If I have to come off as forceful in an area, I can use the smile to counterbalance it so I won't seem so hard." Like Karen, the thirty-two-year-old director of advertising whom we met in Chapter 1, women may even smile when the situation appears to be at odds with their facial expression, such as when they're in the midst of an argument or giving bad news or expressing unhappiness. Inappropriate chuckling and giggling go along with the perpetual smile.

Let's all bear in mind that when a baby girl emerges from the womb, she is not pulled out smiling or giggling excessively. Yet research shows that women will smile anytime, to anybody, anywhere. I remember a client who couldn't punctuate a sentence, no matter what its import, without a giggle. This laughing softened and counterbalanced the verbal message; the stronger the message, the more the giggling. Most men, on the other hand, smile as if they're spending $1,000 bills.

Women have learned excessive smiling during their socialization process. They are the caretakers and nurturers; they learn that they shouldn't rock the boat. Harriet Lerner explains in her book *The Dance of Anger* that nice girls don't engage in conflict or anger. They're supposed to act happy. Even pensiveness, pain, and neutrality are considered unacceptable. Just like my experience at the airport, a serious woman will be asked, "How come you're not smiling today?" But such behavior is rarely demanded of men.

The female sex role prescription that women should be continually cheerful is concretized at work in the role of office cheerleader. This duty is assigned to women; they maintain the peace. In *Room with No View: A Woman's Guide to the Man's World of the Media*, Ethel Strainchamps describes how the women working at NBC in the 1970s needed to behave:

> The duty of the morale booster is assigned to NBC women, and the role is essential in keeping male producers, executives, and brass on their feet. The unspoken command is: "Smile!" And the woman who doesn't smile each time her boss enters the office

(or elevator or cafeteria), and who doesn't smile regularly (god forbid she should actually frown in the presence of her boss) is chided with "Don't look so sullen," "Whatsamatter, sourpuss?" and similar remarks.

Obviously, the situation hasn't changed all that much in the last thirty years.

Women may also smile excessively, not for any immediate or conscious purpose, but because of pressure they feel to fulfill the sex role expectations. Their smiles could reflect nervousness, which is a consequence of this pressure. When women are ill at ease, they'll exaggerate the behavior that was emphasized as appropriate for them while they were growing up. These kinds of smiles may not be genuine. In fact, women often exhibit what I call the "Miss America smile." This is a contrived expression that says, "I aim to please." This plastered-on smile is especially prevalent in corporate America, where I see women slap it on as if they're flipping a light switch. As soon as a woman comes across someone and meets his or her eyes, boom, the smile turns on.

Although excessive smiling is endemic to women in our society, research has shown that the smiley-face syndrome is less prevalent among African-American women, who generally do not smile as much as white women. This reminds us that requirements for femininity vary by culture. As one female African-American engineer told me, "When I attended my first staff meeting, I could not believe how much white women smiled. It's an Uncle Tom issue for me." She was proud of her Ph.D. in engineering and did not feel she needed to placate anyone, especially not white men!

Although smiling serves its purpose, it can become one of the major credibility robbers for women when there is inconsistency between facial expression (in the form of smiling or giggling) and verbal expression when they deliver bad news. This incongruence undermines the message and is confusing, especially to men.

My advice to women who have fallen victim to the smiley-face syndrome? Of course, they should not stop smiling altogether—especially if they're happy about a situation, and the context calls for a grin. Smiles have value. Just the act of smiling creates a sense of internal well-being, and makes others feel good too. But smiling all the time? No! Women should become aware of and manage more assiduously their tendency toward *excessive* or *inappropriate* smiling. No one is relentlessly happy; women who smile continuously aren't taken seriously. (Those who always have smiles plastered on their faces end up looking like the town idiot!) Serious, intense messages deserve congruent facial expressions. If a woman finds herself in a conflict situation and is upset and angry, she is best served by exhibiting her true emotions in face, voice, and gesture.

How does one become conscious of the automatic or excessive smile? In my years of teaching communication, I would send my female students out in the world with instructions to smile only when they genuinely felt happy. This often felt foreign to them, but it did make them focus on the behavior. In *Gendered Lives,* Julia Wood reprints the journal entry of a female student carrying out a similar assignment. Here is how Elaine described her experience, which you might try too:

> I never thought it would be so hard not to smile. When you challenged us in class to go one day without smiling except when we really felt happy, I thought it would be easy. I couldn't do it. I smile when I meet people, I smile when I purchase things, I even

smile when someone bumps into me. I never realized how much I smile—all the time.

What was most interesting about the experiment was how my boyfriend reacted. We got together last night and I was still working on not smiling. He asked me what was wrong. I told him nothing. I was being perfectly nice and talkative and everything, but I wasn't smiling all the time like I usually do. He kept asking what was wrong, was I unhappy, had something happened—even was I mad.

I would follow Shulamith Firestone's recommendation, as described in *The Dialectic of Sex*:

In my own case, I had to train myself out of that phony smile which is like a nervous tic on every teenage girl. And this meant that I smiled rarely for in truth, when it came down to real smiling, I had less to smile about. My dream action is a smile boycott at which declaration all women would instantly abandon their pleasing smiles, henceforth smiling only when something pleased them.

Botox Beauty

Today's women sometimes don't use makeup to hide the signs of aging, but rather Botox (botulism neurotoxin), which paralyzes tiny facial muscles and consequently erases wrinkles, at least temporarily. I find it ironic, however, that while these injections minimize signs of aging, they have the unwanted consequence of reducing one's repertoire of facial expressions—the female animated face. A woman who has received Botox treatments to her forehead or the corners of her mouth, for instance, may have difficulty frowning or showing displeasure, smiling or acting surprised. Dr. Nancy Etcoff, a Harvard psychologist and author of *Survival of the Prettiest,* has said that in a Botox nation we look at wrinkles the way we regard cracked and discolored teeth, as remnants of the past. "It's as though we have given up authenticity," she explains.

Maureen Dowd, a columnist for the *New York Times,* recently noted, "Five years ago, Anna Quindlen wrote there are three stages in the life span of a woman: pre-Babe, Babe, and post-Babe. There are now four: pre-Babe, Babe, Botox-Babe, Cher. Baby Boomer Babes don't want to be post anything, even if it means freezing their faces into freakish death masks." Actor/director Robert Redford is even less generous toward women who use these treatments. He recently called expressionless beauty just plain ugly. "You end up looking body-snatched," he explained, referring to the 1950s cult film *Invasion of the Body Snatchers,* in which aliens took over people's bodies and made completely expressionless duplicates of them.

The power of our expressions is worth considering especially in this era of face-lifts and Botox injections. One of psychology professor Carroll E. Izard's studies at the University of Delaware suggests that we eradicate lines and wrinkles and the expressions that cause some of them at our own peril. Researchers in Izard's lab asked mothers to smile while playing with their three-month-old infants. The women were then asked to assume a neutral face. The lack of expression disturbed the babies in the study who responded with sadness and anger. Adults may react the same way. "Emotional expression is an essential part of our social communication." Izard explains. Often we are more influenced by what we see than by what we hear from others. So diminishing expression has serious implications for the nonverbal messages we send.

Perhaps the deeper irony here is that the use of Botox can influence how women and men relate to each other. The lack of facial animation renders women more like men. And, as Maureen Dowd sees it, it can even cause interpersonal clashes between the genders: "After all these years of trying to train men to respond better to emotional cues, women are making it even harder by erasing the emotion from their faces."

At First Blush

I was conducting one of my "He Speaks, She Speaks" seminars on gender communication when a male participant began talking about the obvious biological differences between men and women, including their genitalia. I picked up the thread, and continued to discuss how genitals are one obvious marker of the differences. I was on my way to an elaboration on body size and how "big" men can get, meaning how much personal space they can take up. "Men have a tendency to get big," I began. But the audience was still stuck on the idea of genitalia. Another male participant chimed in, "Yeah they get big. They better get big. Isn't that what she wants?"

I blushed with embarrassment. I was center stage; there was no escaping. I took a deep breath and threw the hot potato back at the audience. "I know where your mind is," I said, "but I'm not there." And then I went on with the rest of my discussion, reminding myself that if I could bring the discussion back out of the gutter, my blush would disappear. Several times in my career, I've found myself in situations like this one that caused me to blush—usually when the discussion turns sexual. Although the blush is discomfiting, I also know that it makes me seem more human and approachable to my audience—it's not necessarily a bad reaction.

Virtually everyone blushes at least once in a while, and research evidence shows that women report a higher propensity for blushing than men. Indeed, social blushing is both a common emotional response and a communicative signal. The blood rushes to our faces when we're self-conscious. And as if that weren't bad enough, our red faces let others know exactly how we're feeling. It's a one-two punch.

Peter J. de Jong, a psychologist at Maastricht University in the Netherlands, explains that despite its frequency, the majority of people consider blushing highly undesirable, and they often try to stop or conceal it—though that's impossible since blushing is a function of our autonomic nervous system. We have no control over this response. However, de Jong points out, "some individuals experience so much distress associated with blushing that they may develop a blushing phobia and apply for treatment."

Why do people blush in the first place? They are likely to redden if they violate social rules that they share with someone observing them.

1. The blusher is assumed to communicate that he or she is sensitive to the judgment of the observer.

2. Blushing is a display of embarrassment.

3. It may serve as an appeasement function—you caught me red-handed!

Sometimes a blush betrays anxiety. In fact, Carla's blushing always gave away how nervous she was when speaking in front of an audience. She flushed bright red down her neck and on her chest whenever she had to give an oral presentation (this included performances, teaching a class, or talking about her research). The situation was exacerbated by the fact that she always wore plunging necklines. Then one day, a kind colleague pointed out that her attire was inadvertently divulging her nervousness; until that point, Carla had had no clue that gigantic red splotches appeared on her neck and chest when she spoke in public. She eliminated the décolletage, and her stage fright was less readily apparent.

Blushing is a relatively frequent occurrence in women who might feel a bit embarrassed by it. Still, it makes us real and vulnerable. Besides, we're used to expressing our feelings. But blushing is a major loss of face for a man; it's equivalent to his crying in public since it conveys a loss of control. And it also undermines his strong need to mask his emotions.

Just like we can't control our heartbeat, we can't stop ourselves from blushing. It's an autonomic response. But a verbal comment might be in order—"Whew, this is awkward for me. I am embarrassed!" When we admit the feeling of embarrassment, it makes us more real and human to others.

Who Is That Masked Man, Anyway?

Francine has a bone to pick with her husband. Eddie comes home haggard and stressed, night after night, unwilling to share the drama that's obviously going on at his office. When she asks him how he's feeling, rather than welcoming her concern, she senses that he tenses up. Eddie's face seems to turn to stone as he grunts, "I don't want to talk about it." If she badgers him further, he turns his head away, becomes absorbed in the newspaper, and withdraws all eye contact, leaving Francine feeling left out in the cold and probably angry.

This scenario repeats itself night after night in millions of households. Yet it might help to understand that whereas a cardinal rule for female nonverbal behavior is, "Thou shalt be animated," one of the Ten Commandments of masculinity is, "Thou shalt not be vulnerable." Rather than revealing their emotions on their faces, men have learned to internalize them. They mask.

Face management is paramount to many men. It is the corollary to control, and control is a bedfellow to power. The male monotonic face conveys, "You can't move me, you can't shake me; I'll decide if I let you in (and I probably won't). I'll decide who is in control of my emotions." The masked man is a mystery. Does that mean men don't have feelings? Of course not. But they don't show their emotions. Whether in a business situation or a marital dispute, a man's stone face can become incendiary.

The male lack of eyebrow activity is a case in point. Whereas the brow lift is an integral element of a woman's nonverbal repertoire, its absence is part of a man's monotonic face—nothing moves. Men report the political value of this kind of facial management: it prevents anyone from knowing what they think and feel, which, although detrimental to interpersonal relationships, is often key to survival on a job. They don't want to let others see that they're afraid or doubting themselves. It behooves men in the workplace (but rarely in intimate relations) to hide their true emotions. As one man explained, "If everyone really knew what you thought or felt about your job, you wouldn't have it."

Indeed, men can keep a straight face when something strikes them funny, they can hide attraction to another woman when their wives are present, and they can suppress anger at their bosses. To do this, they substitute, de-emphasize, or neutralize their facial expressions.

- *In substituting, men might think:* "I'm really angry, but I'm going to act happy;" "I think the proposal stinks, but I'm going to act like it works;" "They offered me a raise that knocked my socks off, but I'm going to act unimpressed." Lance Armstrong used substitution in the 2001 Tour de France to fool the competition. He grimaced and appeared to struggle during the early sprint portions of the race (at which he was most skilled), leading the other teams to believe he was a weak competitor that year. The racers let down their guard, and Armstrong shot to the lead.

- *In de-emphasizing, men might think:* "I'm overjoyed by the price I've been able to negotiate for this car, but I'm going to act mildly pleased;" "I'm really angry, but I'm going to act vaguely perturbed;" "I'm frightened that my girlfriend will leave me, but I'm going to act confident."

- *In neutralizing, men might think:* "I don't want my wife to know what I feel. Period." And they stonewall.

And these days, Type A men are even resorting to Botox to reinforce their masked faces. According to a recent *Wall Street Journal* article subtitled, "Wipe That Smirk off Your Face. It's Bad for Business," "growing numbers of salesmen and lawyers, bankers and stockbrokers are fixing their facial expressions with Botox—freezing and sculpting their faces into semipermanent serenity." A survey conducted by the American Society of Plastic Surgeons found that about 12 percent of Botox devotees don't use the stuff to combat wrinkles and signs of aging but rather to address a "severe/angry facial expression."

Apparently, the frozen face gives men an even greater competitive edge. One patient—a forty-four-year-old principal at a real estate investment firm—attributed the 10 percent to 30 percent boost in his real estate deals to his treatments. "When you look strong and tough and not afraid," he explained in the article, "people respect you more. Showing less expression really makes a statement." Now that's downright scary!

Masking behaviors seem to operate more frequently in male-to-male interactions. In a book chapter titled "Who Can Resist a Smiling Baby?," Dick Pathier, a writer for the *Philadelphia Inquirer*, reported on research with women and men shown videotapes of cute babies and puppies. Women smiled a lot regardless of whether a male experimenter was around during the test. The men apparently suppressed their emotional reactions when another man was in the room. But when men watched the tapes alone, their facial expressions softened too. The researcher commented, "We think there are certain cultural rules among men that inhibit some emotional responses in men; especially a response of tenderness or affection. This may all sound theatrical or academic, but I think there is some practical significance to this finding. The one thing it seems to indicate is that you can change the behavior of males in all male groups, which is often boorish, crude and insensitive, by adding the presence of a woman."

For cultural or social reasons, a man may show either an inability or a reluctance to express gentleness in the presence of another male, though he may feel more comfortable doing so in front of a female. Again, it's a question of vulnerability. Men may give the impression of having no feelings when they are truly experiencing emotion (I sometimes have a hard time convincing my female audiences that men do feel). We also know that boys become increasingly skilled at inhibiting emotions as they move toward adolescence because impression management becomes more important as they near adulthood.

The most dramatic example of masking in my consulting practice occurs when I work with all-male teams of engineers. For six hours at a stretch, I talk to a group of deadpan faces. Nothing moves, nothing changes in their faces regardless of the stories I tell, the examples I use, the jokes I relate. My fantasies run wild as to what I can do to evoke some response from them. I imagine telling them, "Gentlemen, I'm getting ready to take off all of my clothes." But I predict nothing will happen. Or maybe their seats are wired with electrodes; I have the control panel up front with a button for each seat. I can push a button, and say, "Yo, Bill, what do you think of this idea?" and then send him a few volts. That's the only way I'll get a reaction from him.

Under the most extreme pressures, men will intensify their need to mask. However, it's also true that while men seek to maintain the stone face, it can develop stress fractures during times of crisis. Paul Ekman, a professor of psychology at University of California, San Francisco, talked in a January 2002 interview in O, *The Oprah Magazine* about how the man's face can break down sometimes and leak micro-facial expressions (quick involuntary flashes of emotion, lasting a fifth of a second or less, which appear on a person's face when he or she is trying to conceal something), especially under duress. Kato Kaelin's testimony during the O. J. Simpson murder was a textbook example: "He tried to present a calm, cool exterior, but there were several moments during cross examination when anger flashed across his face and it was clear there was some conflict between what he was saying and what he was feeling."

And President Bill Clinton lost control of his facial expression during the grand jury testimony over Monica Lewinsky and in his nationally televised speech later that evening after the testimonies. What America saw was a grim, grudging, tired man who was brimming with sullen anger. According to *Time* magazine reporter Peggy Noonan, "While the speech will live in infamy, Clinton dropped his Presidential mask, and for the first time the real Bill Clinton was being seen."

Mirroring: The Female Advantage

One of the advantages women have in communication is their ability to mirror—the nonverbal equivalent of paraphrasing. A woman may not repeat verbatim the person's facial expressions, but her expressions are similar and convey empathy. If, for instance, a woman is sad at the loss of a boyfriend, her good friend might also wear a sad expression. If a friend weeps over the death of a parent, she weeps with her. Among women, this is an unconscious, spontaneous behavior. Because it's spontaneous, it is perceived as authentic. It becomes most obvious when you observe mothers interacting with their babies, cooing and smiling when the baby is happy, and looking concerned when the baby cries.

In his best-seller, *Unlimited Power*, motivational guru Anthony Robbins gives advice about how to mirror another person:

Start with his voice. Mirror his tonality and phrasing, his pitch, how fast he talks and what sort of pauses he makes and his volume. Mirror his favorite words and phrases. How about posture and breathing patterns or eye contact, body language, facial expressions, hand gestures, or other distinctive movements. . . . What if you could mirror everything about another person? Do you know what happens? People feel as though they have found a soul-mate, someone who totally understands, who can read their deepest thoughts, who is just like them.

Robbins gives such explicit directions it would be hard for a person to be spontaneous in this interaction. Nevertheless, I can't help but believe that these instructions are directed toward men, who because of their masked faces have much more difficulty showing empathetic nonverbal expression. Mike, the grumpy student in the back of my classroom, is a great example of this. Although he told me he enjoyed my course, he certainly wasn't mirroring my enthusiasm. A man may be feeling sad for his friend—it's not that men don't feel—but he may have a hard time showing it because mirroring is not part of his training or experience.

Even though it may seem forced, Robbins's advice is what some men need to get started. They can "act out" the behavior, and eventually over time, it will become a part of his behavioral repertoire. Practice makes perfect.

Imagine Betsy, in the throes of a hairy divorce, approaching an attorney with her problems. If he doesn't exhibit much mirroring as she spills her guts, she might wonder:

- Is he paying attention?

- Does he care about my problems and me?

- Does he believe me?

- Will he watch out for me?

- Is he the lawyer for me?

You could almost make the argument that through mirroring, women exhibit superior interpersonal skills. But mirroring can also help in persuasive endeavors. It's a marvelous sales tool that can apply to your daily life.

The Poker Face: The Male Advantage

Poker might be thought of as a training ground for developing the masked face. Boys who play this game learn not to give away their hand with their nonverbal expressions, thereby tipping others as to how to bet. Over time, they develop the poker face, which can be a great advantage to them in adulthood during negotiations.

According to matrimonial attorney Eleanor B. Alter, men are "a lot less frightened by negotiating. They're not afraid to offer whatever they think they can get away with. Or they'll say, 'I'll offer very little and wait them out.' Women have a hard time with that." The poker face helps men seem as if they're maintaining their cool, even if they're not. As Alter explains, "Emotional detachment can be productive."

In a context of a negotiation, a woman can borrow and employ the poker face because it doesn't always behoove her to let others know what she feels. Suppose she's in a union negotiation with a union representative she dislikes. It would be smart for her to hide her disgust. We're all in situations when we're with people we don't like. What to do? Women can be more conscious of "controlling" their facial expressions (also other nonverbal cues like posture and gestures). They must watch for overly reactive facial expressions and maintain an air of neutrality. They practice the face they want to wear in the mirror!

The Clash of the Nonverbals

We expect emotionlessness from men. For women, however, the opposite is true. Our expectation is that women should be the happy, cheerful sex, which is reflected in the smiley-face syndrome. Many miscommunications can occur because female and male facial expressive styles vary so profoundly.

Although men might take on an air of neutrality, there is, in truth, no such thing as neutrality in communication. Women perceive blankness negatively. Men's masking of facial expressions causes uneasiness in women, just as it did in Carroll Izard's previously described study of infants with their mothers. This is why women often interpret men's monotonic facial expressions as punishing and admonishing or as negative feedback.

The monotonic face is one of the reasons women feel uncomfortable with men. Males can appear unavailable and emotionally inaccessible because it has political value to them; this is the ultimate nonverbal way for them to express their masculine control. (Indeed, Senator Bob Dole consciously tried to smile more during the 1996 presidential campaign to dissociate himself from his image as "Nasty Bob." On the other hand, the "naughty frat boy" smirk hurt George W. Bush's credibility with some voters during the 2000 presidential campaign.)

When a woman can't take a read on the man with whom she is

talking, it makes her anxious. She becomes confused and begins to doubt herself. She might even become more animated to spark a reaction, but the man will hold fast to his stony demeanor. Indeed, when a woman increases her expressiveness in this situation, the man may believe that she's becoming overly emotional. This undercuts her credibility. This is one of the occasions that prompts women to complain, "I get in trouble when I'm excited." As a consequence of male facial stonewalling, the woman may cut short the conversation, explode in a rage, or avoid personal contact altogether.

Some men love the stone face because they know that it makes the other person feel uncomfortable and throws them off balance. It puts them in control.

What should a woman do when she encounters this stratagem? I recommend that she recognize this ploy and then hang tough, refusing to be influenced by it. Or she can use the verbal package to expose the nonverbal, by saying, "I'm not getting a read right now on how you feel about what I'm saying. What do you think?" It's a powerful approach to let a man know that he is not intimidating her.

Face Reading and Misreading

In my seminars, to illustrate the importance of nonverbal communication and how much we rely on the face for our interactions, I ask audience members to pick a partner, form pairs, sit back to back, and carry on a conversation. Invariably, within fifteen to twenty seconds, predominantly the women will begin turning around to look at their partner. The men, on the other hand, tend to be less inclined to make that connection. In fact, when we debrief, the women in the audience express the most anxiety about breaking the rules—no peeking—that I'd set up.

Why should this be so? Not only are women better senders (encoders) of nonverbal messages, but they are also better readers of other people's facial expressions. Indeed, judging from my little exercise, women rely on these nonverbal cues to help make meaning of their interactions.

This has been borne out in cross-cultural research in the United States, Germany, Japan, and South Africa. These studies show that women are the more accurate interpreters of facial expressions, especially in stressful situations. They also have a superior capacity to recognize and decode micro-behaviors, the subtle momentary loss of control of facial expression that is often the truer, more accurate indicator of what a person is really feeling than what they say. Men miss the micro-behaviors and often focus on the verbal.

When men interact with women, their difficulties in accurately reading facial expressions may cause them problems, especially in the sexual arena. In my work with sexual harassment cases and also interpersonally among my friends, I have found that men often interpret a woman's nonverbal cues as sexual interest when, in fact, the women are merely being outgoing and friendly. Take the case of college classmates Jason and Wendy. One day they run into each other in the student union and decide to have coffee. Jason may perceive Wendy as seductive since she engages in a lot of smiling, eye contact, and possibly an occasional touch on the arm as they discuss their literature assignment. But Wendy may actually feel that she is simply being amicable.

Because Jason perceives Wendy as displaying more sexuality than she is feeling in reality, he also believes that she has more desire to see him again than she does. The difference in interpretation may confuse both of them. He makes his move, but she seems startled and rebuffs him. How does the story end? With Jason calling Wendy a tease and Wendy calling Jason arrogant. We can all see where this is going—straight to the dust heap of relationships.

I believe men read what they want in nonverbals, and especially in the sexual area, they may perceive seductive cues where there are none. One of the best ways to avoid this pitfall is for the man to become more observant before he makes his move. Jason, for instance, might watch Wendy as she interacts with other men. If she displays the same kinds of nonverbal behavior with them that she does with him—smiling a lot, touching—then he can ascertain that he's not unique. She does this with everyone! He can also use the verbal area to validate his perceptions—"Are you with anyone?" "Would you like to go out?" Going on record is riskier, but it prevents the kind of crash and burn that can occur when the wrong assumptions are made.

If we had to draw a continuum, we could say that a small amount of smiling indicates friendly behavior while large amounts are part of flirting. Constant smiling occurs during seductive interactions.

Gender Prescriptions

In surveying the information about gender differences in facial expressions, we can see that we are caught on the horns of a dilemma. In our culture, men are discouraged from expressing their emotions (other than anger), but at the other end of the continuum, women are required to—indeed expected to—be highly expressive and animated (except when it comes to anger). Both camps have advantages and disadvantages.

The masked face may be effective in certain situations when calling attention to one's feelings is dangerous or detrimental, but it can be perceived as off-putting and cold. Even though it's a norm in male culture it may make women feel that men are "inaccessible" and/or "unresponsive" to their communication. Women often report to me a low level of comfort with men who mask because they can't get a read on how they are being perceived or interpreted. They don't want to talk to stone-faced men and find themselves avoiding future interactions. This can be particularly injurious in intimate relations as well as when the offended female is one's boss, patient, or client.

For its part, the animated face is open and appealing, but it can betray too much information, and when done to excess, it can undermine power and credibility. There are times when it is unwise to be an open book; a woman may not want everyone to know (or they shouldn't know) what she is thinking or feeling. She might want to conceal her emotions so as not frighten her child about the gravity of a situation. Or if she's negotiating for a salary and the opening offer is more than anticipated, she may not want to reveal her glee. If she's savvy, she might be able to throw in more bargaining chips and sweeten an already great deal.

What to do? Some schools of thought advise women to become more like men, especially because the female nonverbal style can perpetuate an inferior position and lower status. Unfortunately, there are several risks to this prescription. For one, it may be hazardous for a woman to deviate greatly from her "proper" female role. Even more important, however, is the fact that in adopting a male style, a woman will also sacrifice perfectly usable skills and a certain advantage. Being seen as approachable is *not* a bad thing. Appearing interested is also beneficial in any interaction. We are finally beginning to value women's skills such as smiling, and it can be considered a welcomed relief in the dog-eat-dog world of male competition, violence, and alienation!

That being said, however, I believe both women and men can learn and borrow from each other. That is the essence of gender-flexing, and the first step is self-awareness.

GENDER RX

- Men need to monitor their facial expressions, especially those that seem overpowering or unavailable. Once they have some sense of how much they rely on the stone face, they can incorporate more facial expressions and smiling to facilitate interpersonal communication and interest!

- Men can also learn from women how to mirror the expression of others, thereby conveying empathy.

- Women should monitor their credibility robbers: the timing and congruency of their smiles (are they smiling too much, and especially, do they smile when they are angry about something?).

- Women can learn from men how to mask when it is appropriate. This kind of inhibition is a complex social skill that develops gradually, but with time, practice, and a good deal of self-awareness and monitoring, women can learn to control some of their facial expressions if they have to.

CHAPTER FOUR

The Eyes Have It

An eye can threaten like a loaded and leveled gun; or can insult like hissing and kicking; or in its altered mood, by beams of kindness, make the heart dance with joy.

—RALPH WALDO EMERSON

Ralph Waldo Emerson wrote, "The eyes of men converse as much their tongues." We all know this to be true. A doctor with an excellent bedside manner once told me that when he enters a treatment room, he immediately looks his patient in the eye. "This helps me understand my patient's level of stress," he explained.

From birth to death and all occasions in between, the eyes have it. While women and men differ in their eye behavior and what that behavior means, eye contact is the strongest form of nonverbal communication. A study headed by Stephen Janik and Rodney Wellens at the University of Miami in Florida found that 43.4 percent of the attention we focus on someone is devoted to their eyes, with the mouth running a poor second at 12.6 percent. (The mouth and the eyes together account for 56 percent of our attention.)

We attend to others' eyes because these organs are highly expressive of emotions. Why would we want to look into another's eyes if not to assess what that person is feeling? Think about the sentiments conveyed when a loved one's eyes are dulled and flat, when they're sparkling with joy, when they're softened by passion, when they're filled with fear or surprise, or when they're brimming with tears. How about the images or songs that accompany the following descriptions: shifty eyes, laughing eyes, wild eyes, lying eyes, and Bette Davis eyes. Here are just a few of the wide range of human emotions that the eyes convey:

1. *Downward Glance.* Modesty in a woman or remorse for bad behavior in a child.

2. *Wide Eyes.* Wonder, naiveté, or terror.

3. *Raised Upper Lids.* Displeasure.

4. *Rolled Up.* Fatigue, impatience, or a signal that something is weird.

5. *Eye Flash* (eyelids widened for less than a second). Emphasizes a word (usually an adjective) and acts as a quick greeting or silent communication between intimates. (At the end of a social evening, a couple may signal "let's go" by this gesture alone.)

6. *Bedroom Eyes* (a woman's soft, drooping lids). Seduction.

7. *Sidelong Glance.* Deference, desire, or deceit.

Sometimes an eye expression can have several meanings. Excessive blinking and fluttering, for instance, may signal anxiety, hesitancy, lack of confidence, and/or shyness. Because blinks increase as anxiety levels rise, experts have studied presidential candidates' blinking rates to determine who prevailed in televised debates. Some researchers have concluded that blinking even varies with sobriety. Small doses of alcohol increase the number of blinks temporarily while large doses slow the blinking to a dead stop. Too much blinking can even betray deceit, though there are probably easier ways than counting her husband's blinks for a wife to discover whether he has been philandering.

Given that the eyes are so expressive, it's not surprising that averted eyes can be a dead giveaway if you've got something to hide.

Of the attention we focus on someone, almost half (43.4 percent) is devoted to their eyes.

When my son was in the second grade, I got a call from the principal's office asking me to come to school—a parent's least favorite chore. The principal said a group of boys, including my son, had engaged in kicking other boys in the groin "for fun" during recess. When I walked into the office and spotted Armand sitting with his accused classmates on a bench, he immediately looked down in shame and began to cry. Guilty by lack of eye contact. I didn't even need to exchange a word with him to recognize that he was an unfortunate member of this little gang of groin kickers. His eyes had ratted him out.

The eyes have been associated with power and mystery for centuries and have rightly been called the windows into a person's soul. The Greek philosopher Empedocles explained vision as a flow of fiery corpuscles that pass from the eye to an object of vision and back again. The description of the glance as a molten stream can also be found in French Renaissance love poetry. There, the eyes are said to shoot arrows, daggers, or swords and project fiery beings, which, according to literary scholar L. Donaldson-Evans, "burn the soul and kindle love's flame." Pretty hot stuff!

Women have always sensed the eyes' alluring power. They do more to enhance their eyes than men. Cleopatra was well known for eye adornment; she used kohl makeup to outline and accentuate her eyes. In India, women place jewels around the eyes to draw attention to them. In our culture, we have our own methods: think concealer, false eyelashes, eye shadow, eyeliner, and mascara.

Of course the eyes can be used negatively as well. Consider the following common expressions and phrases: "He could kill with a glance;" "She shot daggers across the room;" "He gave her a withering look;" "She fixed him with an icy stare." The Bushmen of South Africa believe the glance of a menstruating girl's eye is so powerful, it can transfix a man and turn him into a tree!

After the attack on September 11, flying became an interesting event. Travelers seemed to study one another more closely, especially their co-passengers boarding the plane. I was standing by the check-in counter at the gate of my flight to London about a week after the attack—one of the first international flights allowed to leave the country—when an elderly woman approached the airline agent to report, "That man over there has a *funny look in his eye*." The agent asked who it was so he could also size up the degree of "strangeness" in the passenger.

As it turned out, the suspicious man was no terrorist. He had been imbibing at the airport bar, most likely out of anxiety, and his eyes were glassy. We could attribute the "funny look" to too much bourbon and a newfound fear of flying. Nevertheless, he was classified as too inebriated to board the plane, and we took off for London without him. Again, the eyes had it.

What Is Eye Contact?

Eye contact is one of the primal ways of communicating. As I explained in Chapter 2, it serves a crucial role in mother-child bonding. In fact, research conducted by by R. A. Spitz and K. M. Wolf in the 1940s showed that the image of two eyes is the minimal visual stimulus infants need to elicit a smile. We also know that eye contact increases adults' brain activity and heart rates.

However, before we go any further, I'd like to distinguish between gazing and making eye contact. Gazing refers to looking at different points on the person's face besides the eyes; we might be distracted by a mole on the right cheek or caught by the peculiar way he turns up his mouth. Eye contact denotes looking into the other person's eyes. Patricia Webbink, a psychologist who has studied the eyes and their place in human communication for more than two decades, defines eye contact as, "The mutual interaction that occurs when two pairs of eyes meet." It plays a powerful role in interpersonal bonding, she explains. "In a world characterized by mechanization, threats of violence, and social alienation, the need for increased interaction between people is apparent. The power of eye contact is very real: the mutual gaze is a major form of communication that promotes intimacy." In fact, many people who are deaf insist on eye contact in interactions; they depend heavily on the emotions expressed in the eyes to supplement the vocal intonations they miss in the conversation.

Although we may crave eye contact with others, it is an unwrit-

> *We sustain eye contact approximately 60 percent of the time during interactions.*

ten rule of nonverbal communication that no one maintains it exclusively or continuously. We sustain eye contact approximately 60 percent of the time during interactions. That means most normal everyday interactions are a combination of gazing and eye contact. In the course of a thirty-second interaction, research tracking the eyes has shown that people will gaze at fifteen different spots on or near the face, including the unusual design on the frame of a friend's glasses, an ear popping out of her hair, her nonverbal affect, the peculiar way she moves her lips—along with her eyes.

We can predict you will engage in more eye contact if:

- You are discussing easy, impersonal topics.

- There is nothing else to look at.

- You like or love your partner.

- You are interested in your partner's reactions; you're interpersonally involved.

- You are trying to dominate or influence your partner.

- You are from a culture that emphasizes visual contact in interaction.

- You are an extrovert.

- You have high affiliative needs or inclusion needs.

- You are listening rather than talking.

- You are a male and are more physically distant from your partner.

- You are female!

We can predict you will engage in less eye contact if:

- You are physically close to your partner.

- You are discussing difficult, intimate topics.

- You have relevant objects, people, or backgrounds to look at—you're at the museum or the zoo.

- You are not interested in your partner's reactions.

- You are talking rather than listening.

- You dislike your partner.

- You are from a culture that imposes sanctions on visual contact during interaction.

- You are shy or an introvert.

- You are low on affiliative or inclusion needs.

- You're embarrassed, ashamed, sorrowful, sad, submissive, or trying to hide something.

It is also true that people make eye contact more at women than they do at men. There are two possible explanations for this phenomenon:

- Women are considered nicer and are more likely to respond nonverbally. They smile more and are more receptive, engaging, and expressive.

- Women are considered weak. They can't prevent the violation of their privacy by others' prying eyes.

Continuous eye contact for ten seconds or longer—staring—is disconcerting and can make the receiver feel uncomfortable. The recipient will inevitably start wondering, "Do I have spinach in my teeth?" "Do I need to wipe my nose?" "Is that guy challenging me?" On the other hand, the avoidance of eye contact also sends meaningful messages. Looking away contributes to a sense of psychological distance, and may even be a function of anger—"I'm so mad at you, I can't even look at you;" "I wish I'd never laid eyes on you;" "Get out of my face." And the expression "Talk to the hand" has the unspoken subtext "because I don't want to look at you."

We associate minimal eye contact with deception and lying. A study by University of Georgia communication professors John Hocking and Dale Leathers found that police interviewers believe eye behavior is the single most important clue to lying behavior. President Richard Nixon, for example, made repeated attempts to eliminate shifty-eyed behaviors that reinforced the public perception that he was "Tricky Dick."

However, don't put all your lie detection eggs in the eye basket. Deception researchers have also found that accomplished liars know that shifty eyes are a "tell" and therefore learn to control their eye behavior. Remember the fallen executives at Enron? Paraded before congressional committees for their corporate misdeeds, they exhibited a well-coached, self-assured air, maintaining eye contact with their interrogators even when proof of their offenses was irrefutable. They never looked down or glanced away, but always directed their gaze straight at the committee members. This conveyed credibility, power, arrogance—though in the end, their confident gaze couldn't cover the evidence of their crimes.

Bold or Downcast Eyes: The Influence of Culture

The maintenance of eye contact can also be influenced by cultural norms in intimate as well as businesslike situations. In some societies, the "evil eye" as embodied by the direct stare is one of the worst social and/or supernatural offenses one can perpetrate. We also know that the lowering of the eyes in many Native American tribes and among the Japanese is a way of honoring somebody. Having direct eye contact would be a competitive challenge and a disrespectful thing to do.

This is also true in the African-American culture. For instance, growing up in the newly desegregated schools of the South during the 1950s and '60s, I witnessed many an uncomfortable scene between a young black classmate and our white teacher. It usually went as follows: Suzy's cookies are missing. Mrs. Clark quizzes Roger with, "Did you take the cookies out of Suzy's lunch box?" In Roger's culture, to honor his teacher's status and show her respect, he looks down. He acknowledges Mrs. Clark's power in the hierarchy; she's an elder and has more power and status. His downward look is accompanied by a shake of the head and a "No, ma'am, I didn't take the cookies." But the verdict from the teacher is guilty by lack of eye contact. For the verbal message to be congruent for her, it had to be accompanied with the nonverbal maintenance of direct eye contact. Because nonverbal cues override verbal ones, she draws the conclusion that Roger is lying.

University of Colorado, Denver, communication professor Linda Manning has shared with me many stories about her cross-cultural eye contact experiences, especially when teaching international students. "Asian and Latina women would often avoid eye contact with me in interpersonal situations," she told me. "I recall a young woman from China who would alternate between watching me attentively during lecture and furiously writing down everything I said. In the public forum, she showed her respect by looking at me. However, when she would visit me during office hours to ask for assistance or clarification on a course project, her eyes remained downcast—a sign of respect in our interpersonal communication context."

Linda also recalls the culture clashes she had with young men. "The assertive and confident eye contact I made during lectures and office hours was often perceived as too bold for a 'nice' woman," she explained. "And my 'bold eyes' seem to get me into trouble when I travel. Men in Egypt and Mexico have met my gaze with the comment that they have 'always wanted to marry a woman with green eyes.' If my eyes had been properly downcast, I would not have invited these comments. But think of all the sights I would have missed!"

In certain European cultures, such as France and Italy, a woman initiating eye contact with a man can also be construed being sexually interested. These cross-cultural confusions can be disconcerting to someone accustomed to making eye contact when interacting. My advice: when in Rome, do as the Romans do. If the code of prolonged eye contact means sexual interest, it's best not to engage in it. What do you do? Look straight ahead and look away when a man looks at you, signaling that you're not interested. Give a blank expression. Under no circumstance should you smile.

Catching Your Eye

Eye contact is more than a one-way street and plays many roles in our day-to-day nonverbal communication. We simultaneously send and receive information when we look into another's eyes. In fact, experts would say that eye contact behavior exerts a "regulatory function" in our interactions. By that they mean that it helps us organize the maintenance of social connections, and it also governs the exchange in conversations and turn-taking.

Let's look at the first function. We use eye contact to connect to people, to catch someone's eye for our own purposes. When you're in a restaurant, and you want to grab your server's attention, you try to make eye contact before you resort to a more aggressive or rude behavior like waving a hand or calling out. In return, servers also use eye contact to acknowledge their readiness to take your order or to avoid you. A glance accompanied with a nod and a blink will tell you, "I see that you want me, but I can't get to you right now. I'll be there in a minute."

One of the most important functions of eye contact is bonding when we first meet someone new. The critical behaviors in first impressions and bonding behaviors are:

- The smile

- The handshake

- The making of eye contact

All three taken together create a bond, but of the three, eye contact is the most important. We don't trust or like it when people avert their eyes. Eye contact with another transforms that person from an "it" (an object) to a "you" (a person). How often have you averted your eyes from panhandlers on the corner or along a busy street? Part of the efficient metropolitan façade—the metro-look—is the blank stare that doesn't connect with anyone.

Eye contact also regulates the flow of an interaction. It signals with whom, when, and for how long people are going to speak. People generally look more and longer at the other person when they are listening than when they talk themselves. In studying listening and eye contact behaviors, communication experts Janet Beavin Bavelas, Linda Coates, and Trudy Johnson found that listeners tended to respond when speakers looked at them and that speakers looked away soon after the listener responded. "Together speakers and listeners created and used the gaze window to coordinate their actions," they explained. Eye contact helps to regulate whose turn it is without anybody actually saying, "I'm done; you can talk now." A man, for instance, may focus his eyes on the other person's face at the end of his message to signal to the other that he is ready for a response.

Eye contact can be a regulator in conversation in this informal way or it can be used more precisely, as for example when the chairman of the board signals a member of the committee who is asking for the floor. A look in the eye can telegraph, "Okay, it's your turn."

The Politics of Eye Contact

We were having a serious malfunction with our Volvo, so my ex-husband, Adam, and I took it to the mechanic, Dave. Even though this was my car, and I had experienced the problems firsthand, Dave never made eye contact with me. In fact, he acted as if I were not even present. During the entire conversation, he only made eye contact with Adam. Sensing that I was being ignored, I physically moved closer into the circle, almost forcing Dave to look at me. He briefly glanced my way but then turned right back to Adam and carried on.

It wasn't until I made a verbal command, "Well since I am the driver of the car, I can speak to the problems with it when it broke down," that he actually directed his gaze at me.

The moral: we give more attention to and make greater eye contact with people we consider our superiors and less to those whom we feel are inferior to us. All of us unconsciously play these power games with our eyes, even using eye contact to manipulate a social situation in order to get what we want.

Communications experts Robert H. Gass and John S. Seiter describe experiments in the advantageous use of eye contact. In one investigation, "persuaders" were instructed to approach people at an airport to ask for money. Some targets were told the money would be used to make an important phone call. This was considered a legitimate request. Others were told that the money would buy candy or gum—an illegitimate request. Those who thought the persuader needed to make a phone call gave more money but only when the persuader looked at them. On the other hand, eye contact decreased compliance when the persuader requested money for a treat. Perhaps looking away while making an illegitimate request renders a person more humble or embarrassed, thereby winning the sympathy of others. Numerous other psychological studies confirm that looking into a person's eyes while performing a certain task will influence its outcome. In some cases it will cause the individual to repeat the task, and in others it will make him stop what he's doing.

In his book, *The Man Who Listens to Horses,* Monty Roberts tells of how as a child he learned the nonverbal patterns of hierarchies in herd behavior by watching horses. He observed an alpha mare use her eye with a renegade bully colt that was kicking old mares and new foals. The mustang's behavior was getting out of hand. The mare picked up her head and looked at him a couple of times, but he kept on. So she then approached the colt, squared off to him, caught his eye, and gave him direct contact—an aggressive stare. It worked, and the colt settled down. These patterns translated into training methods Roberts later used with animals.

Eye contact is also indicative of where one feels one stands in a social hierarchy. People who have less power or who are dependent are relatively more attentive than those with high power. The corollary is also true. Studies have found that people give more visual attention to those in high status positions than to those who are not. In research with ROTC candidates and officers, for instance, investigators found that people who are more dominant break a greater number of mutual gazes than those who are more submissive or in the power-down position. Individuals in the superior position may look less because they don't need to read their subordinate's feedback. It may also be true that they don't care what their inferiors think or how they are responding to their message.

We know this to be intuitively true as evidenced by attitudes and expressions such as, "I'm in the driver's seat," and "I'm in charge here," which imply, "Why do I care what you think or how you feel? You have no control over me." Or, "He didn't give me the time of day."

We also know from research that high status individuals feel free to stare more at others, to look less as they listen, and to command a larger visual space. (They can look outside, down the hallway, at everyone in the room as they have a wider range.) People with less power and status do the opposite: they will avert their gaze when stared at, look more when they are listening, and assume less visual space. We can see these behaviors exhibited between men and women, between the executive and the secretary, and even between various racial groups.

Perhaps the most instructive example of the power and eye contact link occurs when I conduct training for law enforcement groups, particularly sheriffs. Many leave on their sunglasses even indoors, and some wear mirrored lenses. The glasses allow the officers to stare freely at others while those they're looking at cannot see their eyes. This one-way eye contact intimidates others by creating an uncomfortable power imbalance. Of course, that's right where the officer wants the individual—uncomfortable—so he or she can remain in the driver's seat.

Because of all of these factors and the power differentials in gender relationships, we know that women and men tend to use their eyes differently to communicate. Let's look at those differences more closely.

Eye Contact: The Female Advantage

Research has shown that women make more eye contact than men do. Why should this be so? There are many possible reasons:

- *Connection.* Women are other-oriented. They seem more interested in affiliation, bonding, acceptance, and social maintenance. Consequently, they look more.

- *Intimacy.* Intimacy is important for women, and making eye contact is one way a woman tries to get close. Think of a couple out for their anniversary dinner, gazing into each other's eyes. In conversation with people they like, women tend to increase their looking while talking.

• *Sincerity/Deception.* Women try to take a read on the authenticity of their interlocutor. Consider the mother who admonishes her child, "Look at me when I'm talking to you." She would be seeking out cues of lying such as averted or downcast eyes. Now imagine a wife who believes her husband is cheating on her. When she asks him why he came home so late at night, he looks away. She surmises from his eye behavior that her suspicions are true.

• *Continual Feedback.* Women self-monitor. They look to the other person's expression for validation: Is my message okay? Does he understand? Does she approve? They make eye contact to observe if the other person likes what they are saying—"He just grimaced. I'd better change my message." This kind of scrutiny gives them a chance to self-assess and edit their message. Harriet is an engineer, making a presentation to a group of peers. It's a complicated topic, and she's looking for approval for her budget request. When she hits certain line items, she can see that several of her listeners are shaking their heads, rolling their eyes, or grimacing. She knows that she has to go back and make her case another way. Sometimes she'll even verbally acknowledge it—"I'm feeling that this is confusing. Let me go back and reframe for you."

• *Information Gathering.* Since women are often excluded from informative interactions with men, and men tend to use the stone face to mask their feelings, women must be more attentive during interactions in order to glean as much as they can. They are often "checking in" with men for the appropriateness of their behavior. In a study conducted by R. V. Exline, men and women were asked to conceal their feelings. Interestingly, given these instructions, women looked more at their conversational partner, but men looked less. The women were trying to detect from the men's reactions whether their emotions had leaked out. Perhaps women have more reason to be "on guard" when concealing or denying their true emotions.

• *Monitoring Group Interactions.* I've sat in on many a management team meeting in corporate America. As the speaker is talking, I observe the women at the table glancing around the room, checking others' facial expressions, and using eye contact and gaze behavior to collect information and gain a read on the group. I have never noticed this kind of work in men to the degree that I have observed it in women.

Female superiority in eye contact gives women a decided advantage. At social gatherings as well as business meetings, women judge with great accuracy all coalitions and alliances just by tracking who is making eye contact with whom at certain critical points or when certain topics are raised. Most men don't have the skills to do this. Information is power, and many men may feel handicapped and threatened by the fact that women glean more information from these unspoken interactions. Because of their increased use of eye contact, women are more sensitive to the subtle nuances in communication and can glean where the coalitions are.

The Stare-Down: The Male Advantage

Not only do men routinely make less eye contact than women, they also barely even set the stage. Eye contact requires face-to-face communication. It's a prelude—how can you look into another person's eyes if you're not facing him? Women tend to orient toward the other person's face, but men actually stand shoulder to shoulder when conversing. These patterns are learned early in childhood.

Why would men face away when speaking to one another? It might be because they fear their direct gaze would be construed as a stare or stare-down. In fact, staring is almost exclusively the province of men. When one man squares off and faces another, he communicates that they are in competition with each other. This is meant as a challenge or to assert status. It's powerful behavior—one of the most confrontational eye-facial expressions that exists—and often the prelude to a fight. "You lookin' at me?"

Ethologist Desmond Morris, who attempts to draw parallels between human and animal behavior, hypothesized in *The Naked Ape* that a stare lasting longer than ten seconds can be traced back to man's biological origins—the aggressiveness and hostility signified by an ape's stare. I can certainly vouch for this in a real way. When I was working my way through school as a waitress in a bar, I saw two men several feet away from me engaging in a long mutual gaze. I signaled the bartender to get the bouncer because I was sure a fight was about to erupt. And it did!

I also had my university students run informal nonverbal experiments to test out various theories I'd raised in class related to eye behavior. In one trial, I asked the young men to stare at an oncoming male as they walked across campus and then observe what happened (with the proviso, of course, that they not duke it out or otherwise get into trouble with the guy they were staring at). My guess was that a man must return another man's stare or he will lose face and appear cowardly.

In reporting the results of their little investigation into male eye contact behavior, my student Jeremy explained, "Sometimes, when the guys would meet my eyes and I locked into holding the stare, it meant that they had to look back. It reminds me of the game we used to play—you know, the one who blinks first loses." Ah, the old stare-down game. "You would probably be perceived as a wimp if you don't return the stare," Jeremy continued. "If another guy stares at you and you look away, the macho component enters in."

In male culture, continuous, steady eye contact is considered an aggressive act and a warning. In board meetings, I've seen one guy give the other the eye. The unspoken message: "I'm dissatisfied and angry. You'd better stop right there." Although a man can look long and lovingly into his significant other's eyes, prolonged eye contact with a woman in a business situation could indicate dominance and convey messages such as, "You should be quiet now," or "I'm getting ready to attack your project."

Eye contact is one of the ways men assert their power and authority and establish their position within the hierarchy. They tend to increase eye contact with other men they have an aversion to. Perhaps this is the result of heightened vigilance or to intimidate, as in, "I don't like you. I'm going to watch you, and I am going to let you know I am watching you."

What should you do if a stare-down is directed at you? You don't have to cower under this withering gaze. You can decipher the non-verbal behavior and try to get under it by putting it on record. You might say, for instance, "John, you're giving me a pretty intense look. Do you disagree with what I'm saying?" Or you might not acknowledge the behavior. You can simply say, "John, what do you think about what I said?" His expression will already tell you that he's not happy, but at least you're getting it out in the open.

The stare is almost exclusively reserved for men. Very rarely will you see a woman use that kind of aggressive eye contact unless it's with her children. Women will seldomly glare back. Instead, most are trained to lower and avert their eyes and to communicate submission. It is socially accepted that men will stare but that women will at the very least turn away before a man's gaze. A fascinating study conducted among college students found that when a male student stared at a female classmate, not only did she look away, but she also quickly left the area. Males, on the other hand, would look more intently when a female classmate stared at them. A woman, of course, may stare at a man, but will often do so in a subtle, acquiescent way by slightly tilting her head. Or she may interrupt her stare by glancing away or by taking a quick look and then casting down her eyes.

What if you find yourself glaring back at an angry, staring man? Men expect other men to challenge them in this way because they exchange stares all the time, but they do not expect a stare-down from a woman. The sex role expectation is that men compete with men, and women should be in support of men. In fact, men can feel more threatened when a woman challenges them than when other men do. It's perceived as an affront to a man's masculinity. This occurs in leadership emergence. If a woman tries to emerge as the designated leader even in a social situation—as, for instance, when several couples try to decide where to go for dinner—and dominates the group, the men will feel more competitive with her than they would if another man were attempting this feat.

A man will sometimes take a challenge from a woman more intensely than he will from another man. It's important to recognize that if you make a stand, men may not always meet it favorably. This is the ultimate testimony that sex roles are alive and well; many men expect to be dominant in leadership positions. You need not acquiesce, but recognize that if you stare back, you may not always be popular. Others, especially men, may call you aggressive or bitchy or tell you that you're coming on too strong. Unfortunately, that's the price you may have to pay to be in a leadership position.

Why Don't You Look at Me When I Talk to You?

Until this point, we've examined the advantages of good eye contact and the disadvantages of aggressive eye contact. But now, it might be helpful to consider the opposite problem—not enough eye contact.

It is clear that men and women handle their eye behavior differently. Take, for example, standing face to face when making eye contact. For a woman, eye contact serves the purpose of information gathering, but it's also for bonding and intimacy. She's looking for reactions to her messages, but also building a connection. For a man, direct eye contact is a challenge and a sign of competition. The genders attach two entirely different meanings to the same behavior, giving rise to communication disconnects.

When someone becomes embarrassed, both genders tend to look away, but during a positive interaction, men tend to decrease their eye contact as time elapses whereas females tend to increase theirs. Research also shows that women tend to look at members of their own sex more than at those of the opposite sex, at least when paired during lab experiments. Two businesswomen at lunch will look at each other more than a businessman coupled with a businesswoman, and they'll certainly look more than two businessmen who barely meet each other's eyes. Woman seem to feel more comfortable making eye contact with people of their own gender.

Eye contact behavior reveals the balance of power, and all of these power-play behaviors have gender-based implications. If a woman is interacting with a man who is masking, she is desperately gazing for any crack in the façade in order to glean clues about his reaction to what she's saying. Lack of eye contact can also be an indication of sex bias in an interview—a subtle nonverbal indication of general disinterest. You are not being taken seriously for the position.

Recently, I attended a board meeting of an organization where there is an entrenched good-old-boys mentality. Three of the fifteen board members were women. I observed that the chairman of the board (who had the most air time) made absolutely no eye contact with these women. Later, I asked the women if they had noticed this. "How does it make you feel?" I wanted to know.

"Oh, this is so commonplace," Linda admitted, as the two others nodded in agreement. "But it still makes me feel invisible, as if I'm not in the room. And it also makes it difficult for me to get the floor when I want to make a point. Frank never looks my way so I can never signal my intention to say something. I can't tell you how frustrating it is!"

In the twenty-five years that I have been a trainer and consultant in corporate America, lack of eye contact is the primary nonverbal cue that women mention when they tell me that they are not being "taken seriously by the opposite sex"; this is one of the top complaints women have about men. Janice, a corporate vice president, for instance, may perceive that when she is in a face-to-face interaction with her counterpart Ed, and he does not look at her, it's because he doesn't care about her message. This is understandable.

It may be, of course, that Ed doesn't make eye contact because he wants to avoid any suggestion of the aggressive stare and that Janice interprets his lack of eye contact as diminishing her credibility. On the other hand, it also may be true that Ed uses the dearth of eye contact to manipulate the situation and assert dominance. As linguist Deborah Tannen has pointed out, a person who withholds information establishes a more powerful position. If Janice wants to access that information, she has to do whatever she can to analyze Ed's nonverbal cues. That means she may have to look at him more to discern what his intentions are.

The Wink: What You See Isn't Necessarily What You Get

We can't leave our discussion of eye contact without also mentioning the wink. A Chinese novel written in the early Ching period describes a murder trial in which a secretary signals the prefect with a wink: "He realized that the Secretary obviously wished to communicate something of importance to him." Frequently, the inflection and the accompaniment of winks impart special meaning to our ordinary words. I am reminded of an old *Seinfeld* episode in which the character George completely invalidated everything he was saying because something had flown into his eye, causing him to wink at particularly inopportune moments.

A wink is a potentially dangerous tool in the nonverbal communication toolkit. Winking also serves different functions for men and women. For men, it's employed in primarily in three ways:

1. As a pick-up cue, usually exhibited by men forty or older (winks are uncommon among teenage boys or young men in their twenties or thirties).

2. As a reassuring sign that everything is okay.

3. As a way to signal that he doesn't really mean what he says.

Most important, a wink is rarely directed from one heterosexual male to another, for fear of coming across as a homosexual. Many women perceive the wink as patronizing. Men must be aware that a wink can connote sexual interest.

On the other hand, women wink at both men and women. The female wink helps to maintain social connections and build relationships and bonding. It's a sign that everything is okay. However, a woman also must be sensitive that men could perceive her wink as a come-on. She experiences the same risk of misinterpretation as men.

Both genders must take into account the context of their winks! At a board meeting with others present and accompanied with a verbal statement such as, "We can get it done!" it is perfectly acceptable. But after hours at a dimly lit restaurant, it can have a different meaning altogether—"Ma, he's making eyes at me!"

I Only Have Eyes for You

I have observed that couples who have been together for a while maintain less eye contact—this is true for myself as well as others—than those who are just falling in love. Although we are intimates, we know each other well and are no longer in the courting phase. But I recently witnessed a scene at a local restaurant that brought home to me how important eye contact can be in a romantic context.

I watched a young couple having dinner, noting that the whole evening passed without them looking at anyone else in the room. She did a lot of "gender signaling"—tossing back her head, and smiling and laughing a lot, acting as though she found her young man profoundly entertaining.

Just as I got ready to pay the check, a guy sitting only two tables away came up to the young couple. "Hi Michael!" he said with some excitement. "You didn't even notice we were sitting right there!" He pointed to his wife and baby in close proximity.

It turned out that this man was Michael's brother. For his part, Michael's gaze was so locked into his date's face, he was completely unaware of his family's nearby presence! This group created quite a stir. And as I walked out, I couldn't resist adding my two cents. "This has got be your first date!" I proclaimed.

"How did you know?" they asked with incredulity. Although this couple was totally unaware of the signals they were sending, once again the eyes had it.

Eye contact is one of the first components of a sexual relationship. It communicates the intensity of our feelings. Just watch people on a date. They will "make eyes at each other." Often during flirtatious interactions, there is a moderate degree of eye contact while more seductive behaviors are usually characterized by more gazing—the "look of love" immortalized in Burt Bachrach's song. Sexual attraction is generally communicated through extended eye contact. *Body Language* author Julius Fast claims, "Most men direct a three-second-plus look at attractive women; and attractive women are usually not surprised by the duration of the look. If it is held for longer than three seconds, however, the signal that is conveyed is that of sexual interest." Such an extended look suggests a wish for further involvement.

Additionally, flirtatious behavior for a woman can also include the demure glance downward. Bedroom eyes—a woman's soft, drooping lids—are quite seductive, and sidelong glances can indicate deference.

In fact, eye contact is so important, it can be the first step toward making a connection—"Just one look, that's all it took." In the courtship ritual where the norm generally is that the man is the initiator, eye contact provides a face-saving function. It's off-the-record nonverbal behavior. Ken can glance at Marla across a crowded singles bar without going on record and opening himself to her rejection. He tests the waters by looking at her. She notices. If she's uninterested, she averts her gaze, and usually contact is ended. But if she returns his look, this indicates that she might be attracted to him. Emboldened by their mutual gaze—now seen as an invitation—Ken may initiate further interaction by moving closer and striking up a conversation—"Haven't I seen you somewhere before?"

Among intimates, gazing into each other's eyes is perceived as a loving act. Communication professors Lawrence Rosenfeld and Jean Civikly suggest that lovers communicate almost at subliminal levels, with an eye glance, a flick of the head, or another almost unnoticed gesture that conveys great meaning.

Women may rely on the man to be the sexual initiator, however they don't take kindly to unwanted wandering eyes—a man who looks them up and down in preparation of a sexual advance. I call it "elevator eyes." In a work situation, such a leer could be grounds for a sexual harassment complaint. Yet I know it is quite prevalent based on my work as an expert witness and on the countless reports I receive from women attending my seminars. "He's not making eye contact with me," the female participants gripe, "he's looking at my breasts!" Women attending my seminars in the late 1970s and 1980s would threaten to hang notes on their blouses saying, "Don't look here; look at my face!" You will rarely hear the reverse, men protesting that women are ogling their crotches.

Again, this lack of eye contact and sexual looking is "off record" which allows some men to think they can get away with it. If you find yourself in this uncomfortable situation, put the nonverbal message on record. You might say, "Tom, you seem distracted. Is there a better time for us to talk?" Almost instinctively, the men will catch themselves, and look you in the face. It is company policy in most Fortune 500 companies that you document these off-the-record non-verbal harassing behaviors in writing—for example, "Tom stares at my breasts when I talk to him instead of making eye contact." It often has to get to that extreme for men to understand the offense and use some self-control!

That having been said, I also have to admit that this issue is more difficult for men. Visual stimulation turns them on sexually—as compared to women who respond more intensely to touch. Probably one of the reasons that *Playgirl* magazine failed! Nevertheless, this is no excuse for them to have those wandering eyes! Our society has established a variety of eye-related norms. One is that we are *not* supposed to look at certain body parts except under particular conditions (such as when we're making love). It's best that we all adhere to these norms to avoid misinterpretation and conflict.

Gender Prescriptions

When we try to interpret sex differences in eye contact and gazing behavior, there seem to be competing themes of affiliation/approachability on the one hand and dominance/power on the other. It seems clear that women use eye contact to check in and read how they are being perceived. They also try to bond with others and incorporate them into an interaction with their eyes. Women will also lower their eyes in submission.

In contrast, men employ eye contact to mark status and dominance (men stare more than women). They use less eye contact with an individual as a way to communicate—"You are unimportant. I have a higher ranking than you."

Awareness of these divergent nonverbal styles will help you better understand the signals that you're sending, and how they can be interpreted and misinterpreted. Pay attention to the behaviors that go on autopilot out of habit or socialization. I think it's important for men and women to self-monitor. Women should pay attention to lowering their eyes, a behavior that sends the message, "I'm the doormat." Keep your gaze steady and straight as an equal and participating member of an interaction. Men need to understand that they should also participate in some of the social maintenance that occurs during interactions by looking more to get more information on how they're being received. They need to understand that women misinterpret their lack of eye contact as lack of interest.

GENDER RX

- In some cultures, a woman initiating eye contact can be construed as being sexually interested. Women who find themselves in this situation should look straight ahead or away, signaling their disinterest.

- A woman who becomes the object of a male power-oriented stare-down can put it on record by saying, "You're giving me an intense look. Do you disagree?" or "What do you think about what I just said?"

- If a man withholds eye contact, a woman might have to look at him more intently to discern his intentions.

- A woman who finds herself the object of a man's sexual ogling can put it on record by saying, "Tom, you seem distracted." If the behavior continues, she should file a report.

- Men can miss critical communication nuances that contribute to the meaning and interpretation of a message by not looking. They can get more information if they maintain more eye contact.

- Men should, in the correct contexts, make conscious attempts to engage in eye contact to send the message, "You are important; the topic is important."

- Men must monitor more aggressive eye behavior, such as the stare. Power moves are useful in certain contexts but should be invoked sparingly.

CHAPTER FIVE

The Power of Touch

We often talk about the way we talk and we frequently try to see the way we see. But for some reason we have rarely touched on the way we touch.

—DESMOND MORRIS, MAN WATCHING: A FIELD GUIDE TO HUMAN BEHAVIOR

T he automated trams to the gates at Denver International Airport were down for fifteen to twenty minutes. The anxious crowd kept growing and growing. Determined to board the very next tram to make our flights, we all jammed on the first one to arrive. Imagine 200 people touching everywhere—front, back, side. Human sardines. Most of us looked up to increase the "psychological space" that would ease the level of discomfort we endured in having such close encounters with strangers.

As we exited, a man in the crowd employed humor to ease the touch violations we had all just experienced. "I don't know," he quipped, "but it sure feels like I was just unfaithful to my wife on that tram!"

We all laughed in agreement and relief as we hurried off to catch our respective flights.

Just think about the many kinds of touch we might engage in each day: patting, holding, bumping, stroking, shaking, massaging, squeezing, kneading, groping, grabbing, grooming, guiding, poking, prodding, rubbing, hugging, caressing, embracing, cuddling, kissing, licking, linking, fondling, tickling, scratching, flicking, flipping, tapping, slapping, punching, kicking, pinching. The list seems endless. Not only is touch a multifaceted nonverbal communicator, but it is also quite powerful. According to Albert Mehrabian at the University of California, Los Angeles, touch is often considered the single most influential nonverbal variable to impact the tone of an interaction. It instantly changes the message, even when the interface is relatively trivial.

In fact, researchers now consider the skin a "communication system" among humans. It is a sensitive organ; its surface area has a tremendous number of receptors that receive stimuli of heat, cold, pressure, and pain—all touch. In fact, some physiologists consider touch to be the only sense. Hearing begins with sound waves touching the inner ear; taste begins with a substance touching the taste buds; and sight begins with light striking the cornea. All the other senses are therefore derivations of touch.

Researchers also believe that the skin has its own capacities for sending and receiving information, often subliminally. In one study, clerks at a university library either did not touch students or they made light physical contact by briefly touching the students' palm when handing back library cards. After the books were checked out, the students were asked to rate the quality of the library. Interestingly, those who were touched evaluated the facility much more favorably than those who were not.

Skin Hunger

Still, psychologist Sydney Jourard claims that America is a touch-starved culture. We take great care not to bump into one another and express regret when we do—"Oh, pardon me." Unless we're jammed into airport trams, we don't touch strangers—"Keep your hands to yourself!" A flight attendant on a recent trip I took, in a nod to our touchiness about touching, announced during her safety demonstration, "If any of you have been on the road too long and are feeling lonely, you can pull that seat belt tight and give yourself a little hug." We are circumspect about whom we hug and for how long. Indeed, newspapers have reported that we touch our pets more than we do each other. "More Than Other Folks, Pets Get Loving Strokes" was the title of one such article. Anthropologist Paul Byers claims that senior citizens suffer the most from touch deprivation. He speculates that people are afraid to touch the elderly because somehow they worry old age is contagious.

Advertising campaigns such as "The Midas Touch" for the muffler shop and "Reach Out and Touch Someone" for the phone company demonstrate how marketing departments use touch as an important element of selling. I believe these slogans wouldn't work in Italy; Italians are not as touch-phobic as Americans are. Communication researchers Judy Burgoon and Thomas Saine claim that compared to other societies, American culture is "restrictive, punitive, and ritualized" in regard to touch.

In their book, *Will I Ever Fit In?*, Emory University psychologists Stephen Nowicki Jr. and Marshall Duke give their recommendations for touching people in the United States—especially to those who touch too much or inappropriately: "Don't touch anybody, anywhere on their body at any time. . . . We are not a people who like to be touched by anyone other than friends or family, so a good rule of thumb is simply not to touch other people. This way you are safe from misinterpretation of offense."

This may be fine advice for people who are a bit too touchy-feely, but a poignant "Dear Abby" column published in 1982 describes the potential consequences of a strictly hands-off policy:

> Dear Abby, I am a 14-year-old girl. My problem is that nobody ever touches me. My parents haven't hugged or kissed me for a long time, except when I go away for a long time. Close friends outside of the family don't touch me either. I am outgoing to a degree and sometimes when I really want to hug someone I just go ahead and hug them, but they always just stiffen up or back off. No one ever reaches out to me first. I need someone older to talk to. I feel like nobody cares about me or loves me. I am intelligent. I don't have a mental problem, I don't smell bad and I am not ugly. I am so confused—please help me.

This poor girl's situation seems extreme, yet many families develop patterns of not touching. If I were to answer this teenager's letter, I'd tell her that she's not alone and shouldn't feel abnormal—many people experience touch deprivation. How might she help herself? She could initiate hugs and kisses with her parents upon greeting or leaving them. That would be a courageous act. She could also hug her girlfriends; women embrace each other readily when they get together. She might also volunteer to help young children. That would provide opportunities for her to extend the kind of touch she craves—hugs and other kinds of physical contact.

Anthropologist Desmond Morris, author of *The Naked Ape* and

The Human Zoo, says we have all become far too cautious and inhibited in our social contacts. We even hire "licensed touchers" to take care of our need for bodily contact. Although we may touch our babies, generally our impulse to touch seems to decline from early infancy on. We know, for example, that in elementary school the amount of touching steadily decreases, but it still surpasses most adult tactile behavior. The trend continues in junior high with about half as much touching as in the primary grades.

That most Americans don't touch each other is, of course, not entirely true. We do touch our children, family, and friends. Our noncontact culture may explain the rising popularity of various forms of bodywork, manicures, and other hands on treatments—Morris's so called "licensed touchers." Also, certain ethnic and racial groups employ more touch than others. Communication experts Barbara Bate and Judy Bowker cite the testimony of a young woman of Filipino-American heritage who experienced a culture clash because people in her ethnic group are much more physically demonstrative than those in her adopted country:

> When I was growing up it was not uncommon to show affection to the members of my family and friends. I was brought up to hug people, hold hands, and kiss friends on the cheek to show respect and affection. These nonverbals are prevalent in the Filipino culture; it is normal for brothers and sisters in their young adult age to hold hands in public. In the Western culture, that is almost unheard of. Even friendships have more affectionate physical activity than in the Western culture. Growing up with this cultural difference, I have picked up the idea that it is okay to show unconditional affection toward other people.

However, when touch is used against the backdrop of a culture that generally refrains from it, it stands out and becomes highly significant. You can move closer to another person, but if you touch, the message is more powerful.

The Importance of Touch

Touch is so significant in our lives that the lack of it can cause us to become ill or otherwise disordered. According to Sarah Trenholm, a communications professor at Ithaca College, "People deprived of touch may develop physical, mental, and social disorders. In fact, studies have linked touch deprivation to depression, alienation, and violence." In talking about his book, *Intimate Behavior: A Long Look at What Society Has Done to Our Need for Physical Contact with Other Members of the Same Species,* anthropologist Desmond Morris chalks it up to our prenatal experience: "In a way, do you think man needs this contact because of the 'uterine bliss' we experience prior to birth? Certainly that's part of it. The fact is that we do have total comfort inside the womb. There is one thing that intrigues me to no end about that, in the womb, experiencing this 'total embrace.'"

Think about it. The first thing most parents want to do the moment their child is born is nestle the infant in their arms. Of course this has psychological implications for bonding, but researchers have also found that touching and stroking babies helps them grow. Child development specialist and nursing professor Susan Ludington-Hoe carried out an experiment with 120 newborns demonstrating just that. The babies were given more than an hour and a half of extra stroking during the first three days of life. Surprisingly, they gained weight faster and performed motor movements earlier than expected. Fascinated by these findings, Ludington-Hoe investigated why the stroked babies lost less of their birth weight than those who were not stroked. She found that the former had more glycogen in their bodies, a chemical that is important in energy and weight gain. Such rhythmic skin-to-skin stroking may enhance nerve development and has also been shown to be effective with premature infants.

"How complex we human beings are," Ludington-Hoe wrote in *How to Have a Smarter Baby.* "It's a miracle that stimulating your baby's sense of touch with gentle, rhythmic stroking definitely can enhance his digestive functioning and growth." Perhaps cats, mares, and other mammals lick their newborns in part because touch provides stimulation that actually starts the heart and the digestive system in their offspring.

Sadly, the reverse is also true. Mortality rates during the nineteenth and early twentieth centuries, especially from a disease then called "marasmus" (which translated from Greek means "wasting away"), were devastating. Communication professors Ron Adler and Neil Towne note, "In some orphanages the mortality rate [from this disorder] was nearly 100 percent. Even children from the most progressive homes, hospitals, and other institutions died regularly from the ailment . . . they hadn't had enough touch and as a result they died." Today this disorder is known as "failure to thrive." Experts in this field estimate that 50 percent of the children who suffer from it do so because they have not received enough parental attention. We need look no farther than the horrible scenes televised from orphanages in Romania and more recently from North Korea to understand the physical, emotional, and developmental devastation that lack of touch can wreak on a young child.

Touching is an important cue that indicates liking and acceptance. We know that even when it contradicts other nonverbal cues such as posture, position, and words, it still determines the total impact of the message. For instance, the phrase "I love you," devoid of loving touch, will ring quite hollow. In short, touch is one of the most powerful ways to communicate.

All Touches Are Not Created Equal

Although we all need touch, not all tactile behavior is the same. Touch can communicate varied emotions from one end of the spectrum (extreme hostility and aggression) to the other (comfort, intimacy, and love). Its meaning is a function of a number of factors: how long it lasts, how intense it is, where you are touched, the other person's intentions in touching you, and the relationship in which it occurs—the context.

The very same behavior can have myriad meanings depending not only on who does the touching, how, when, for how long, and where, but also who is being touched. For instance, a recent news story reported on Kenneth Abraham, a University of Virginia torts professor who gently taps the shoulder of a random student in his class to show that even negligible unwanted contact can be costly if the individual is vulnerable in ways no one could have expected. Unfortunately, unbeknownst to him, the person he tapped in one of his classes was a recent rape victim.

It's natural to lightly touch a student on the arm or tap her on the shoulder. I did this when I was in the classroom. Abraham probably had no intention of harassment. I am sure he had a history of tapping students on the shoulder while making this point, but unfortunately, the woman he touched interpreted unintentional innocent touch as traumatic because of her history. She claimed that Abraham's unwanted touch retraumatized her, and she filed a $35,000 lawsuit against him for assault and battery.

Touch is an inherently ambiguous form of nonverbal communication. It can't be separated from its context or from the words or the other nonverbal cues that accompany it. Touching a woman lightly on the outside of the arm sends quite a different message than touching her on the inside. And when your husband tucks in the label of your blouse at the nape of the neck it feels entirely different than when the veterinarian's assistant does so. As Robert H. Gass and John S. Seiter explain, "What one person may interpret as friendly . . . another may see as flirtatious. Can the brushing of one employee against another be interpreted as accidental or as a form of sexual harassment? Is a pat on the back a sign of encouragement or an attempt to demonstrate dominance?"

To help clarify these issues, psychologist Richard Heslin categorized touch by the relationship with the person touching you:

• *Functional-Professional.* Many professionals—nurses, dentists, doctors, personal fitness trainers, manicurists, tailors, masseurs, hairdressers, physical therapists, and the like—touch people in the normal course of work every day. This has been referred to as the "cold touch"; people are touching you in order to achieve a goal or provide a service, not because they want to be friendly with you.

However, just because professional touch is called "cold" doesn't mean it can't affect our behavior. Psychologists Allen H. Crusko and Carol G. Wetzel conducted an interesting study similar to the one mentioned previously involving the librarians. In this investigation, waitresses fleetingly touched their customers either on the palm, on the shoulder, or not at all when returning the change or credit slip after the meal was eaten and the bill paid. They found that customers who were touched for a second or less—whether on the shoulder or hand—were more generous in their tips than those who were not touched at all. Reach out and touch someone, indeed!

• *Social-Polite.* Heslin explains that we use this kind of ritualistic touch to "affirm the other person's identity as a member of the same species, operating by essentially the same rules of conduct." This is the kind of everyday touch that we enact with acquaintances and even strangers. You might tap someone on the shoulder to ask for directions or to tell him he's standing in the wrong line or that her purse is open. You might guide someone out the door by putting an arm around her. Handshakes fall into this category as well as leading someone by the arm as you give directions—"Look, it's over here."

• *Friendship-Warmth.* This kind of touch sends a message that the person being touched is unique and unlike anyone else (in contrast to the social-polite touch that's more anonymous). We may communicate our closeness by grasping the arm of the person, putting our arm around his shoulder, taking someone's hand into our two hands, or even covering a handshake with our free hand. CBS reporter Morley Safer once said that President Clinton was adept at using such subtle changes in handshakes to communicate warmth and friendship to those he met.

There can be a fine line between social-polite and friendship-warmth touch. I recently returned for a second year to speak at a conference of emergency services workers. (These people do a lot of touching in high-stress situations. They are supreme emergency caregivers.) When I arrived, I ran into Stuart, the man who had been tending to my room arrangements. I extended my hand for the expected social-polite greeting. He shook it and then hugged me. Although most men do not hug, because Stuart is in a caregiving profession, this friendlier contact is a part of the unspoken code and may have even been a job requirement.

Hugs and consoling pats on the arm—even rubbing a friend's arm in gratitude—show friendship and warmth. One of my friends explained how she used this kind of touch with her cleaning lady, who had come to work despite the fact that her father had died just three days earlier: "I was up in my home office working when suddenly I heard sobs coming from the kitchen. I ran downstairs to see what was happening, and there was Maria, her face buried in her hands. 'I feel so sad,' she told me through her tears.

"I didn't know what to do. I'd never touched Maria before, but how could I stand there mutely and not comfort her? For a second or two, I watched myself debating how to respond. Finally I just threw my arm around her shoulder and hugged her. Her grief was so profound that I even started crying too. Somehow my gesture helped her regain her composure, and we talked some more about her loss. When she left that afternoon, she smiled sweetly and said, 'Thank you for *everything*.' That's when I knew I'd done the right thing; I'd treated her like a friend in her moment of need."

• *Love-Intimacy.* According to psychologist Sidney Jourard, touch is the primitive language of love. It is the gatekeeper of intimacy—the final bond between people even when words fail. In intimate situations, touch is welcomed and necessary. Hugging, handholding, caressing, kissing, and side-by-side snuggling is usually reserved for family members and significant others. With intimate touch, many more parts of the body are allowed to be touched in private than in public. According to Desmond Morris, all intimate touch if used appropriately serves to sooth and comfort us. We will explore this kind of touch more fully below.

A colleague of mine whose husband travels a lot for business gets her touch needs met by going to the manicurist, getting a massage, and/or having her hair cut when he's gone. That helps reduce her feelings of loneliness and prevents her from feeling touch-starved during his weeklong absences. Still, I have always been concerned about people who don't have an intimate partner. I have children, so even when I was single, at least I fulfilled some of my intimate touch needs with hugs and kisses from my kids. But how do childless, single people cope with the lack of touch when they are not involved with someone? Some may use pets as a substitute. Others might engage in contact sports or other behaviors that involve touch such as karate, square dancing, or ballroom dancing. Or, like the young "Dear Abby" correspondent suffering from touch deprivation, they could become involved in volunteer activities with children or the elderly—where hugs are required.

A Woman's Touch: The Female Advantage

My women friends and I all greet each other by hugging hello and goodbye. I can't imagine seeing one of them without such a quick embrace. That's a real contrast to what men do. I rarely see hugging among male friends. In fact, research shows that as with eye contact and smiling, women are more inclined to touch their communication partners than are men. Perhaps nurturing and the urge to create closeness motivate women's heightened use of touch. We also know females are the initiators and recipients of more hugs than males. Men rarely hug other men, but we frequently see women embracing one another, even at work. In fact, studies suggest that women are more comfortable with same-sex touching than men. The latter use comforting, reassuring touch to address their need for rapport, bonding, and orientation toward others.

It's also interesting to note that touching can enhance other forms of communication. For instance, there is a relationship between self-disclosure and touching. Self-disclosure refers to moments when we reveal private information that people would not otherwise know about us. We have strong evidence that women are the recipients of more self-disclosure than men. Indeed, both men and women would prefer to divulge their personal stories to a woman than to a man. We know this for a fact.

Why are women the recipients of others' secrets? One of the big answers (that we'll explore further in Chapter 10) is that they are better empathic listeners. A recent study of 4,000 people nationwide conducted by researchers at California State University in San Diego found that touch actually prompts recipients to talk about themselves; there is a relationship between self-disclosure and touch. Women give more nurturing and empathic consoling touches. They'll be the first to reach out and hug someone or squeeze a hand, when they need it. Why are we surprised, then, that others open up more easily to women? It only seems natural, given their propensity to touch more.

The Untouchables

Men live in a different universe when it comes to touch. They don't employ as much touch as women do. This is especially true in the office, and often it's not because they fear being accused of sexual harassment, being politically incorrect, or being self-conscious. (In the last two decades, the reports of sexual harassment have increased tenfold from what they had been in the past.) For men, touch in the workplace is almost exclusively motivated by power. Nancy Henley analyzed nonverbal behavior in Fortune 500 companies and found that touch among men tends to be directed from the top down as a status marker. A manager can pat an employee on the back and say, "Good job," but the employee will think twice before returning the favor. Whoever initiates the touch has the power. Beyond this sort of power-touch behavior, men in our culture have not been avid touchers. To wit: the term "touchy-feely" is used to ridicule.

Someone has to die (funerals are basically it) for men to hug others, especially other men. American men can be so homophobic that certain of them in my audiences actually cringe when I tell them that in Italy men stroll arm in arm and kiss each other on the cheek. A pat on the fanny is acceptable in the context of sports, but not when you're walking down the hallway at work! Context is critical!

Men do engage in banter touch or play touch, which is delivered in the spirit of teasing and having fun. Banter touch would include a gentle slap on the cheek, a high-five (or other hand ritual that evolved from the high-five, which can involve up to a dozen or so hand or arm touches), a *Three Stooges* noogie on the noggin', a head butt, a clip to someone on the chin, pinching, roughhousing, or slapping. This is really not the arena of women except perhaps in team sports, where both men and women will engage in banter touch.

My son has a great lacrosse coach who used this kind of touch to motivate his players. The team was losing, and the coach tried to fire up the boys. As the parents stood agape, we watched as he walked down the line of players—some had their helmets on and some didn't—and butted heads with every single one of them. He got in their faces exhorted each of them to play harder. "Do you want to win?" he shouted with each head butt. These must have hurt him more than the players—after all, he kept doing it twenty times. But it was symbolic of, "I'm tough. You're tough. Get out there and win."

Banter touch becomes the domain of men within and outside the sports context. I believe it is a man's way of showing connection, friendship, and camaraderie—especially in male-to-male relationships, where it becomes a sanctioned touch, free of homosexual interpretation. However, according to psychologists Linda M. Kneidinger and Perry L. Maple at Georgia Institute of Technology, "the contact being made with those body parts [is] aggressive in nature, slapping, shaking, grabbing and rubbing. . . . Perhaps," these researchers suggest, "aggressive contact removes this intimacy or should be conceptualized as a different type of intimacy." I believe the latter to be true.

Young males (and females) also use banter touch to get the attention of a member of the opposite sex they like. My son's first girlfriend and her father were to meet us at the end of Armand's lacrosse game on a field of about a hundred parents and kids. Suddenly Armand got a tap on the shoulder. It was Mary. She did that trick where you tap and jump away, leaving the recipient to wonder who did the touching. It was cute and playful. You'll also often observe a pre-adolescent boy pulling the hair of a girl he's attracted to (and then running off before she can figure out who did that to her). This, of course, evolves as boys mature. A man will display intimate and sexual touch toward his girlfriend (hug her, squeeze her, try a little tenderness), but he'd be wise not to go after her ponytail.

Power Touch: The Male Advantage

Touch is also a marker of power within relationships, especially among men. A person of higher status is more likely to touch a lower status person than vice versa, and an older person is more likely to initiate touch with a younger person than the reverse. Touch can be perceived negatively when it is employed unilaterally; the boss has access to touch the employee but the employee cannot exercise the same privilege. This is an indicator of status. Communication expert Judy Pearson lists several examples of unilateral touching: "doctors touching nurses, customers touching waitresses, teachers touching students, managers touching subordinates, police officers touching accused persons, counselors touching clients and ministers touching parishioners." It is clear that touch in these contexts is a demonstration of power and status.

However, touch also can be used as a power equalizer. Those in inferior positions may initiate touch with a person in a superior position in an effort to balance the power between them. However, sometimes these bottom-up touches can constitute power-touch violations and can generate uncomfortable feelings.

My friend, communications professor Sonja Foss, had an encounter with a student that demonstrates how power-touch violations can be unsettling. "I was teaching a doctoral seminar at the University of Denver," she told me. "The class ended, and several students and I stood around talking. I made a joke, and one of the male students reached up, patted my face, and said, 'Good joke, Sonja.'" I doubt he would have done that if I were a man. I tell this story in my gender classes to illustrate how those with the most power can touch those in lower power positions, but not the reverse. It really felt like my student had violated a norm, because I had more power in that situation."

Sonja's experience demonstrates the use of power touch among people who are unequal in status. But what about those who hold relatively equivalent levels of power? A recent National Public Radio report on touch behavior among U.S. Senators elucidated "Capitol Hill's unique silent vocabulary of body language and touches, a vocabulary that lawmakers use to bond with each other and also to assert power," as NPR host Bob Edwards explained. David Givens, an anthropologist specializing in nonverbal communications, viewed a videotaped scene during a Senate floor vote. On a high-speed playback, Givens said, "It reminded me of an ant colony."

He was especially intrigued by one scene, a conversation among several Democrats—what reporter Peter Overby called "a 75 second display of most of the Senate's vocabulary for acceptable power touching." Tom Daschle, then the Senate Majority Leader, stands at the center. "The others approach and touch him, but he doesn't approach anybody. Christopher Dodd, another powerful Democrat, pats Daschle on the shoulder and then leaves his arm draped there. Daschle responds by putting his arm around Dodd's waist. This could raise eyebrows in other settings, but not here on the Senate floor."

According to Givens, Dodd is trying to temporarily reverse the power structure "and get dominance himself just by virtue of reaching out and touching. You can do this with your own boss. Go up, put your hand on your boss's shoulder and temporarily at least your boss has to take the subordinate position, just because of the power of touch." Touch carries unspoken authority "that goes right to the emotional centers of the brain and for that time period where touch is on it makes that person feel a little submissive."

Overby explained the general pecking order of congressional touching: "Congresswomen touch congressmen, but rarely the other way around. Congressional staff might touch lawmakers, for instance, to get their attention at a hearing, but their touches will be tentative, not assertive. Some lobbyists will touch a lawmaker; others think it's beyond the pale."

Also commenting on the Senate video was private consultant Kari Anderson. She suggested that new members of Congress could adopt some of the accepted ways of behaving with some modification. Instead of grabbing someone's elbow and squeezing it in the crook, they could tap at the point: "Do something slightly different which is within the acceptable range and it will signal their attention." This female consultant shows us how to stay within the realm of normalcy and the rules for appropriate touching while pushing the boundaries just enough to get someone's attention.

Stan Jones, retired communications professor at the University of Colorado, Boulder, claims that when the goal of touch is to persuade others to do something, it is associated with influence. He calls this "compliance touch." We know that touching people can be persuasive. Power touch has been found to get others to behave in ways we want them to: to increase the number of people who volunteer, return money, sign a petition, purchase a product, or complete a survey! In a 1977 study, touch increased people's response to requests for help. A researcher left dimes in phone booths at the Boston airport. (Remember, this is 1977, when calls were cheap and cell phones a thing of the future.) When participants emerged from the phone booths, purloined dimes in hand, they were more likely to return the change to the experimenter when his request was accompanied by a light touch on the arm.

We might ask why touch makes a difference. It's possible that people are more likely to feel good when someone touches them, and the "feel good" encourages them to comply with the request! Or, perhaps people who initiate the touch feel confident about themselves. They create a favorable impression on others and open the door to be persuasive—someone we do not like cannot persuade us. We know that touch can have many positive meanings: relaxation, closeness, informality. Finally, touch only serves to enhance the image of power!

Remember, however, that there is a fine line here. Power touch can be excessive, as in the case of the car salesman who is too presumptuous in his physical contact. He is anxious to befriend the potential customer and make his monthly quota! In his eagerness to sell, he crosses the line. It's a question of finesse—to maintain enough touch to be influential without overwhelming and overpowering the other person.

Ritualistic Touch: The Handshake

A student invited Sonja Foss to her wedding. As Sonja made her way down the reception line, she introduced herself to the father of the bride. "Hello," she said, "I'm Dr. Sonja Foss, your daughter's professor." She extended her hand with a smile and continued, "It's nice to meet you."

At that point the father of the bride drew back and said, "Sorry, I don't shake hands with ladies." Although for some people religious faith dictates male-female tactile contact (for instance, Orthodox Jewish men are forbidden from touching women to whom they are not married), I don't believe this father refused to shake Sonja's hand because of his beliefs.

Although disconcerting, it's not surprising that this man refused to shake a "lady's" hand. The use of the handshake among women coincides with their influx into the workplace in the 1970s. Our mothers didn't shake hands with other women or with men, for that matter. Still today, some etiquette books warn women not to initiate a handshake. Only recently have women been permitted this ritual. Yet it's critical. If a woman walks into a roomful of men and fails to shake hands at first, she can't go back and salvage the gaffe later. The handshake is a bonding behavior that must be executed in the first seconds of contact. It is as important as eye contact.

The handshake is the only formalized, ritualistic touch that is sanctioned in the United States. Men have been trained in proper handshake technique since they were boys of four or five. In fact, the first message most received about appropriate physical contact was how to shake hands—"Son, when you meet somebody, you take their hand like this . . ." A homophobic meaning may underlie this training; if you have a wimpy handshake, it means you're a wimpy guy.

In a recent interview in the *New York Times Magazine*, Bill Richardson, governor of New Mexico and negotiator-at-large, discussed his handshakes and other touching behavior while conducting talks with Saddam Hussein some years ago:

> *What's the first thing you do when you enter a room with a negotiating partner?*
>
> I think that at the outset of a negotiation, physical contact is very important, as is small talk . . . a hug even if it's not culturally proper.
>
> *When you were negotiating with Iraq in 1995, did you hug Saddam?*
>
> Yes.
>
> *You didn't have to kiss his armpits, as he's said to make his inner circle do, did you?*
>
> Saddam tried to intimidate me with 16 security guards, who entered the room at the same time he did. I stood up and grabbed his arm and hand. It wasn't just a fish handshake. I put my arm on one of his shoulders.

Handshakes have evolved from Greco-Roman days when men grasped each other at the upper arm to check for hidden weapons and finally shook hands as a sign, "You're clean, I trust you; I know you're not going to hurt me." (Was Richardson looking for a concealed dagger in Saddam's sleeve when he grasped his arm?) Today, the handshake is a critical bonding ritual and a code among men that they reinforce in the business world. No man in the workplace would ever greet another without gripping his hand and pumping three or four times. The handshake is an expected business practice that all men in most industrialized nations engage in.

However, there are some cultural differences. Middle Eastern men may grip your hand gently because they consider a firm grasp to be too aggressive. The French shake hands much more than Americans do—at all of their comings and goings. In *A Year in Provence,* Peter Mayle described Frenchmen as extending their pinkies for a shake if their hands are dirty or full with packages.

For us in the United States, a handshake must be executed in the proper manner: full palm, firm grasp. Yet both men and women will shake a woman's hand with the "limp fish," differential and preferential treatment that conveys one believes she is frail. Indeed, male workshop participants have even voiced the concern, "Won't I crush her hand if I shake it like a man's?" Of course, this is untrue. A man should shake a woman's hand firmly; he should extend the same etiquette to her as he does to another man. She will not break. And by the same token, a woman must sometimes initiate a handshake with a man. It is important that she not be excluded from this business bonding ritual. If a man leaves her out, she can smile, take a step forward, and say, "Hi, I'm Nancy." By this nonthreatening act, she can teach him how to treat her—as an equal.

Men will also execute a power handshake. It is quite firm, and rather than being parallel, one of the handshakers turns his hand horizontally so it's on top. This dominance display occurs strictly among men. You won't see it among women, and will never see a man do it to a woman.

The Gatekeeper of Intimacy

John Lennon and Paul McCartney immortalized romantic touch in their early hit "I Wanna Hold Your Hand." The lyric, "And when I touch you I feel happy inside," sums it all up—touch and intimacy are almost synonymous. How can you be intimate without touching the person you love? Psychologist Sidney Jourard explains, "The metaphor of 'being turned on' describes the experience of physical contact. When part of your body is touched, you can't ignore that part of your body. It becomes a 'figure in your perceptual field.'"

Anthropologist Helen Fisher called touch "the mother of all senses." "Most mammals caress when courting," she explained. "Blue whales rub each other with their flippers, male butterflies stroke and rub their mate's abdomens as they couple. Dolphins nibble. Moles rub noses. Dogs lick. Chimpanzees kiss, hug, pat and hold hands."

Human couples also have many tactile ways to signal that they are together. Our tactile signals of intimacy run on continuum from low to high: the pat on the back or arm, holding hands, rubbing shoulders or arms while walking, the arm-link, the shoulder embrace, the waist embrace, the pat on the behind, the snuggle in the backseat, the full-frontal body hug, and the ultimate expression of intimacy short of intercourse, the kiss!

Other than having sex, kissing is the only exchange of bodily fluids (saliva) in which couples engage. According to Desmond Morris, the lips, mouth, and tongue are the most exquisitely sensitive parts of the body. And the brain, in turn, devotes a disproportionate amount of its resources to processing messages from the lips and tongue and linking them up to behavioral reactions and psychological functions. The space devoted in the brain to messages from the lips alone is far greater than that devoted to sensory inputs from the entire torso.

Finally, as William Schutz explains, "It is significant that the closest adults ever come to touching each other totally is in the lovemaking situation where there is an effort of total acceptance and love of the whole person."

You will also observe couples engaging in banter or playful

touch—grabbing, slapping, nibbling, even pushing or shoving. The latter is especially true among preadolescents who aren't dating yet but are beginning to feel their first sexual stirrings toward the opposite sex. To disguise or eliminate the taboo of touch, they pretend to play tag football so they can wrestle each other to the ground and roll around in the grass for a while.

Morris coined the great term "tie signs" to describe touch behavior that signals a relationship exists between two people. What Morris calls the "waist embrace" (arms around each others' waists) often substitutes for the full embrace when a couple wants to indicate more intimacy than merely holding hands. These tie signs are quite useful. They help me identify who is a couple at parties! On the other hand, when a husband and wife display lackluster or only a few tie signs, I intuit that the relationship is on shaky ground. Married couples also report more positive reactions toward touch and tend to associate it with sex more often than do unmarried people. Unless the touch is in an erogenous area (buttocks, breast, penis), a sexual response is uncommon for the unmarried. Nevertheless, sexuality is most closely linked to the location of touch.

That having been said, there is still an inherent ambiguity in how men and women perceive intimate touch! Sexuality researchers tell us that women are more stimulated (turned on) by touch whereas men are primarily visual—perhaps the origin of elevator eyes. Men may view intimate touch as an instrumental behavior (such as the power touch discussed above) in that it can lead to sexual activity. A man might be more likely to initiate touch during dating to attract a partner or fulfill a courting ritual. He holds hands because it may be a prelude to bigger and better things!

Women may see touch as an expressive behavior that communicates warmth and affection. She thinks he is holding hands because he likes her and is trying to connect. A woman would be more reticent to make the first touch move (only bold women do this!) during a first or second date. However, as the relationship progresses and develops a history of handholding or other intimate touch, she may take the lead.

Although women do distinguish between touch that indicates warmth and touch that suggests sexual intent, and they tend to value touch more than men, there can be many mix-ups in the interpretation of simply holding hands! A friend told me that when she said to her boyfriend, "I feel like snuggling on the couch and watching a movie," he took her "snuggle" to be an invitation for sex. On the contrary! She just wanted to be held. The cuddle muddle can be chalked up to the fact that men think about sex on average from ten to twelve times a day. For women, sexual thoughts may occur only once a day. A man may interpret any suggestion of touch to be a come-on—that she's saying indirectly that she wants to have sex.

In the 1960s, psychologist Sidney Jourard's studied body accessibility and the meaning of touch. He found that there is an ambiguous connection between intimate touch and one's commitment to a relationship. Men inferred significantly less commitment from this type of touch than did women. "Women may be more inclined than men to associate commitment with behavior," he writes in reference to intimate touch that occurs in the context of a couple. "Females judged increasingly greater level of commitment as touch became more sexually intimate when compared to males." Of course this presents a great potential for miscommunication. For her, the increasingly intimate touch can signal a deepening of the relationship, whereas for him, this type of touch doesn't necessarily indicate a commitment. When the relationship is in its early stages, this may not present much of a problem, but as it heats up, the opportunities for mixed signals grow exponentially. Jourard's suggested solution: talking about the relationship and one's commitment level can help clarify these ambiguities.

Taboo Touch: Is It Sexual Harrassment?

One of my friends was sitting at her desk, working at her computer, facing away from the door. Jeremy, a male co-worker, entered her office, came up behind her, and placed one arm on each side of her, resting his hands on her desk. Then he leaned his chest into Charlene's back. Her instant reaction was to stiffen in surprise and sit up straight, knocking him in the face with the back of her head in the process. Wham! Not that he didn't deserve it. Jeremy was known as the "harasser" in the office. He took advantage of any opportunity he could to touch women, often relying on the element of surprise. When Charlene told me this story, she added, "I think this was just his way to cop a feel and look down my blouse." I guess he learned his lesson.

Taboo touch comes at the intersection of intimate touch and sexual harassment. According to communication expert Dale Leathers, "Two of the major factors which affect quality of tactile communication are quantity—how much touching takes place—and region of the body where one is touched." Don't touch me there!

Generally, touching a person's clothing, hair, or body and especially giving a massage around the neck and shoulders would be considered inappropriate touch. For instance, one of my clients complained that a male co-worker reached out and rubbed his thumb over the texture of her leather belt (pretending that he was exploring it) during an interaction in the hallway. By the same token, women should also be careful about the messages they send. Another sexual harassment case I was involved with dealt with this dilemma. When Bonnie complimented Jack on his attire—"That's a nice shirt," she murmured as she gently felt the fabric on the sleeve, touching his arm in the process—Jack thought she meant she was interested in going out. She wasn't.

Men in my workshops are often confused about what constitutes inappropriate touch. I tell them to ask themselves, "Would I touch my mother or daughter this way?" This quickly helps them sort it out. Context—time, place, the nature of the relationship—often gives meaning to touch. If you're wondering whether some touch behavior is inappropriate, you'll need to analyze your situation in light of the prevailing circumstances. In one instance, a forty-seven-year-old white male would touch women in his office when no one else was around or when everyone else had left the building. This was considered harassment. Inappropriate touch is also generally accompanied by a space invasion.

Nonverbal behavior is off the record and works ideally for a man intent on sexual harassment. He can look at a woman's breasts, stand a little too close, brush against her body—all common behaviors I've encountered in my twenty years of work as an expert witness in sexual harassment cases—without going on record. If you're confused about what constitutes harassment, the following are some loose guidelines to appropriate and inappropriate touch:

- Patting on the head or shoulder as in "'Atta girl" can feel patronizing, but these behaviors may have little sexual content. Rubbing and massaging, on the other hand, are considered sexual moves.

• The duration of the touch is significant. A pat feels much different than a lingering caress.

• Who touches whom outside the context of intimate relationships is often an indicator of power. Some of us have worked with the same people for five or six years and feel comfortable with physical contact. Others do not.

• Who hugs whom is also important to discern. Does a man hug only the women in the office or does he hug the men too? Does he hug everyone or only the twenty-year-olds?

• Context is very important; where the touch occurs gives it meaning. If it's 7 PM, 90 percent of your co-workers have left for the night, and the lights are off with the exception of your and your co-worker's respective offices, a co-worker-initiated touch can have an entirely different meaning than if the touch occurs at noon in a heavily trafficked hallway with all the lights on. Public touch in an open context with people around is much safer and leaves less opportunity to be misconstrued than touch that occurs in a more isolated setting.

• What part of your body is being touched is also quite important. Safe body parts include the outside of the arm and the top of the shoulder. Taboo spots include at or below the waist, at the inside of the arm, at the front (in contrast to a pat on the back), and on the leg. Tapping someone lightly on the shoulder to gain his or her attention is fine, but running a finger along the nape of the neck is not!

• Touch is acceptable only when both individuals consent to it and are in an equal relationship. To determine how touch is being used, men should ask themselves, "Is it reciprocal or unilateral?" and then imagine performing the same touch to someone who is an equal, a superior, or someone of the same sex.

• Men must determine if their touch potentially minimizes the other person's status. They must ask themselves, "What costs to the relationship will I incur by the use of dominant/status marker–type touches? Can my touch be interpreted sexually?" On that note, there is a lot of disagreement (I experience it firsthand in my sexual harassment work) if the touch is an act of friendliness or an attempt to assert sexual dominance.

• When in doubt, always use the handshake. The handshake (and seldom an embrace) is the appropriate etiquette for the workplace.

What should you do if you feel you've been subjected to inappropriate hugs? The first step is to freeze—leaving your hands at your sides sends an unspoken message that you don't want to engage in that hug, you don't approve, and you won't reciprocate. The second strategy is to back away, to step out of the two- to three-foot zone that allows for the touch. More aggressive men may keep coming. In that case, put up your hands as a barrier and verbally place the interaction on record. You might say, "Hey Carlos, no hug today. I feel uncomfortable when you greet me with a hug. The only person who hugs me is my husband." The more aggressive the man, the more a woman must step up the intervention. If the touch escalates, and if the man still doesn't get it, the final step should be a memo complaining about sexual harassment copied first to the perpetrator, and if he does not respond, to his superior. It is difficult to go forward with a sexual harassment case unless the off-record inappropriate behaviors are put on-record. Document every unwanted touch in a diary, including date, time, place, where you were touched, and the type of touch. The context and type of touch give the behavior meaning.

Gender Prescriptions

Different strokes for different folks. When it comes to touch, the very same behavior can have very different meanings. Women use touch to create relationships, for social maintenance, to bond, to encourage closeness, and to enhance commitment. Men, on the other hand, employ touch as a status marker, for assertiveness, or in courting rituals. Different kinds of touch can be used by each sex to achieve different goals. Men touch other men with the least frequency, perhaps due to homophobic attitudes.

Touch has many positive and negative attributes. On the positive side, it is essential to growth and development from birth. It is also important to intimacy and is equated with sexual interest. In reciprocal relationships such as co-worker to co-worker, spouse to spouse, friend to friend, touch can be employed to affirm, bond, and solidify the relationship. It is neither sent nor received as an assertion of power, rank, or status over another individual. Women employ touch in the context of empathy to enhance the level of disclosure. They use an empathic touch to express nonverbally, "I feel with you." This sensitivity leads to a greater feeling of closeness and, as Diana Ivy and Phil Backlund claim, "less psychological distance between persons in a relationship."

Touch is the equalizer of feelings. It can serve as a relationship accelerator, and women are champions in this arena. Operative here are women playing out the gender-role norm of maintaining social connection. This contrasts with men's hierarchical world, which is marked more by the constant manipulation of status and posturing to assert dominance.

Women should certainly continue to employ touch in the context of empathic listening and to facilitate interactions. However, they must also be sensitive to the possible ways a touch can be received and misinterpreted. He could be thinking, "Oh, she likes me!" or "Is this a come-on?" when, in fact, she's really only interested in his shirt!

GENDER RX

- We all need to be touched. Without touch, we can become ill or otherwise disordered.

- Childless, single people can fulfill their touch needs using "licensed touchers," volunteer work, pets, contact sports, or dancing.

- People in inferior positions may use touch to equalize relationships, but they must proceed with caution as sometimes touch can constitute a power violation.

- Touch prompts people to self-disclose and provides persuasive influence, but it's a question of finesse—maintain enough touch to be influential without overwhelming the other person.

- No limp fish! Execute a handshake properly with a full palm and a firm grasp. A woman should shake a woman's hand firmly; a woman should initiate a handshake if she is left out of this ritual.

- Men and woman must avoid the kinds of inappropriate touch that constitutes sexual harassment.

- Both men and women must take the following steps when confronted with inappropriate touch: freeze, back away, use hands as a barrier, verbally place the interaction on record, and write a report to superiors.

CHAPTER SIX

Close Encounters

If you can read this, you're too close.

—BUMPER STICKER

onverbal behaviors begin to have a domino effect. In order to touch people, you must get into their personal space, what's called their "body buffer zone." This is an invisible boundary between individuals that is culturally dictated.

How does the body buffer zone work? Imagine a trip to the library. It's nearly deserted; six of eight tables are unoccupied in the periodical room. You chose a quiet place at one of the empty tables. Another patron, a stranger, enters and plops down right next to you, even though there is plenty of space elsewhere. Do you have the urge to get up and move? The same might be true at the movies. How do you feel when a stranger sits beside you in a mostly empty theater? Creepy, right? And I understand from male participants in my gender workshops that when men use a public restroom, they will not take the urinal alongside one that's already occupied. They take pains to use the next stall over.

Although the body buffer zone varies from one person to another, from gender to gender, from situation to situation, and from one society to the next, we all know when our space has been invaded. When someone else stands too close, it makes us feel uncomfortable. In fact, one of the best ways to ascertain someone's personal space is to continue to approach until he or she complains! This invisible boundary is a place where intruders are not allowed.

Personal space also varies in shape. It is not perfectly round, and it doesn't extend equally in all directions. For example, we can handle a stranger coming up to us on the side but not directly in front of us. Young children have no concept of personal space; given the opportunity, they'll crawl all over you. But by the third grade, boys have been found to already be aware of the body buffer zone and to mimic adult behavior.

How Near? How Far?

The study of personal space is called "proxemics." When anthropologist Edward T. Hall was a professor at Northwestern University, his work took him all over the world from the Pueblo cultures of the American Southwest to Europe to the Middle East. His mission was to teach foreign-bound technicians and administrators how to communicate effectively across cultural boundaries. *The Hidden Dimension* and *The Silent Language* were two pioneering books in which he examined how people use space in public and in private. He came up with four spatial relations zones that apply to most social interactions among Americans:

• **The Intimate Zone.** This zone extends from touching distance to about eighteen inches. It is reserved for intimate interactions and very private conversations—when you want to whisper something to a colleague at a board meeting or when you stand close to your sweetheart, spouse, mother, or child.

• **Personal Distance.** This zone extends from eighteen inches to about four feet. It's the space reserved for our casual, friendly, everyday interactions such as when we run into an acquaintance at the supermarket or talk to our daughter's teacher at open house.

• **Social Distance.** This zone extends from four to twelve feet during impersonal business relationships. It's what we use when we are in public places with people we don't know, like waiting on the platform for a subway or shopping in a department store. (I hate it when I'm flipping through a rack of clothes on sale and someone comes up behind me and grabs the garment next to the one I'm holding. That's a violation of my social distance zone.)

• **Public Distance.** This zone extends from twelve feet to the limits of visibility and hearing. It's used for public performances, lectures, and the like.

These distances are also culturally dictated. Communication professors Lawrence Rosenfeld and Gene Savickly offer a quick survey of the cultural disparities in their book, *Words Unspoken: The Nonverbal Experience:* "There are major differences between cultures in the distances that people maintain. Englishmen keep further apart than Frenchmen or South Americans." And in Hong Kong, where three million individuals are crowded into twelve square miles, people seem to have adapted to living in close quarters. Low-cost apartments provide only about thirty-five square feet per person for living and sleeping. Now that's cutting it close from our point of view!

These differences can give rise to intercultural misunderstandings. For instance, Rosenfeld and Savickly explore the difficulties that Americans and Spanish speakers encounter, often due to discrepant expectations about body buffer zones. "When a great many Americans and Spanish speakers meet for the first time they have trouble establishing friendly relationships," they explain. "The Spanish speaker thinks the American is cold and stand-offish. And the American thinks the Spanish speaker is trying to be too intimate too soon. What neither realizes is that the two cultures have very fixed customs on how close two people should stand next to each other during a normal, relaxed conversation."

No matter what their gender, when Spanish speakers converse, Rosenfeld and Savickly explain, they stand about sixteen inches apart. But for the average American, this falls within our intimate zone—the distance sweethearts or those sharing a secret use. In ordinary conversation, Americans employ the personal distance zone—from eighteen inches to four feet. "Until the members of each culture understand this difference," Rosenfeld and Savickly continue, "each gets a wrong impression of intentions of the other, and they have trouble trying to establish a friendly relationship."

Why Is Personal Space So Important?

Personal space acts as protection, a safety device, and a status marker. It was said of President John F. Kennedy that when he walked into a room, it was like parting the waters—the higher the status, the larger the space. Dominant animals maintain a larger buffer zone of personal space; they are not approached as closely as submissive animals. Prison inmates have been found to have huge personal space behind them and actually smaller in front of them, because they prefer to see who is coming up to them. It's also likely that they're afraid of being stabbed in the back.

When people stand too close, their faces become visually distorted. Perhaps this is one reason why lovers close their eyes when they kiss. Have you ever noticed how people instinctively flip their heads back (almost leaning backward) when someone comes up directly into their face? You can't get a fix on a person's face if he or she is right up against you. You can't see it.

Personal space may vary in size for an individual depending on the situation, his or her emotional state, gender, and the relationship with the other person. We stand closer to people whom we like. That's why there is no personal space between lovers and intimates. Sting's song "Don't Stand So Close to Me" is an excellent example of how proxemics can reveal intimacy; by standing within the intimate zone, a female student inadvertently makes public the affair she's had with her teacher. Conversely, a couple experiencing marital difficulties may stay so far away from each other as they walk that they cannot graze each other's arms, let alone hold hands.

Proxemics also interact with other dimensions of nonverbal behavior such as facial expression, eye contact, and touch. If a person's facial expression is inviting (he or she is smiling, nodding, or using an eyebrow lift or head tilt to show concern), we feel we can physically move closer. If the facial expression is masked or appears cold or neutral, we back off. Proximity is a prerequisite to touch: a person can't reach you if he is not in your body buffer zone. When individuals are in a forced situation (in the subway or me on that crowded airport tram), and there is no way to increase physical space, they avert their gaze, looking up or down to increase space psychologically. People riding an elevator will lower their eyes to minimize unwanted interaction.

Marking Your Territory

Sometimes people erect actual boundaries to stake claim to their personal space. According to communication professor Mark L. Knapp and social psychologist Judith A. Hall, this is a popular response to encroachments (or predicted encroachments) of our territory. Leaving an occupied sign on an airplane seat, draping a coat over the back of a chair in a restaurant, arranging a towel and sunscreen on a hotel poolside lounge, or spreading books at a library desk indicate this place is mine, and I will be returning to claim it—*so keep off!* In fact, most people get pretty peeved if someone deigns to move their markers—"Hey, I was here first!"

People often mark where their territory begins or ends. A fence may separate one yard from that of a neighbor, just as painted lines demarcate parking spaces and the bedroom door clearly delineates that area from the rest of the residence. You may also formally mark your territory with your name or a representative symbol such as a club's emblem or your initials. "This room belongs to . . ." is a popular sign for those who need to make it clear that trespassing will not be tolerated.

Female markers in bars or restaurants—sweaters, purses—tend to be less effective than male markers—a coat, cell phone, pack of cigarettes, or newspaper. Women's boundaries are not respected and are invaded more easily. Consequently, a woman's territory is over-taken more quickly than a man's. In fact, I have observed people touching and moving women's markers but keeping their hands off the male stuff! If another man moves a man's marker, watch out. The situation could escalate into a territorial contest. Also, personal markers such as a coat or briefcase are more effective than nonpersonal items like magazines or coffee cups.

It is possible for women to "grow" their space using these kinds of markers. Communication professor Linda Manning recalls that even though it's not in her nature to take up a lot of space, when she was president of a foundation board, she purposefully chose her seat at the head of the table and spread out her papers, day planner, and other paraphernalia over a larger area. "I suppose it was my nonverbal way of saying, 'I'm in charge here because look at how much territory I have marked with my possessions,'" she explained to me. Tactics like these can actually work to a woman's advantage for the purposes of influence and persuasion. The message conveyed: "I will allow you into my space to create a bond, but I am still in control and have power."

The Politics of Personal Space

The politics of personal space can be reduced to one sentence: subordinates yield space to people of higher status. Theodore H. White described such a scene in his analysis of John F. Kennedy's presidential race in *The Making of the President, 1960*. Kennedy was talking with his brother Bobby and his brother-in-law Sargent Shriver when it became evident that he had garnered his party's nomination. At first, the other people in the room surged forward to congratulate him:

A distance of about 30 feet separated them from him (Kennedy), but it was impossible. They stood apart, these older men of long-established power, and watched him. He turned after a few minutes, saw them watching him and whispered to his brother-in-law. Shriver now crossed the separating space to invite them over. First Averell Harriman, then Dick Daley, then Mike Di-Salle; then one-by-one, let them all congratulate him. Yet no one could pass the little open distance between him and the uninvited.

Of course, the reverse is also true: dominant individuals can intrude on the space of those who are perceived as subordinates. This came clear to me during my first consulting job with a Southern California police department. The all-male group of interrogators told me that they intentionally invade their suspects' personal space. There is no protective barrier—no table—between them. By coming uncomfortably close, they gain power and control over the interrogation.

Indeed, how we seat or arrange ourselves is often used as a status marker in relation to others. Over the years, police officers have told me that during a traffic stop, they insist that the driver stay in his or her car. Obviously, there's a safety reason for this; it reduces the chances of an accident or for the detainee to make a run for it. But the police also want the alleged speeder in a lowered position, looking up at them. That position helps the officers maintain control and enhances the deference shown them.

A recent Dilbert cartoon is equally instructive. The pointy-haired boss is behind his desk with Wally sitting in front of him. The boss says, "I'll come around the desk so it appears that I consider you an equal." He pulls his big executive chair around, but that still elevates him above Wally, who is seated in a small chair that's low to the ground. Literally and figuratively, the boss continues to talk down to Wally.

This is not as far-fetched as it seems. Former FBI director J. Edgar Hoover was known for having his desk placed on a wooden platform to elevate him above the people who came to his office. What's more, he provided his visitors with a soft leather chair. They would sink lower so he could peer down on them.

Virginia Valian, professor of psychology and linguistics, was interested in how gender stereotypes shape perceptions, but her work is also instructive when it comes to understanding the politics of space and positioning. In her book, *Why So Slow? The Advancement of Women,* she describes an experiment she conducted to discover whether college students are equally likely to perceive women and men as leaders. The students were asked to identify who was the leader in photos of people seated around a conference table. If the photo depicted all-male or all-female groups, the students overwhelmingly chose the person at the head of the table as the leader. Where you sit apparently makes a big difference in how others perceive you. Interestingly, however, this was not so in mixed-gender groups. When a man was seated at the head of table, the students participating in the experiment selected him as the leader, but when a woman was at the head, they believed she was the leader only half the time.

Reams have been written about President Clinton's use of proxemics. Maureen C. Minielli, professor of speech communication at St. Cloud State University, examined why Clinton's first administration was plagued with chaos, the former president being chronically late for his appointments. Part of the problem, it seems, had to do with how comfortable he was in the space he was occupying:

For the first two years in office, Clinton held many public meetings in the Oval Office. These situations found Clinton conversing much longer than was necessary causing him to be late for other meetings. Although it was Clinton's ability to listen and converse with the common American that got him elected, it was also the main cause of his Administration's faltering during his first Presidential term. The staff decided to switch meetings to different parts of the White House. Clinton's aides moved many of his events out of the Oval Office and the Roosevelt Room where he was inclined toward harmful kibitzing and into a more formal setting in the East Room and the Rose Garden. "When he stands up," noted an official, "he is more careful about what he says; when he sits down he just talks more."

Apparently, Clinton's political advisors took advantage of this bit of information about him, scheduling nationally televised interviews with news anchors Dan Rather and Tom Brokaw in the Roosevelt Room. He clearly looked relaxed and self-assured in that setting. As Minielli explains, "Clinton's use of space supports . . . the argument that physical use of space influences communication. It suggests that Clinton has created personal and public persona partially based on his surroundings, and his comfort and confidence levels can be linked with his use of space."

Male and Female Space

I live in Boulder, a college town. The University of Colorado football team is often bussed to local movie theaters the night before a game to keep players relaxed and out of trouble. But I've noticed that when they enter the theater, the guys settle themselves one seat apart, never next to each other. This could be due to their impressive bulk—the bigger the person, the larger the body buffer zone. However, not all the team members are enormous linebackers—some are average guys. Still, they give themselves wide berth.

Contrast that to women's behavior. I would never sit one seat away from a female friend at the movies. It would be socially unacceptable. In fact, were I to separate myself from her in this way, she would surely ask me, "What's wrong, Audrey? Are you mad at me?"

The genders certainly behave differently when it comes to defining comfortable body buffer zones. The smallest personal space occurs in female-to-female interactions, whereas the largest space occurs when two men get together. (Male-female interactions fall somewhere in between.) This becomes clear when I conduct minipersonal space exercises in my gender seminars. I ask participants to choose a partner and stand ten to fifteen feet apart with no obstructions like tables or chairs between them. Partner A is to remain still while Partner B slowly walks toward him or her. Partner B is instructed to continue walking until Partner A says stop. Once they reach this point, Partner A will have defined his or her personal space.

Male pairs participating in the exercise usually stop when they're four to five feet apart. In fact, some men begin this activity with a joke. After they get into position and I say, "OK, start to walk slowly toward your partner," Partner A will yell "Stop!" before Partner B can take his very first step. A woman would never do that. In fact, some women get so close they actually embrace! When I ask why their personal space is so small, they'll say, "Jeannie is my best friend" or "I've known and worked with Mary for ten years." This never happens with men. (On the other hand, as communication professor Linda Manning explains, "When I do this exercise, when an attractive woman approaches a man, he almost always lets her invade his intimate space, to the great amusement of the rest of the class.")

We know that men and women of all ages have differing preferences for interpersonal space. Men set larger distances toward others than do women. Why? No one knows for sure, but it is theorized that women are more affiliative and concerned with bonding than men. As part of their being other-oriented, their job includes social maintenance. Women prefer what communications expert Judith Hall terms "the positive-affect connotations of closer distances." They like standing closer to others. Of course, by maintaining less distance, women encourage others to approach them more closely too. This could explain why women's space is invaded more (and even why they're touched more often). They initiate the closer proxemics, inviting people into their space, creating an interactive effect.

In contrast, men's nonverbal training is often directed specifically toward showing strength, not weakness. Allowing someone too close or into his space would render a man vulnerable. A man can better control his environment by creating more space around him. Boys are told to "stand tall" in order to show confidence and assertiveness, and even occasionally aggressiveness.

Women cannot command as large a personal space as men. Consequently, they are often perceived as having a lower status. We can better understand this when we observe common sidewalk etiquette. Generally, we have a built-in radar that tells us how to walk down the street, allowing space so two people can comfortably pass each other. In fact, if the space is too narrow, one person defers to the other and moves aside. (This is also true on a hiking trail. We turn side by side or step off the trail so we don't bump into the hiker coming from the opposite direction.) Sometimes both people do a choreographed maneuver where they simultaneously move to the left or right. Invariably they start laughing and one may ask the other, "Do you want to dance?" joking about their faulty radar.

But here's the issue: in the United States, men rule the sidewalks (and the hallways). A woman is expected to step out of the way to give him space to pass through. To prove this to my skeptical students, I would send male and female pairs to observe sidewalk etiquette on campus especially during busy times between classes. I would ask the woman to hold her ground and walk straight down the sidewalk. "If a man comes toward you," I instructed, "just continue down the path. Don't alter it. Look straight ahead and be determined." Their male partners would observe the behavior and note the reactions.

"My shoulder almost got dislocated," one female student complained. "One guy bumped into me, and my books spilled," another confessed. Unless they are "gentlemanly" and abide by etiquette rules dictating "ladies first," clearly some males expected the females to step aside and let them through. I believe that this expected deference is a power issue; some men see it as a contest. The male has the power and the status to command the path, and he should not defer to anybody. I hear about this dynamic on factory floors as well as on college campuses, in corporate corridors, and at shopping malls. It's unconscious—an unspoken code that women give in to men's space.

Men claim that when a man passes another man, they both try to move or adjust their gait to accommodate each other on the path equally. Generally men do not show deference to other men. Unless there is a known status difference, one man is not going to completely move out of the way for another! They share the power of the path!

Physical factors may also contribute to gender differences in personal space. Men tend to be bigger (taller, larger) in body size than women, and we know that the bigger you are, the more space you control. For example, obese people are given more personal space (this is especially relevant with all the recent press on the alarming numbers of Americans who are considered to be overweight) than those who are thinner. Height is another major determiner of the space we maintain when interacting with others. When a tall person converses with a shorter person, it is necessary to back up and increase space so the shorter person is not craning her neck. Men tend to be taller than women. The greater the height difference (a five-foot-tall female interacting with a six-foot-four inch man, for instance), the more space is required to interact comfortably.

Side by Side or Face to Face?: Male Versus Female Communication Style

Posture and position—how we hold, carry, and orient our bodies—also convey myriad nonverbal messages. Psychiatry professor Albert Scheflin organizes our sense of personal space with the concept "frames." He believes that when people carry out reciprocal activities (conversing, for instance), they frame those activities in space and time by the way they place their bodies when sitting or standing together. Here are his categories of frames:

- *The Vis-à-Vis Frame.* When two people come together, they greet and address each other in a face-to-face position. They will adjust the distance between themselves according to their ethnicity, their level of intimacy, their prior relationship, their business together, and the available physical space and circumstance. The vis-à-vis frame is a prerequisite for making eye contact—you can't see the other person's eyes unless you're looking at his or her face.

• *The Side-by-Side Frame.* Often, this is a communication choice, especially among men. It precludes eye contact. However, sometimes unrelated people assume a side-by-side position by accident or because of the physical nature of their circumstances. They happen to be walking in the same direction or they sit down on the same bench or the same seat on a bus. In this case, they may have no other relation to each other.

• *The Terminal Marker.* People indicate that they have finished their activity in a group by discontinuing their postural frame. They step back, look down and away, turn out from each other, and then go on to other things. (In communication, we also call this "leave taking behavior.")

Scheflin's categories have to do with what we in communications call "shoulder orientation." Interestingly, men and women differ in this area too; they have completely different shoulder orientations when conversing. When women talk with other women as well as men, they orient themselves toward the other and tend to use the vis-à-vis frame, maintaining eye contact. According to Deborah Tannen, women also display more general immediacy behaviors than men such as leaning forward, nodding the head, smiling, and touching.

Why do women stand face to face? There are many possible reasons:

- The vis-à-vis frame allows women to get a fix on the face, and because they have a full view, they get more information.

- It enhances and encourages more eye contact, which creates more bonding and connection. It keeps people focused on each other.

- It creates a gatekeeping function; when someone is standing directly in front of you, it is easier to keep him or her engaged. You are more connected in the interaction. (The side-by-side position opens the door to outside stimuli and people, allowing for interruptions.)

- It signals that they are listening.

- It helps women read emotions, convey their own feelings more directly, and maintain the social connection.

In contrast, men are more apt to stand side by side when they speak. They don't look at each other or use more signals of power, and are less immediate in conversations with other men. Why do men favor the side-by-side approach? There are several possible explanations:

- Direct eye contact can be construed as challenging among men; a face-to-face frame is a more competitive posture and stance.

- The side-by-side frame increases men's comfort level and eliminates the feeling of "competition."

- Men are not as interested in looking at the face or maintaining eye contact. It is not always high priority for them to be able to read the other person; therefore, they do not take a direct body posture.

• A person in a dominant position (we assume the male in this scenario) usually makes less eye contact than one in a subordinate position.

Sociologist Harry Brod surmises that the side-by-side shoulder orientation is a way for men to seek intimacy: "Numerous studies have established that men are more likely to define emotional closeness as working or playing side-by-side, while women often view it as talking face-to-face. Men, for example, derive intimacy from playing and watching sports."

However, the side-by-side position can have negative consequences on communication. It makes it difficult for one to scrutinize the other person's face for emotion-laden micro-behaviors. This is true for women as well as for men. Imagine the following scenario: Three friends are out for lunch. Mary, seated next to Jenny, can't see her face. Sherry faces both of them. After lunch, Sherry pulls Mary aside. "Boy, Jenny was pretty upset about what's happening with her parents," she says.

"I didn't get that," Mary replies.

"Well you should have seen her face!"

Whose style is adopted when men and women talk to each other? Anthropologist Helen Fisher suggests a bit of gender-bending androgyny. In *The Anatomy of Love: A Natural History of Mating, Marriage, and Why We Stray,* she writes, "A woman should probably adopt at least one nonverbal, side-by-side leisure activity that her spouse enjoys, whereas men could improve their home lives if they took time out to sit face-to-face with their mates to engage in talk and active listening."

In business situations, however, this may not be so easy, especially if a man insists on shoulder orientation. In that case, a woman may perform a highly coordinated dance: she tries to stand face to face, but her male colleague orients away. Does she keep moving around in circles? Does she acquiesce to his style and stand side by side, missing those all-important nonverbals that she's used to receiving?

A woman can accommodate this in several ways. I am not suggesting she throw the baby out with the bath water, but if her goal is to be successful in her communication with men, she can make some minor adjustments that will facilitate her success. There are other ways to get that nonverbal information. She can ask questions. Or she can invite the man into a conference room or office where they can sit face to face. Most men will not rearrange furniture to maintain the shoulder orientation. This dilemma only arises when standing.

Whether seated or standing, a woman may consider negotiating a "corner" position. At a ninety-degree angle, she's neither side by side, missing important facial cues, nor is she face to face, rendering the man uncomfortable. The corner position still allows her to see the man's face and establish eye contact without adding the competitive edge. And, while standing, she can also move in and out of a direct face-to-face position. Men attending my seminars have told me that they can tolerate this, but not for long periods. One participant said it beautifully: "Audrey, when anyone, man or woman, stands face to face with their feet planted and it seems like they are not going to budge, I feel like I am back in the military with the sergeant in my face!"

Although no one can argue the interpersonal advantage women have by facing those with whom they are interacting so they are able to read facial expressions and maintain eye contact for bonding purposes, they must also be aware of the impact these skills may have on men. Men don't have a high tolerance for direct, face-to-face orientation. It feels competitive and disarming to them.

By the same token, men must understand that women are attempting to bond and connect when they stand face to face. They want to gather information and have the ability to read male reactions. This feedback is critical for them to make adjustments in their communication. Men must value these skills and honor them. They can make minor adjustments by making sure to check in with the woman they're talking to by turning toward her occasionally. In Chapter 10, we will explore the implications of men's indirect shoulder orientation on women. But for now, understand that a woman perceives a man is not interested and not listening when he orients away from her.

The Incredible Hulk and the Shrinking Violet

Late-night TV host Johnny Carson once said of Dr. Joyce Brothers, "She sits as if her knees were welded together." The genders have differing body buffer zones; a man's territory is larger while a woman's is smaller. Posture is most reflective of gender, and many behaviors separate boys from girls; males make themselves larger while females attempt to contract.

A male workshop participant once said to me, "You're pretty tall, aren't you?"

I confirmed that I'm nearly six feet tall.

"Well it's okay that you're tall," he continued, "because at least you have small bones." His message: I'm tall enough to be bumped into the masculine category, but I'm still in the feminine niche because my bones are small. If I were tall and big boned, I would be in trouble—consider former Attorney General Janet Reno's image problems. It's no mistake that the eating disorders bulimia and anorexia affect women by a ratio of ten to one. These illnesses are a hyperbolic example of "How petite can I become?" Emaciated celebrities such as fashion model Kate Moss and actress Calista Flockhart also convey the image that tiny means feminine. In fact, some parents, fearing that their preadolescent girls will grow "too tall" have been dosing them with high levels of estrogen to arrest their growth. Unfortunately, according to a recent article in *Health,* keeping girls at a "ladylike" height with this controversial method may jeopardize their health, potentially causing blocked fallopian tubes, heavy periods, miscarriages, and the like.

Men make themselves bigger to seem more masculine while women compress, condense, and coil up, even in dating situations where they want to accentuate their femininity. Novelist Marge Piercy's description in *Small Changes* is apt:

> Men expanded into available space. They sprawled, or they sat with spread legs. They put their arms on the arms of chairs. They crossed their legs by putting a foot on the other knee. They dominated space expansively. Women condensed. Women crossed their legs by putting one leg over the other and alongside. Women kept their elbows to their sides, taking up as little space as possible.

The large-small dichotomy is evident in the differing ways the genders walk. Men take bigger strides, exuding greater confidence and a sense of self-assurance. Their nonverbals convey, "I'm getting to where I need to go with determination and conviction, and I'm getting there faster." Women, on the other hand, have learned to walk little. They take small, mincing steps. Consider Chinese women with bound feet—the most extreme example. American women in tight skirts and high heels, however, are similarly (if not permanently) handicapped.

Men often expand to stake their territorial rights through the posture and position they maintain. Imagine the following scene: a person leaning back, hands behind the head, feet up on the desk. The message here: "This is my meeting. I'm running the show." Is it a man or woman? Status and power markers are indicated by how laid-back we are and how much space we take up; the more relaxed and expansive, the more power we have. We see this kind of male expansive behavior in the office. As one woman complained during a workshop, "I find that when many men speak to other people in the room, they put their feet up on the desk or table. I do not like looking at the soles of their feet; I feel it's a barrier."

The converse is also true: the more restricted, tight, pulled in, and tense, the less power we have. This is evident during a job interview. The interviewer is in a power position, relaxed and at ease; the interviewee looks like a private in the military, sitting in a straight-backed, full-attention position. Similarly, women in the workplace are more rigid and men are more relaxed. The former even keep their upper arms close to the trunk to create a barrier for protection. I once witnessed a woman giving a presentation with her arms by her sides, followed by a man who was much more commanding because he moved around with ease. (I later had a dream that the female speaker's elbows were surgically attached at her waist, and I kept wanting to help her!)

When women assume the condensed posture, it sends a message they may not want to send. Do they get bigger than men? No. But they can learn from men to be expressive and to use more space. They need not be so rigid; they can stand at ease.

These postural elements carry over to how we sit and stand. American women and European men cross their legs. This is a condensing posture. It would be considered effeminate for American men to cross their legs, especially at the ankle. Instead they most often take the seated military stance, with legs apart. Another accepted seated position is to have the ankle squared off on the knee. This could be considered a genital display. Some of these male behaviors may be driven by homophobia.

While standing, men also take a military stance—both feet on the ground, legs spread, chest out, chin up. The hands can be clasped at the crotch, another genital cue. Again, men seem to be staking out their territory, signaling, "I'm confident and in control." Women are often in awe of this posture. "Look at those men," they may say. "They act like they own the place."

Females' nonverbals, on the other hand, often look as if they are asking for permission. The feminine stance is third ballet position, legs together. Their heads are somewhat bowed, eyes lowered, in a demeanor that is submissive and demure. Men, in contrast, hold their heads up, take up more space, and are open.

It's best to become aware of how you're standing. Women can assume the same kinds of relaxed positions men do. Their legs don't have to be welded together, and they don't need to become little in their posture. As for men, it's useful for them to become aware of the impact of their position and whom they're crowding out when they take up so much room.

Space Invaders

I was at the airport, waiting to board a full flight. Just about all the seats at the gate were taken when I got to the terminal. The last vacant seat was next to a man who had set up his laptop computer and was already working away. The cord to his computer draped across the back of this empty seat and the armrest. I hesitated before I sat down, my cue to him to "please move your cord because this is now going to be my territory." Even though I gave him the signal, he made no move to reposition the equipment as I sat down. In fact the computer cord remained on my seat the whole time we waited for the flight to be called.

We call this a **"territorial marker."** Men tend to mark their territory with their coats, an arm flung across a chair back, documents, computer cords, coffee cups, or whatever else is handy.

The ground crew began loading the passengers. When this man's row was called before mine, he simply reached over behind me and tried to grab his cord.

"Do I know you?" I asked with great irritation for his lack of regard for his invasion of my space.

He made no attempt to adjust. No apology was forthcoming. "Oh, excuse me," he simply muttered. And that was that!

Unfortunately, both men and women often discount and actually violate women's personal space. It becomes a power and control issue. Do people invade their space because the woman invites them into it by smiling or otherwise indicating interest? Or, do they have a low regard for women's status and therefore have no compunction in crowding her? It is a chicken-and-egg issue. We could argue that societal forces and sex role norms encourage women to use small distances, therefore perpetuating their oppression.

My friend Pam recently had such an experience at a bulk discount store. No one likes waiting in long grocery lines, but the wait can seem intolerable when someone crowds you too. Pam had written a check and was waiting with the cashier for approval from a supervisor. The customer behind her in line moved into her body buffer zone such that he hung right over her, peering directly into her checkbook. The cashier asked the impatient shopper to back up, but he didn't budge. Finally Pam turned to him and said, "Please, sir, I need some more space," to little avail. He merely muttered something about wanting to get out, as if crowding Pam would speed the process along. She, of course, couldn't wait to get out of the situation.

The popular term "in your face" is an aggressive reference, usually to a style of behavior. We use the space invasion expression to indicate violated boundaries and belligerent attitudes or acts. When a man gets in another man's face, it's perceived as a challenge and a prelude to a physical fight, even among white-collar workers. When a man gets too close to a woman, however, she does not experience it as a challenge. Rather, she feels threatened or scared. Invasion of personal space signals a disregard for an individual and her personhood.

Invasions of space can send the message, "I can take liberties with you." It may be the prelude to touch and possible sexual harassment. Imagine the following scenario: Keith stands too close, Sarah backs up. He keeps advancing, she feels uncomfortable and possibly frightened. Many women don't know what to do when facing this perturbing situation. These sorts of encounters fall within the purview of sexual harassment, as discussed in Chapter 5.

Women must take some responsibility for allowing people into their space. I am not suggesting they discontinue this practice altogether. We can choose to let certain people close if we want to—when we sidle up to friends or lovers, when we wish to share something in confidence and need to speak in a low volume, when we want to touch someone to facilitate empathic listening.

However, the issue arises when we do not want someone in our space. In certain contexts, such as when interacting with men who are dominant or who have a reputation as potential "womanizers" or "harassers," women may consider being more standoffish. That means maintaining more space when these men are around by taking a step back or moving away. Also, they can counteract their need to allow people into their space by using other, more assertive nonverbal cues—keeping their voice firm and their hands to themselves and employing bigger gestures. Finally, they can always take the off-the-record act and put it on record. For instance, Sarah, finding herself in this predicament, might say, "Keith, I only feel comfortable when my husband stands this close to me. Please back up."

This reminds me of an incident that occurred when my daughter, Alexandra, was about three. We were in a store when a boy toddler came up to her and tried to hug her. She wanted no part of this strange kid. When she pushed him away, he almost fell over. The mother came running to his defense. "Jason only wants to hug her," she said, as if he did not need Alex's permission.

"Well, she does not want him to hug her," I replied. The mother was obviously offended by this, but her son's violation of my daughter's space went right over her head. She actually got into it with me. Finally, I had to tell her, "Alex has a choice about who is going to touch her!" That's something we want young children to know. Strangers—not even cute little boys—should touch you when you don't want them to. Isn't this where gender dynamics begin?

Men also must take responsibility for spatial invasions. Since getting into another's personal space is the prerequisite to touch, this is a potentially potent and dangerous territory for men. Given that 90 percent of sexual harassment cases are filed by women against men, most men should consider how their invasion will be interpreted!

Of course, men aren't the only gender to invade women's space. Other women do it too. Women need to respect one another's personal space and not perpetuate the lowering of another woman's status and the undermining of her credibility. Moreover, hospital patients often complain that nurses, doctors, and other medical personnel violate their personal space, further reducing their dignity.

Social psychologists have conducted some interesting experiments in the 1970s on elevators to gauge when and how space invasions occur. They found that eye contact behavior played an important role and that gender differences are apparent in the dynamics of eye contact and violations of personal space. In one study, for instance, women entering an elevator were more comfortable standing next to women (but not men) with whom they had made eye contact, whereas men stood closest to a person of either gender who had not looked at them.

These elevator experiments that all of us practice in real life suggest that eye contact serves as a type of permission or a sign of possible closeness for women. On the other hand, women find a man's look to be more threatening, while men seem less sensitive to the gender of the other and prefer to stand closest to a nongazing person. The lack of eye contact increases their level of comfort.

Violations of personal space can also be used as power and control moves. In *The Man Who Listens to Horses,* Monty Roberts describes how he modeled some of his horse training techniques on the invasion of personal space that he observed of an alpha mare (she's the lieutenant to the stallion in the herd) as she tried to control a wild and abusive colt.

Using a technique Roberts called the "advance-retreat," the mare practiced an intentional invasion of space. When the colt charged her, as he did the older mares and his peers, not only did she charge him back but she got into his face and kicked him to the ground. In fact, she knocked him down three times. She then pushed the offending colt out of the heard. He literally walked along with his head hanging down, following the other horses. He had to stay a physical distance away from the others until the mare granted him permission to ease back in again.

What happens during an interaction between a man and a woman when he begins to display dominant and aggressive behaviors by advancing into her space? She certainly can't kick him to the ground, though she may feel like she'd want to. Suddenly she finds herself on the horns of a delicate dilemma. If she constantly retreats, she is granting permission, enabling him to continue this kind of wrongful invasive behavior. Does she hold her ground, cementing her feet to the floor and refusing to budge? Again, I recommend that a woman who finds herself in this uncomfortable situation use the verbal channel. "Sam what are you doing?" she might ask. "I know you're trying to make a point, but you don't need to get in my face to do it."

Close to You

Standing face to face is not a competitive or challenging cue when one is interacting with one's sweetheart or wife. In mixed-group parties and dating situations, people expect some invasion of personal space. It's permitted if it's reciprocal. In fact, potential couples use off-the-record nonverbal signals to indicate their availability to and interest in each other. Getting up close and personal is the prerequisite to touch, eye contact, and the ability to see facial expressions, all of which constitute signals of interest.

Imagine the following two scenarios at a local coffee shop:

1. Maria and Ron are sitting across from each other at a small table. They are both leaning in toward each other. They don't break eye contact. In fact, they rarely take their eyes from one another's faces as they talk. They smile as they clasp hands.

2. A few feet away are Renee and John. Renee is leaning earnestly toward John, but he slouches back in his chair and gazes around the café. Neither is smiling, and no one is touching.

We can infer much information—what I call "intimacy signaling clues"—from these scenes that hint at how close each couple is at the moment. We can assume, for instance, that Maria and Ron are enjoying one another's company; each is very interested in what the other has to say. On the other hand, it appears that Renee and John are having a hard time tonight, and that John is withdrawing. That we can make these inferences is a testimony to how informative and revealing the use of space (and the resulting domino effect on facial expressions, eye contact, and touch) can be to involvement.

Mutual gaze, touch, and the close observation of facial expressions are all predicated on entering another's personal space. Men and women who care about each other sit and stand closer to each other than those who are disinterested. In *The Anatomy of Love*, Helen Fisher describes "intention cues" such as "leaning forward, resting one's arm toward the other's on the table, moving one's foot closer if both persons are standing . . ." (this is what we call "playing footsie," right?)—all proxemic cues that let the other person know we're interested.

A man and a woman will enter one another's personal space as a sign of interest or if they wish to express intimacy. If a man ignores a woman's overture (and withdraws nonverbally like John does from Renee), creating more space, the "pickup" is over, or for established relationships, the intimacy has declined. The spatial relationship must be in total body synchrony; one member of the couple cannot be leaning forward and the other back.

Gender Prescriptions

There is more than enough space to go around! Men and women employ personal space and territory differently. People also react and respond to women's and men's personal space and territory differently. Becoming aware of how we use and react to the opposite sex's personal space and territory is critical to interpersonal effectiveness.

GENDER RX

- Personal space acts as a protection, a safety device, and a status marker. If there is no way to increase personal space, people will avert their eyes to create space psychologically.

- We all use markers to establish the boundaries of our territory. Women can grow their space by taking up more territory.

- Subordinates yield space to higher-ups, and dominant individuals may intrude on the space of those perceived as subordinates.

- Men relate side by side but women relate face to face. To practice gender-flexing, women can adopt one nonverbal side-by-side activity with their partner and men can spend some face-to-face time with theirs.

- In business settings, women can circumvent the male shoulder orientation by sitting or standing in a corner position, moving in and out of a face-to-face orientation, asking questions, or sitting face to face in a conference room.

- Women should become aware of whether they're coiled up. They can assume a more relaxed position.

- Men should become aware of how much space they are occupying. Are they crowding others? Invading their space?

- A woman who feels crowded by a man should put his nonverbal behavior on record.

CHAPTER SEVEN

Talking with Your Hands

We respond to gestures with an extreme alertness and, one might almost say, in accordance with an elaborate and secret code that is written nowhere, known by none, and understood by all.

—EDWARD SAPIR

Whether our intent is to deceive, intimidate, attract, avoid, or express our emotions, men and women are constantly communicating with their hands! Sigmund Freud once claimed, "He that has eyes to see and ears to hear may convince himself that no mortal can keep a secret. If his lips are silent, he chatters with his finger tips; betrayal oozes out of him at every pore." We can tell a lot about how people feel from their gestures!

But it's also important to be able to read gestures properly. In an essay titled "A Little Louder, Please," Woody Allen describes a character who was poor at receiving gestures. This character had been invited to a theater performance. Unfortunately for him, it was a mime performing a skit called "Going on a Picnic." Allen describes his

181

character's impressions of what he thought the mime was trying to communicate:

> It all began when a wisp of a man walked on stage in kitchen-white make-up and a tight black leotard. . . . The mime now proceeded to spread a picnic blanket, and instantly, my old confusion set in. He was either spreading a picnic blanket or milking a small goat. Next, he elaborately removed his shoes, except that I'm not positive they were his shoes, because he drank one of them and mailed the other to Pittsburgh. I say Pittsburgh, but actually it is hard to mime the concept of Pittsburgh, and as I look back on it, I now think what he was miming was not Pittsburgh but a man driving a golf cart through a revolving door—or possibly two men dismantling a printing press.

Allen's humor illustrates why it's important to interpret gestures accurately. An Associated Press account of an incident on an airplane headed to Salt Lake City about six months after the September 11 attacks demonstrates just how powerful gestures can be. We were all still pretty jittery about potential terrorism. A new FAA regulation had been passed prohibiting airplane passengers from leaving their seats during the last thirty minutes of flights into and out of Salt Lake City where the Olympics were about to take place. However, despite two warnings from the captain, Richard Bizarro, one of the passengers on a flight from Los Angeles, decided to get up twenty-five minutes before landing to use the restroom. When a flight attendant instructed him to return to his seat immediately after using the lavatory, the six-foot-two, 220-pound Bizarro ignored her and used the hostile stare-down that I described in Chapter 4. In fact, he stared at her for a full minute.

Unbeknown to this unruly passenger, however, two undercover sky marshals were also on the flight and observed his behavior. One of the marshals even reported seeing Bizarro give what looked like a thumbs-up signal to another passenger on the plane. As a result, the air marshals took control of the cabin and ordered all of the passengers to put their hands on their heads for the rest of the flight. Bizarro was arrested and could face twenty years in prison. His use of menacing gestures was perceived as interfering with the flight crew, which is a federal offense.

The Unspoken Word

The term "gesture" can have many different meanings to us, such as a head nod or shrug, but in the field of communication the term refers specifically to movements of the hands and/or arms that convey an attitude, feeling, idea, or intention. Gestures perform many functions in interactions. They can replace speech—a teacher, for instance, bringing her index finger to her lips to silence her class, a pickpocket in Florence drawing an index finger across his throat because he did not like me staring at him, or an angry father shaking a fist at his wayward son. Gestures can also regulate the flow of conversation, help speakers maintain their listeners' attention, accentuate speech (to illustrate the intensity of the feeling), take up space, signal the intent to speak, and provide clarity (How big was that fish?). They can even illustrate or represent the thought process, as when you snap your fingers to create the impression of immediate knowledge or draw an object in the air with a finger.

Actually, there are two kinds of gestures. The first are what communications professors Mark Knapp and Judith Hall describe as "speech-independent." Psychology professor Paul Ekman also refers to these as "emblems." Like a teacher's shushing behavior, it is an autonomous behavior that conveys meaning without words. Other speech-independent gestures or emblems include holding the thumb and index finger in a ring to indicate okay; waving the hands to say come in, goodbye, or hello; circling the index finger by the temple to indicate crazy; giving a thumbs-up or thumbs-down; and rubbing one index finger over the other to say shame on you.

Just as there can be a slip of the tongue, there can be what Ekman describes as an "emblematic slip." Ekman has developed a reputation as an expert in deception—how nonverbal cues betray our real intent. He cites a situation that occurred when a person of high status subjected a woman to a stressful interview. During the encounter, both the woman and her powerful interviewer were unaware that she displayed "the finger" for several minutes during the course of their time together! She was hostile and subconsciously telling this powerful male interviewer to "f— off."

Children can decode several speech-independent gestures by age three, and their ability increases dramatically by five. In a study conducted by developmental psychologists George Michael and Frank Willis, four-year-olds of both sexes accurately decoded the emblems for "yes," "no," "come here," "quiet," "goodbye," "two," "blow a kiss," and "I'm going to sleep." Generally, children at this age can understand more speech-independent gestures than they actually use. By adulthood, we are fluent in both sending and receiving gestures that have a direct nonspeech meaning. We have developed a full repertoire of understood emblems.

The second type of gesture is not independent of speech but actually related to the words we use. I think of these as referential gestures. Based on their research, Mark Knapp and Judith Hall have summarized and categorized the most common types:

1. *Gestures depicting concrete reference points,* such as pointing to a specific person or in a direction while showing someone where to go.

2. *Gestures indicating the speaker's relationship to what he's discussing* by characterizing the thing or commenting on the speaker's orientation to it. An oscillating hand movement, for instance, can suggest that a speaker "isn't sure" or that a situation "could go either way." The former president of France, Charles DeGaulle, often used a grasping gesture when he spoke. Many people perceived this as his desire to grasp an idea or control the subject.

3. *Gestures acting as a visual punctuation for a speaker's words.* Pounding a fist on the table or into one's other hand help make a strong point.

4. *Gestures regulating and organizing the dialogue between two people.* A wave of the hand in front of the speaker can signal, "I want to interject here!" when the listener wishes to speak.

These referential gestures clarify and provide additional information to what the speaker is saying.

Watch It . . . I'm Biting My Beard!

Like other nonverbal cues, gestures vary culturally, and much miscommunication can occur when we are unaware of culturally sensitive behaviors. Beckoning (a wave to signal come hither) is a case in point. Psychologists Paul Ekman and Wallace Friesen have observed that North Americans will raise a hand and/or wave to get a waiter's attention. Latin Americans, on the other hand, beckon others with a downward arc formed by the right hand, looking for all it's worth like the North American gesture signaling, "Go away."

Gestures are highly culturally variable. A single behavior can have multiple meanings in different cultures and can get us in trouble! For instance, the ring gesture (the circle created by the thumb touching the index finger) with which Americans convey "okay," means "You are a zero" in France and Belgium. In Japan, it denotes "money," but in parts of southern Italy, it stands for "asshole." In Greece and Turkey, the same gesture can be a sexual invitation.

Signs of contempt (giving someone the "finger" or signaling "up yours") are another area ripe for miscommunication, as they too vary from culture to culture. For instance, male Pitta-Pitta aborigines of Australia bite their beards to indicate their displeasure, while the females insult others by thrusting their abdomens forward and vibrating their thighs. (Cool!) Making a V over the nose with the forefinger and middle finger as the palm faces inward toward the face is considered obscene in such disparate countries as Saudi Arabia and Mexico.

President Nixon committed a major faux pas in Brazil when he deplaned with hands upraised in the American peace emblem—fingers held in a V. This, it seems to me, this was his favorite gesture. Unfortunately, for Brazilians, this is the equivalent of flipping someone the "bird." Nixon had not done his nonverbal homework!

According to Roger Axtell, author of *Gestures: The Do's and Taboos of Body Language Around the World,* in Belgium, the country where my mother and I were born, "If a woman wishes to shake hands, she will extend hers first." Also, "Standing with your hands in your pockets while conversing is considered bad manners, and snapping your fingers when others are present is also frowned upon." I remember my mother also constantly insisting that my hands be on the table, not in my lap, at the dinner table. I guess in Belgium they need to see your hands.

Children may use gestures such as thumbing a nose or putting their thumbs by their ears while sticking out their tongues. This is probably the extent of their obscene gesture repertoire. However, by adolescence, a sex difference emerges. In middle school, boys will begin to employ "the finger" and the "up yours" gesture using the arm in an upward motion. Preteen girls would rarely engage in such behaviors. It would violate a feminine prescription. At this age, children are already learning that certain gestures are acceptable for one gender but not the other.

Gendered Gestures

A number of frequently used gestures either undermine or expand one's credibility and power. As we have seen with the nonverbal behaviors explored in previous chapters, men are more likely to use those gestures that augment their power, whereas women are apt to use gestures that diminish theirs. As communication professors Virginia Richmond and James McCroskey explain, "Males tend to use more dominant-type gestures and movement when communicating with females, as compared to their female partners. Similarly, as compared to their male partners, females tend to use more submissive-type gestures."

What are dominant and submissive-type gestures? Men are more apt to be expansive and powerful in their hand movements. We know, for example, that anger is the one emotion men are permitted to display publicly. A clenched fist will communicate tension, irritation, and anger. When my father would lose his patience with us, he would say, "Get in here and clean up your room." If his words were combined with a clenched fist, we knew he meant business! Pounding one's fist into one's palm is an especially effective show of power.

Studies have revealed that women tend to put their hands in their laps or on their hips, tap their hands on the table or on their leg, and pull in their gestures as if their elbows were surgically attached to the waist. They also incorporate more bonding gestures. These are "openness" behaviors such as the hands and arms being outstretched toward the other person as if to say, "I invite you to participate and be my partner." These are meant to facilitate interaction and invite the listener to participate. And women are more expressive. Just as they incorporate more facial expressions, they are or can be equally animated in their use of gestures, especially when they become excited.

Communication professor Judy Pearson claims, "The differences between the use of gestures by women and men are so evident that masculinity and femininity may be distinguished on the basis of gestures alone."

Here are some examples:

• *Adaptors.* These gestures learned in childhood (often involving self-touching) are a form of self-soothing, such as pulling on an ear, rubbing the nose, tapping on a leg, twisting fingers, chipping off nail polish, twirling hair, or even shaking a leg. We can also engage in adaptors with objects if we adjust clothing or play with jewelry, a pencil, or pocket change.

Adaptors are distracting. Imagine Carmen, sitting in on a board meeting, twisting her rings and shaking her leg. Some people will pay more attention to the adaptors than to Carmen's words, because her activity not only draws their gaze but also conveys anxiety. We also know that people who engage in these kinds of self-adaptors are generally perceived as less persuasive. The behaviors erode credibility.

As we've already discussed, men do not want to convey that they are out of control because this is synonymous with losing power. They are also good at body management. Consequently, men don't use adaptors as frequently as women do. Indeed, women generally employ more self-touching and other adaptors more often than men. As a result, women are at greater risk for undermining their own credibility. The most common adaptors that women use? Playing with their hair; rubbing, squeezing, or wringing their hands; cracking knuckles; picking at their cuticles; touching or adjusting their clothing; and picking or pinching flesh of an arm or hand.

• *Steepling.* This refers to holding the hands together, fingertip to fingertip. It's often done at eye level, as one stares at the other through hands placed on the nose or bridge of the nose. Steepling is a control, power, and status gesture employed primarily by men. The hands cover the face, so facial expressions are obscured.

• *Hand-to-face.* Chin and beard stroking are pensive gestures. These are closely married to control. Hand-to-face gestures could communicate, "I'm thinking, I'm contemplating, I'm judging." They are also employed primarily by men—especially the beard stroking!

• *Pointing, Fist Shaking, and Table Pounding.* Men use these aggressive power behaviors almost exclusively. In my consulting work I have seen many such displays during heated arguments, and when a man is trying to make a point. I was once involved in a meeting between labor and management regarding a union dispute where these behaviors came into play. The labor representative's gestures toward a manager escalated from a pointing of the finger to a pounding of the fist on the table and an angry and abrupt exit—the union rep actually got up and stormed out of the room.

In my twenty-five years as a business consultant, I have never seen women employ these kinds of aggressive gestures. It is not that women are incapable of using them (they may, with their children), but they usually do not engage in them outside the home.

Living Large: The Male Advantage

As we have seen in Chapter 6, the division between large and small, aggressive and condensing, applies to how we take up space and mark territory. These themes also hold true to male and female gestures. Men stake their claim by using large gestures and are rewarded for doing so—"These are my ideas and they are good ideas. Don't question me on them!" Men convey these sentiments while stretching their arms, and generally use larger, more sweeping gestures than women do. Big gestures take up more space; they are more commanding and aggressive.

Bob, the CEO of a telecommunications company, was making a presentation to the management team. I was seated up front. It was a lengthy exposition, and at some point, I had to excuse myself to make a run to the ladies' room. As I quietly got up to leave, he inadvertently hit me with an outreached hand. He had been flailing his arms in harmony with his enthusiasm for a new project. Caught by surprise, I actually stumbled, and everyone laughed. Bob apologized for almost decking me. "I was trying to bowl everyone else over with my new project, but I guess I got you in the process," he chuckled.

Enthusiasm: The Female Advantage

Women also use gestures to their own advantage. Sometimes they even evolve a secret code to communicate with one another. This happened with a management team I was working with. The women in the organization had identified Dave as the problem guy. He was the source of a lot of their complaints as he had little empathy or understanding for working women's issues.

The women in the management group developed a code among themselves. They made the letter "L" for loser with their thumb and index finger and displayed it on their cheeks every time he spoke, giving the appearance that they were holding their chins. This they saw as a humorous outlet for a difficult situation. Unfortunately, they let me in on their little game, and I became very distracted by this gesture. Sometimes, the women themselves had to work hard not to laugh. After a while, I could not even look at them. I was afraid others on the management team would begin to feel something was up!

In general, women's animated gestures add value to a charismatic presentation—a necessary component of the persuasive process. An audience member once told me, "Your gestures alone communicate the enthusiasm you have for your work. I don't think you could talk without them. I bet if we tied your hands together, you couldn't talk. But your enthusiasm is contagious. You get me excited and on board with your ideas. I actually start to believe and I am convinced of what you say!"

Since gestures are important in conveying enthusiasm, women whose communication style is gesture-deprived (elbows pinned to their sides during public speaking) should develop a more expressive approach to their presentations. They can practice in private and/or in nonthreatening settings incorporating appropriate gestures into their nonverbal vocabulary.

However, there is the possibility of going overboard in this arena. Women should pay attention to the level of animation conveyed in their gestures when they become highly energized. Unfortunately, when the excitement takes over, messages may be lost. Wild gesticulation can be distracting. A highly animated woman runs the risk that her listeners pay more attention to and maintain more eye contact with her hands than with her and her ideas. What should she do?

I suggest she videotape herself talking with a willing colleague or friend to observe how she uses gestures. She can monitor herself, making sure that her gestures closely accompany her speech and that her enthusiasm for her ideas is congruent with her behavior. She should also observe her other nonverbals. If her vocal cues are also becoming overly animated (see Chapter 8), it might be all too much!

Women's business fashions are at times modeled on men's attire; a woman could similarly modify masculine gestures to fit her feminine form. Petite women have license to use bigger gestures. Indeed, it's often the only way for them to get attention. But women must also recognize the quandary they find themselves in if they choose to use more masculine expansive or aggressive gestures. Some people will react negatively. However, if women condense and coil up, they will lose credibility. On the other hand, lively gestures can covey passion and enthusiasm, commanding the attention of one's listeners.

How to resolve this difficulty? It's a balancing act. I suggest that if women must come on strong in one nonverbal area, they can back off in another. So, for instance, they may use expansive gestures but also wear a pink suit to appear more feminine. Softer speech, smiling, or humor will counterbalance the dominant gestures and lighten things up. One caveat here, however: when women counterbalance in this way, especially with smiling, they risk contradicting their message and falling into the smiley-face syndrome. The way to remedy this is to come on verbally and nonverbally strong, then move to a softer but congruent verbal/nonverbal style. Whether powerful or more submissive, the point is to remain consistent in your verbal and nonverbal cues.

Also problematic are women who learn new gestures to expand their repertoires, but do not integrate them smoothly at first. For instance, women taking assertiveness training learned new ways to behave, but they hadn't yet assimilated these into their collection of acceptable behaviors. A woman might say, "I'm so upset with this," but then let too many beats pass before pounding the table; the gesture, when it finally comes, is way out of sync with her words. If a woman's nonverbal gestures aren't timed to flow compatibly with the verbal, she will appear awkward. Moreover, she will be sending incongruent messages that hurt and undermine her credibility and that even prompt others to laugh at her social ineptitude. She must develop awareness that not only should the flow of her verbals and nonverbals be congruent but they must also be synchronous.

Crossing the Boundaries

We don't usually associate men with grooming or preening gestures. That's women's work and considered feminine. However, on our daily commutes, many people forget they are in full view (at least from the waist up) of every passing motorist around them and believe they are isolated in their cars. Consequently, I often see men fixing or combing their hair in their rearview mirror or adjusting their clothing much the way a woman might. We all know what happens to a man who uses more feminine gestures in our society. He may be ridiculed and ostracized. Indeed, we are so tightly bound by socialized gender norms that men who use feminine gestures are often labeled or perceived as gay—yet another indicator of our homophobic society.

But what happens when a woman uses more masculine gestures? Women have been socialized not to stand out and most feel uncomfortable doing so. Yet, a recent article in *Executive Female* described how Carly Fiorina used relatively masculine gestures while engaged in a highly publicized proxy fight with board members of Hewlett-Packard. "Photos printed of HP's Carly Fiorina grew increasingly fierce," the article explained, "with fists clenched or index finger pointing." She was fighting for her corporate life, and she won the battle. Former British Prime Minister Margaret Thatcher was named the "Iron Maiden" and was notorious for aggressive gestures such as pointing her finger during a political speech or when Parliament booed her.

A woman who employs dominance gestures—she is expressive and uses big arm movements because she's excited about what she's discussing—takes up space and makes her presence known. One who uses more aggressive gestures such as finger pointing or table pounding can be perceived as being hostile. Both kinds of behavior can render a woman the target of taming campaigns by men and other women who don't like that she's acting like a man. Feminine means little, but such an expressive woman is getting big—too big, in some people's opinion.

While these are more extreme examples, we all need to become more self-conscious of what gestures we are employing and the impact they have on others. Both men and women can make minor adjustments to fit the needs of the context and the opposite sex, especially within the framework of gender-flexing. They can begin first by observing how others react to their gestures. Look at people when you are talking to them. Are they crowding into your space? Are they backing away from you to allow room for your expansiveness?

A male friend of mine was infuriated when he discovered the tire mechanic did not properly secure all the lug nuts on his SUV when replacing the snow tires. This carelessness endangered Geoff's safety. When he stormed into the tire dealership hot under the collar to report his frustration, the female store manager and the male assistant manager both took a couple of steps back to get out of firing range of Geoff's big gestures.

It's clear that men will continue to employ power gestures such as pointing, shaking a fist, and pounding the table, and there is a time and a place for these bold behaviors. If it is in the context of persuasion and they want to use them to make an important point, of course they should. But we must also become aware of and understand the overpowering effect aggressive gestures can have. Sometimes these grand gestures can shut out the listener, especially if the listener is a woman. She doesn't want to go up against his bold gestures. She can't match them—or she chooses not too. Literally and figuratively, he takes up too much space, and there is no room for her! But if she backs off, he loses out too, as he will not have the opportunity to receive input or valuable feedback from her. I suggest that men monitor themselves more closely to note how others (especially women) respond to their gestures.

Should a woman act or become submissive because a man uses power gestures? Does he cue her to be acquiescent with his expansive, powerful, dominating behaviors? Also, consider the size of men's hands, which are usually much larger than women's. These might be frightening to some women.

What's a woman to do under these circumstances? First, she must pay attention to her reactions when she encounters large male gestures. She should ask herself, "Do I feel overwhelmed by them?" She must also remember that she has choices. She should consider the context and short- and long-term goals of her response. It's important to be aware of becoming reactive to a man's power gestures, and I would advise not to respond in kind by acquiescing or by becoming "big" herself. However, if a man gets steamed up in public (in front or around other people), it may be more useful for a woman to stay calm. Later she might confront him in private where his loss of face would be minimized. There, she could explain the impact his gestures had on her.

Finally, a woman does not have to react by also using big gestures, and she also does not need to grow small and submit. She can simply hold her ground and send the verbal and nonverbal message, "You may be using big gestures, but I am not going to be intimidated or back down from my position." It's best to be neither aggressive nor submissive, just assertive.

Gender Prescriptions

Gestures go unnoticed because they flow with speech. Becoming more self-aware of one's gestures takes great concentration. Most are exhibited unintentionally, so women and men have a challenge to overcome. Both must ask themselves what impact or goals they are attempting to achieve. If it's to convince and persuade or to demand, power gestures are in order. If you are a woman, monitor the other person's reactions and be aware that you can control other verbal and nonverbal channels of communication to counterbalance a more masculine behavior. A man will need to assess his goals as well. If he wants to build interpersonal relationships, overpowering gestures will minimize his effectiveness and could distance others from him.

GENDER RX

- Gestures can convey emotions, replace speech, and regulate the flow of conversation.

- Men are likely to use gestures to increase their power while women are apt to use them to diminish theirs.

- Women use adaptors, a type of gesture, more frequently than men. Because these can be distracting and can rob credibility, women should monitor this behavior.

- Female gestures can convey enthusiasm, but women must be careful not to overdo it. Women who wildly gesticulate as well as those who are gesture deprived can practice moderating extreme behaviors in front of a friend or on video.

- To balance expansive gestures, women should come on strong in one nonverbal area but back off in another.

- Women must be sure that their gestures are congruent and contemporaneous with their verbal messages.

- Men should monitor themselves closely to note how women respond to their gestures. If women retreat, men should modulate their behavior.

- A woman confronted by a man's power gestures should stay calm and not respond in kind. It's best to be neither aggressive nor submissive, just assertive.

CHAPTER EIGHT

Don't Look at Me in That Tone of Voice

Her voice was ever soft,
Gentle, and low, an excellent thing in a woman.

—WILLIAM SHAKESPEARE, KING LEAR, ACT 5

"**H**ey!" you might be thinking. "I thought this book was about nonverbal communication. Why are you covering voice? Isn't that verbal?"

It's easy to get confused in this regard. But this chapter is not about the "what" of words but the "how" of voice. Benjamin Disraeli is credited with having said that there is no index of character so sure as the voice. Indeed, it's not what we say, but how we say it that's important. When we open our mouths we reveal all kinds of things about ourselves that have nothing at all to do with the words we are uttering.

The importance of this area of nonverbal communication was borne out historically in April 1974 when Richard Nixon sent written transcripts rather than audiotapes of his secret White House conversations to the House Judiciary Committee investigating his possible impeachment. Members of the committee quite rightly complained that written transcripts could not convey the full and correct meaning of an utterance since they lacked the additional nonverbal cues that one derives from the voice—inflection, stress, context, and other such nuances. They demanded the actual tapes because they contained this vital information. The landmark decision to provide the committee the tapes eventually led to Nixon's resignation, but it also legitimized paralinguistic communication—the study of voice and how words are said.

Manipulating the nonverbal elements of our message can completely change its meaning. Take a simple sentence: I will see you at the game tonight! My words give the logistics and plans for the evening, but my nonverbal vocal cues can convey a variety of additional meaning about my feelings:

- The game might be fun or boring!

- I really want to go, or I don't—sigh.

- I want to see you (in a seductive or romantic sense), or this is just business as usual.

- I'm proud to be involved in the game, or I'm dreading it.

- You'd better be there because you haven't come to a game yet!

The list could be endless!

Paralinguistic cues refer to everything having to do with speech except for the words we actually utter. These may be a bit subtler than other forms of nonverbal behaviors in communicating our intent. Certainly a booming, yelling voice is not subtle. However, a firm tone that conveys conviction is more nuanced than a pointing finger, big gestures, or the invasion of one's personal space. Vocal cues include:

- *Rate.* How many words per minute? In the United States, Northeasterners speak with more rapidity than do Southerners and generally men speak faster than women. Rapid rates of speech (and quickly coming up with a retort) have been correlated with composure and self-assurance.

- *Volume.* How loud or soft is the voice? Researchers have found that confidence, assertiveness, and boldness are reflected in louder speech.

- *Pitch.* Is the voice high or low in pitch? A high-pitched voice can sound squeaky and childlike. We associate lower pitches with greater credibility. More men are born with low-baritone or bass-pitched voices. They rarely use the highest level of pitch that women use.

- *Inflection.* Inflection refers to variations in pitch. How sing-songy does one sound? Imagine a storyteller reading a book to children. We would expect inflection. Too much inflection, however, in other contexts such as the business world can undermine credibility. In contrast, we are put to sleep by speakers who employ a monotonic voice, and they are perceived as less charismatic!

- **Quality.** Quality generally refers to those vocal characteristics that allow you to differentiate one voice from another. Is the voice small, feminine, or tremulous; thin, throaty, or fronted (aloof); tense, flat, or orotund; grating, nasal, harsh, or shrill? Is it stentorian or even bombastic (Charlton Heston playing Moses in *The Ten Commandments*), mellifluous (Liv Tyler as Erwan in *The Fellowship of the Ring*), unctuous (Sally Field as Mrs. Gump asking the principal to let her son Forrest into school), or breathy (Marilyn Monroe singing "Happy Birthday Mr. President" to John F. Kennedy)? All of these represent different combinations of rate, pitch, and volume.

- **Intensity.** How emphatic are the statements? For example, "I *really* want you to do it *now!*" The intensity can be a direct indicator of the speaker's passion and commitment or lack of it!

- **Silence.** Silence can speak volumes. It can provide thinking time, hurt another person, isolate oneself, prevent communication, convey feelings, create personal distance, signal respect and reverence, provide greater opportunity for increasing awareness of the self and others, accent or emphasize certain messages, say nothing, allow the speaker to explore his or her own thoughts and feelings, or create interpersonal distance. The Amish call this "shunning." Pausing is a form of silence that can be motivated by anxiety. It also impacts the rhythm and cadence or flow of the speech.

- **Nonfluencies:** These are expressions like "Um" or "Er" "Ah," "Like y'know" that fill pauses. (The latter can be confusing. Although they are words, they are employed as fillers!) They can lower credibility and make the speaker seem less sure of what he or she is saying. Ted Kennedy used many of these in explaining what happened at Chappaquidick, much to the detriment of his political career. We know that women incorporate more nonfluencies or filled pauses in their speech than men.

The way people use and vary these vocal characteristics can have a deep impact on our lives. I was at a political rally featuring two speakers who took opposing views on the then-impending war with Iraq. Both were well prepared. The speaker from the National Republican Party (who favored the war) spoke slowly and used the same pitch throughout. The opposing speaker was from Students for a Democratic Party. He spoke at a lively rate with a good deal of variation in pitch. Was the audience more persuaded by one style than the other? Did their paralinguistics impact the credibility the audience assigned the speakers? Research indicates that these variables do influence the attitudes of their listeners. When applied to this situation, I would surmise that the audience would probably feel less favorable toward the war as a result of the antiwar speaker's superior speaking skills.

Your Voice Speaks Volumes

Paralinguistic cues can give clues to our stress level, age, height, weight, socioeconomic status, anxiety, gender, personality characteristics, and culture. In fact, our voices are so unique that voiceprints can be used to identify individuals today in the same way that DNA has been used for forensic purposes. Take, for instance, recent events in the Persian Gulf. The opening salvos of the 2003 war in Iraq were aimed at a bunker complex in which it was believed Iraqi president

Saddam Hussein was meeting with his sons. When Hussein showed up on television shortly thereafter, there was some belief that a body double was being used to fool the Iraqi population (and the Allied forces) into believing that he was still alive. To verify Hussein's status, U.S. intelligence began analyzing voiceprints of his speech, comparing them to earlier television addresses. Other nonverbals couldn't be trusted. One can manipulate the facial hair, expression, or even appearance, but controlling vocal cues is much more difficult!

We make myriad judgments about people based on their vocal cues alone. Studies have found high correlation among listeners regarding the personality traits of speakers. Whether these judgments are correct is beside the point. Rather, our voices help create in others perceptions of and reactions to us. A friend of mine knew a lawyer, raised and educated in the South, who used this insight to his advantage. Bill moved to Philadelphia to start his law practice but purposefully kept his Southern drawl so as to appear friendlier than your average northeast, big-city attorney. "My voice puts my clients at ease," he once commented. Bill's voice also threw his adversaries off guard. They didn't expect someone with a Southern accent—a country bumpkin—to be very bright or quick, but Bill was.

It's amazing how much information the voice can carry. It has been shown that from voice alone, listeners can accurately distinguish between female and male speakers. In one study, for instance, listeners who heard twenty speakers pronounce six recorded vowels were able to correctly identify the sex of the speaker 96 percent of the time.

Paralinguistic cues also help us distinguish persons of high and low social status; stocky and slender speakers; short and tall speakers; black and white speakers; those with college, high school, or less than high school education; speakers in different age groups, by decade—that is, those in their twenties, thirties, forties, and so on. They even give us clues to a person's occupation or profession, overall appearance, body type, dialect region, and status.

When I did my postdoctoral work in Oxford, England, I learned that the British identify class and education by nuances in accent, possibly a close parallel to our perception of the Southern accent as low in credibility and containing a "redneck" element. Distinguished actor Michael Caine was brought up in a lower-class family in England, and he intentionally kept his cockney accent, even after his rise to fame. Although this pronunciation is poorly regarded—in fact, it's perceived as low class—he was proud of his roots. He claimed he had nothing to be ashamed of. Dr. Henry Higgins's travails in training Eliza Doolittle in the movie *My Fair Lady* show how voice and inflection are influential in determining social class—"The rain in Spain falls mainly on the plain." And O. J. Simpson actually attended voice and diction classes to eliminate accents related to his race. He wanted to sound more like a white person who had grown up in a middle-class home.

The voice can also carry much information about the feelings and attitudes of the speaker. A recent television commercial from AT&T demonstrated this phenomenon: a father spoke to his college-student daughter on the phone, questioning whether she was "Okay" or "Okay," using different inflections to indicate merely all right or really good. Her emails lacked the nuance he was seeking. The only way he could get the information he sought was to talk with her directly—and, of course, use the company's long-distance phone services.

Vroom, Vroom and Sweet Talk

In the first year of life, boys' and girls' speech appear to be almost identical. But girls learn language more quickly than boys, and their verbal expression is more comprehensible at an earlier age. The variety of sounds that babies use is nearly indistinguishable by gender, but as early as age two, girls are better able to control those sounds. They use complete sentences sooner, and they are more fluent than males from about the age of twenty-four months. As a consequence, girls' ability to articulate matures about six months earlier than boys'. It is possible that the advanced maturation of female vocal chords leads to their faster speech development and greater proficiency in articulation.

Socialization may also be a factor here. Research indicates that girls and boys grow up in what appears to be identical environments; however, they are nurtured in totally different social-emotional climates. In one study of three-month-old infants and their mothers, for instance, mothers talked more to their female babies and, consequently, the girls vocalized more in response to their mothers than mother-son pairs. These female infants actually got more practice talking than their male counterparts.

As they grow older, toddler boys may see that parents (particularly fathers) frown upon verbal play for them—it is not manly to talk to dolls or mimic mother's speech, even though she is most frequently the adult speech model at home. Boys' play centers around action rather than talk. What boy talks to his action figures? His toys—trucks, planes, cars, soldiers, Transformers—are for feats of bravery. Not surprisingly, some research shows that preschool boys use more sound effects like engine and motor noises in their speech than girls do. Vroom, vroom.

On the other hand, girls' playthings encourage interaction and verbalization rather than heroic action. Tea sets, stuffed animals, dress-up clothes, dolls (especially those that talk such as Chatty Cathy), and play schools all promote verbal interaction with playmates and the toys themselves.

Also, as young as age two, children can discern discrepancies between the voice and other cues, which results in tones such as sarcasm. When my patience wore thin with the trials of motherhood and my attempts to get my young children to be more goal oriented, I would say in a sarcastic tone, "Maybe someday, we'll be able to get to the front door and leave!" As young as age two, my daughter would remark, "Mom, you're using that sass voice."

The change of pitch—the cracking voice—is an embarrassing but welcomed rite of passage for adolescent boys between the ages of twelve and sixteen. Now a boy's voice is truly different from a girl's. Both quality of voice and pitch change for both sexes during this time, however boys progress to a deeper pitch than girls. According to communications experts Barbara W. Eakins and R. Gene Eakins, "Girls' vocal cords lengthen and the throat lining becomes thicker and softer. Consequently, female voices often become mellower and richer in quality with the coming of adolescence. They have a longer, slower pubescent period and less laryngeal growth, so they have more time to adjust to vocal changes." Unfortunately, boys must endure the rapid growth of cartilage and muscle, and their vocals are out of control! They can swing from high to low pitches and a variety of qualities (hoarseness, softness) all within the same utterance.

Girl Talk: The Female Perspective

Women communicate a level of authenticity through the expressive variation of their vocal cues. They can demonstrate real sincerity, show their true feelings, and exhibit empathy in what they say. The variation inherent in the female voice conveys charisma. This is a great asset for public speaking. Women also talk to bond and connect, to fill up the empty space in order to make others feel more comfortable. Indeed, filling the silence can increase the comfort level for everyone, including the women themselves! If we don't have a good comfort level, we don't have good communication—our interactions become strained and forced. Women engage in "relationship talk" (classically called "chitchat") to help them warm up and ease the conversation into an easy, spontaneous flow.

Unfortunately, this doesn't always go over well with the men folk. In my own family, my sixteen-year-old son, Armand, and even Geoff, my significant other, wave me on to speak faster. My son complains that my voicemail messages go on and on. Geoff will cue me to "Cut to the chase!" or ask, "What's the bottom line?" Incidentally, both of those expressions are born of male culture, and I believe are a result of men's need to be goal rather than process oriented—"Just the facts, ma'am." To a woman, the conveying of the "story" is as important as the story itself, but most men don't care about the details! They want to get to the bottom of things.

We also associate credibility with determined, short speech. My literary agent even cued me to talk in sound bites when I met with prospective publishers for this book. He said, "It's critical for these editors to perceive that you have succinct answers." Time is a premium in today's business world. "If you start going on and on," he continued, "I will nudge you to stop!" Research has shown that a faster rate of speech coupled with fewer words contribute to a more persuasive outcome. People who speak faster are also perceived as more intelligent and knowledgeable.

Sad to say, some women can't tolerate pauses in conversations and will talk about meaningless gibberish just to alleviate their own anxiety or because they crave attention. Unfortunately, in the process they undermine their credibility and validate the airhead stereotype. In fact, several other paralinguistic features of women's nonverbal communication work against them.

Take, for instance, the notion of being soft spoken. How often have we heard this term applied to a man? Almost never. No, it's women who keep their voices small and delicate. Part of that is biological, as explained above. However, when men's and women's voices are compared to the respective size of their vocal tracts, women talk as if they are physically smaller than they actually are. Their voices are pitched to the upper range, the decibel level is reduced, and vowel resonances are thinned. These paralinguistic elements are not the effect of biology but of socialization and learning—the imperative to be soft spoken.

In fact, according to communications professors Deborah Borisoff and Lisa Merrill, "Women, like children, have been taught that it is preferable for them to be seen rather than to be heard." Following this line of reasoning, Borisoff and Merrill point out in *The Power to Communicate* that when not held in check, women's louder voices are considered abrasive or displeasing and referred to as "carping, brassy, nagging, shrill, strident, or grating." And female conversation may be referred to as "babbling, blabbing, gabbing, or chatting"—none very serious endeavors. Unfortunately, however, a woman's quiet voice is rather ineffectual and a credibility robber.

The soft-spoken woman's voice doesn't carry. She threatens no one; she may lack sufficient force and volume to speak up effectively and convincingly. Women who are hampered by the need to sound feminine may adopt a high-pitched "little girl" voice; an artificially "sexy," breathy voice; or a volume so low as to be barely audible. In any case, the soft-spoken woman is at a marked disadvantage if she attempts to negotiate a contract, persuade a jury, or present a report. She risks being perceived as unconvincing.

A *Los Angeles Times* account of South Gate, California, councilwoman Maria Benavides presents a disturbing picture of how the quality of voice affected one woman's political career. Whenever she spoke, residents of this Southern California town mocked Benavides with "meowing sounds—a caustic reference to her soft, cat-like voice." The mayor finally intervened and asked the police to warn residents not to ridicule her. So her critics brought placards reading, "Meow," and waved them at her instead. Of course, the public's political objections with Benavides had nothing to do with her voice; she is the cousin of a mayor accused of corruption. But they found attacking a personal attribute—the soft quality of her voice—as a way to render their objections to her as personal as possible! (By the way, the city has since voted to recall her and the mayor.)

Finally, a woman's use of the linguistic phenomenon called the "tag question" can backfire on her. A tag question involves a seemingly declarative sentence that's punctuated with a question: "Linda, I need this report today, okay?" or "Jessica, clean up this room right now, all right?" What makes these statements so distinctive is the rising pitch that accompanies the question at the end of the sentence, which actually negates the original demand. More confusing still is the use of the declarative statement without the actual question but with an accompanying rise in pitch, as in "Linda, I need this report today?" or "Jessica, clean up this room right now?"

Tag questions can be very confusing; they undermine a woman's ability to get the job done at work as well as at home. A rising vocal pitch at the end of sentences (that is the operational definition of a tag question) leads listeners to conclude they have a choice. In a sense, the female speaker has damaged her own credibility and the possibility that the other person will accomplish the task. She has opened a Pandora's box, unconsciously giving the listener a choice!

In *A Woman's Guide to the Language of Success,* communications consultant Phyllis Mindell describes a scene that took place when two young executive women were on a conference call with her office:

> The person in New York asked the other, "What city are you in?" She replied "Atlanta?" Despite her sure knowledge of where she was, she said it like a question. If your voice ends every statement as if it were a question, then no one will listen to you. Why ask instead of tell? . . . If your intonation turns every sentence into a question, you're sending a clear message: "I don't know what I'm talking about. Don't listen to me!"

However, it also could be argued that this approach is characteristic of a more democratic leadership style rather than one that is authoritarian or direct. It solicits the listener to engage as a team with the speaker to make the decision. If the speaker's goal is to elicit and incorporate others' opinions into decision-making, a rising pitch opens the door for them to respond and feel included.

Women must walk a bit of a tightrope. They can be animated—it pulls in the audience—however, if they get too sing-songy, their voices become inadvertently comical, and they destroy their credibility. They need to monitor their vocal cues such as pitch, inflection at the end of sentences, or softness, especially when they get emotionally charged in a business meeting. It's wise to audiotape (or videotape) yourself to hear *how* you sound. This is especially helpful for women who are given to using too many nonfluencies and tag questions. Communications professor Linda Manning once set up a camcorder in her classroom and recorded herself lecturing and interacting with her students over a week's time. "How enlightening!" she told me. "First of all, I learned that I needed to spit out my gum before I began lecturing. I also learned a great deal about my paralinguistic cues, posture, and use of gesture."

Once taped, women can recognize if their paralinguistic cues are at odds with what they are saying and their purpose in saying it. They could role-play significant interactions in front of a camera. In addition to the feedback they get from watching the videotape, the practice would be beneficial in helping them feel more at ease in difficult situations. They should consider how pairing powerful vocal cues with other nonverbal behaviors can emphasize their intended message. Imagine a woman caught in the smiley-face syndrome who also uses a sing-song voice. How difficult it would be for her to command power and respect in a board meeting.

If a woman believes there are no ifs, ands, or buts about her point of view, she risks coming off as wishy-washy and undermining her credibility if she relies on little girl vocal cues. Barbara W. Eakins and R. Gene Eakins illustrate this beautifully: "There is an old pun concerning a theatergoer complaining about an actor who played the part of the king: 'He played the king like someone else had just played the ace.'" Some women must avoid habitually sounding like the queen limping in after the ace and the king have appeared. The content of their speech must be congruent with the vocal cues that accompany it. Their tone and pitch should reflect confidence, not doubt or what I call "an-asking-for-permission voice". They do not need to seek approval using vocal cues—no pausing, hesitation, or halting speech.

Bottom line: a woman should know her goal. If there are no ifs, ands, or buts about it, she must become aware of and then eliminate the rising pitch. A lowering of the pitch signals that a decision is final—"If you have an opinion, I am not interested." If, on the other hand, a woman wants to incorporate the listener in the decision-making process, she can feel comfortable using the rising pitch.

The Strong Silent Type: The Male Advantage

Consider the late actors John Wayne and Gary Cooper. They were the epitome of what we call "the strong silent type"—men who convey their resolve and power through a sturdy, deliberate silence. Peggy Noonan, former Reagan speechwriter, *Wall Street Journal* columnist, and Fox News political analyst, made this point when she said there is much that women can learn from studying men, from watching how they proceed through the world. "I admire and have often been instructed by the strong silence of men," she said. "They're silent not because they have nothing to say, but because they don't have to fill up the air with words. They don't need to be looked at to dominate. They already dominate, just by looking at themselves, but they're serene about it. Other people wonder what silent people are thinking and respect their silence."

Men often use silence to be in charge and collect their thoughts. They rely on it like they do the masked face. Silence exhibits control.

You know the image: "You can stand on your head, but I will say nothing. I will not let you in and better yet, I will throw you off balance by my silence. I am in control. I have the power!" Employed in this way, silence can be as earsplitting as shrieking.

Of course, as with all nonverbal communication, in the proper context, silence can be most effective. But it may also be detrimental, making men appear distant even when they don't want to be. In *The Right Words at the Right Time,* the famous architect Frank Gehry explained in an essay how his silence got him into trouble in his group therapy. For two years, Gehry attended these twice-weekly meetings with other talented business people, writers, and artists, but shy by nature, he never uttered a word! Finally the group turned on him. "They said things that stunned me," he wrote in his autobiography. "They attacked me . . . saying who did I think I was, sitting there, never talking, judging them, withholding."

Men risk being misinterpreted by their silence. As I have observed in corporate America, its source could be the desire to maintain power and control. Or, as in the great architect's case, it could simply be that they are shy or uncomfortable in a situation that requires the emotional sharing of feelings. Unfortunately, Gehry realized that he was also giving the same aloof impression to his clients: "Projects were falling through not because people did not like my work but because they were uncomfortable with me." Simply put, Gehry's quietness hurt his ability to engage with his clients successfully.

This is not to say that men don't talk. Of course they do. And their paralinguistic cues can convey credibility; they have the edge in the authority department! Deep voices and loudness—male attributes—have been associated with a lack of nervousness or anxiety, and even confidence and boldness. Such strong, certain voices are respected. In fact, a woman at one of my seminars remarked, "How is it that men sound like they always know what they're talking about even when you know they don't?" However, just like women, men must walk the vocal cue tightrope in certain contexts. If a man seems so sure of himself, is there room for anyone else's opinion—"Sounds like Jim has already made up his mind. What's the point of adding my two cents?"

Besides, men can speak volumes when they need to, using vocal variations (some feminine) when they contribute to persuasion. President Bill Clinton was quite skilled in the use of paralinguistics. According to communications expert Maureen C. Minielli, "He is an eloquent public speaker who appreciates the power of language and is not afraid to use it. He often speaks with passion and is comfortable expressing emotion. Clinton is not only well versed in the use of language but he is also a master of rhythm and cadence as well."

Men also use volume in their speech to command attention and authority. They may talk over others by growing louder to keep the floor and squelch other speakers. Whoever can get the floor and keep it usually has the power and control in a conversation.

I witnessed this phenomenon when I was a consultant to a committee that was in charge of constructing a major addition to our local university. The female architect spoke very softly, but the contractors, building inspectors, plumbers, and electricians on the job were primarily used to a male-dominated culture in which whoever spoke the loudest was king. On a walk-through of a building with the men, I noticed that whenever Jodie attempted to get the floor, half the guys never even knew she was speaking! I suggested to her that she not only speak louder, but also manipulate other nonverbals to get the men's attention. "Why don't you stop in your tracks and say, 'Hey wait a minute! I am concerned this won't pass structurally . . .'" I offered. It took a lot of work, but that's what Jodie had to do to command the floor. This was her project!

He Said/She Said

Women often accuse men of missing many nonverbal cues, and my research shows this to be true. However, males *do* focus on the vocal aspects of what is being said—the paralinguistics. And one conclusion that can be drawn from research on vocal quality is that women tend to be more specifically judged on voice traits than are men. Perhaps this is an extension of the fact that women are judged more (and judge others more) on their physical attractiveness. A woman's voice is yet another dimension of her attractiveness.

Men react negatively to female vocal characteristics that undermine authority, such as a high pitch, slow pace, or increased inflection. British Prime Minister Margaret Thatcher spent hours with a voice tutor doing humming exercises to lower the unpleasantly high pitch of her speaking voice. In my survey about female communications weaknesses, men were often critical of female voices, saying, "Women need to speak with more strength of voice and presence," or "Their pitch needs to be lower and their speed is too slow." Indeed, voice is one of the biggest contributors to women losing credibility in the workplace. Some women use their voices like little girls, with attention grabbers at the beginning of their statements—gasp . . . "You'll never guess what happened to me!"

Unfortunately, women's soft voices also often open up the opportunity for interruption. It is feminine to speak in a small voice. I remember watching almost every head turn in a seminar in which a woman with a big, bellowing voice raised her hand to ask a question.

It was as if everyone needed to check out the source of this huge voice. In contrast, one of my clients had recruited what it considered to be the top engineering candidate from a premier university in the country. Lin had a Ph.D. in a specialized area of engineering. She was also Chinese. Because Lin spoke in accordance with Chinese cultural rules, her voice was even softer than that of her American female counterparts. Unfortunately, people could barely hear her. So here was the dilemma: should she talk loudly like American men, or maintain her culturally prescribed soft quality? In consultation with me and a few of her male colleagues, we developed a few strategies for Lin. She could sit more centrally at meetings (literally making her the center of attention), formally place herself on the written agenda, or even have one of the male engineers get the floor for her with questions such as, "Isn't this Lin's area of expertise?" or "Lin, what's your opinion on this?"

Because women are more expressive, they tend to lose standing with men who prefer the voice to be more monotonic. Women often report to me, "He tells me, 'Don't get so excited.'" To counteract this, they must make a greater distinction between their home and work voices. They should use diplomacy, as they are working in a different culture. For instance, they can lower the pitch of their voices when they want to sound more authoritative.

Women, of course, have their problems with male paralinguistics. Often the male silent treatment drives them crazy. They can interpret a man's tight-lipped reticence as judgment, withholding, or a refusal to engage. Women have a high need for affiliation and approval. They need to know what their conversational partner is thinking. A woman who comes face to face with a strong silent type may ask herself, "Why isn't he saying anything? Oh no, he doesn't like my idea. He doesn't like me!" She may see him for something he isn't. Now we have a major communication breakdown!

Silence can affect our interactions with the opposite sex in intimate settings as well. A man's silent treatment can communicate to his partner that he doesn't care about or is uninterested in her or that he's just trying to maintain control and make her feel uncomfortable, even if, in reality, he is shy or uncomfortable sharing feelings. Men must realize that their silences can strain and even destroy relationships. As a woman in my seminar put it so poignantly, "My husband was silent for the first twenty years of our marriage. When he finally decided to talk, sensing our marriage was in trouble, it was too late. He could not engage or open up. I was tired of the silent treatment. My parents did that when I was a kid, and I was not going to tolerate it anymore in my marriage."

Moreover, many men are not terribly adept at managing their vocal cues to communicate feelings. In fact, they may feel challenged and handicapped in this arena. It reminds me of when you admonish a child to apologize for a wrong behavior when he doesn't want to do it. When you force it, the request for forgiveness comes out all wrong. He'll shout, "I'm sorry!" in an angry voice and then run away. The words are there, but the tone conveys the opposite feeling. Similarly, women may not believe what men are saying when they express emotion or they may think their words lack commitment or authenticity.

Men often feel misunderstood in these situations. Why? Because they're sending two messages. On the one hand, they're conveying their feelings, but on the other, they feel uncomfortable doing so. As a consequence, they may be gruff when expressing an endearment, muttering a compliment or yelling an apology. Although the right words may be there, the unfriendly vocal cues indicate the degree of discomfort they may feel in articulating sentiment.

Finally, women often feel intimidated by a man's loud voice. It slams them. They back down, feel downright fearful, and shut up in response! Unfortunately, that may be just the result the booming man is looking for. This is a common tool bullies use! When faced with a loud blast, it's important for women not to respond in kind. They need not be loud back. Rather, it's best to remain assertive, calm, and steady in their vocal style with enough volume to be heard but not overpowering.

Big Boys Don't Cry

Recently, televised sports showed two major setbacks for one university's teams: the men's and the women's basketball teams both experienced big losses on the same day. The male players walked off the court with heads hung down and fists shaking in disbelief and disappointment. Then the sports coverage cut to the women's loss. A female player had thrown herself to the gym floor, belly down, put her head in her hands, and cried! These were two entirely different reactions to the same event—a loss! The woman expresses her disappointment by crying, which many would regard as unsportsman-like behavior.

Crying is extremely context bound. We would feel odd to attend a funeral at which no one cried. I, for one, would wonder, "Did anyone like this person?" But in the arena of sports, crying is rarely okay! You win some; you lose some. It's perfectly acceptable to feel disappointed, but may not be suitable to display tears in a sports context.

During informal surveys in my seminars, I frequently ask my audiences the following question: "How many of you have seen a woman cry at work?" Both men and women—actually everyone—raise their hands. Then I ask, "How many of you have seen a man cry at work?" Maybe 10 percent of the participants respond. Do you remember when former Colorado Congresswomen Patricia Schroeder formally withdrew from the presidential race? After she gave her concession speech, she put her head on her husband's shoulder and began to cry. Presidential? Hardly.

Women are more expressive. They're taught that it is acceptable to show their feelings even through tears, and many can shed a tear on a moment's notice. Crying is natural for them; it's a way to release stress. But not for most men! The expressions "Big boys don't cry" and "Don't be a crybaby" come to mind! Men need to have someone die before they weep. As Mary Ritchie Key claims, "Even when tears appear to be a spontaneous reaction to sorrow, there are still cultural controls and stipulations as to when the tears may be shed, and where, and in front of whom." Instead of crying, men may use humor or even hostility to vent their emotions.

Big boys don't cry, but unfortunately they also hate it when women do. When a woman stockbroker lost her biggest client—the one that had made her a top producer in her office—she did what any woman would probably do. She fled to her cubicle, put her head in her hands, and cried like a baby. Everyone in the office heard her weeping, including her boss. Within moments, he came in, put his hand on her shoulder, and said, "Linda, take it like a man. Just go in the bathroom and throw up."

Men may either perceive crying as emotional blackmail, or they can believe that the weeping woman is weak and out of control. One woman in my seminar said to me, "If you are crying and older, they think you are menopausal. If you're younger, they ask if you have PMS." In either case, a woman's tears increase a male intimate's or coworker's discomfort and can diminish her effectiveness. Katy Sparks, executive chef at Quilty's in Manhattan, has adopted a more stoic attitude as a way out of the crying dilemma: "What I've learned from men is to keep disturbing emotions away from the workplace. I don't share my trepidation if I feel it at work."

So why do women cry? When a man is confronted with a crying woman, he mistakenly believes she is sad. Wrong. The majority of the time, anger is lurking underneath those tears. Anger is not a "feminine" emotion. It's the only sanctioned emotion men can display publicly, but not women. So an angry woman reverts to tears. Nice girls don't get angry, they cry. That's the norm. And that could explain why a man is often shocked and confused when he approaches a crying woman to soothe or comfort her and she snaps at him! Watch out.

Women face a credibility problem when it comes to crying. What should they do? Short of squelching their emotions, I believe precuing can reconcile this dilemma and protect a woman's image. It's helpful for a woman to know her weaknesses. If she recognizes that she is given to crying when faced with a confrontation, she should prepare herself—bring tissues, wear waterproof mascara, or even announce that she might cry.

Here is how Heather began to set the stage for a difficult interaction. She told her boss Sam, "Look, I am very concerned, and have been thinking a lot about what we are going to talk about. It's been on my mind constantly, but I want you to know that I may get upset." In this way Heather takes responsibility for what she is saying as well as her tears. When she tells Sam (cues him) that she may lose control, it prepares him. She looks like she's in control because she can anticipate that she might go out of control. She also signals to him that she wishes to continue the conversation although she may cry.

When a woman prepares for a worst-case scenario, the situation often does not arise. Advance preparation and acknowledging the potential situation give her the sense that she is more in control. In fact, women often report that just the act of announcing they may cry somehow prevents it from happening.

Sweet Nothings

Anthropologist Desmond Morris calls the distinctive paralinguistics involved in courting and dating as "grooming talk." Helen Fisher says that this kind of idle, often meaningless conversation is "distinctive because voices often become higher, softer, and more sing-songy— tones one also uses to express affection to children and concern for those in need of care."

Grooming talk starts with such benign statements as "I like your shirt" or "That's a neat car." The best leads, according to Fisher, are either compliments or questions because both require a response. She claims, moreover, that "*what* you say often matters less than *how* you say it! . . . The moment you open your mouth and speak, you give away your intentions with your inflection and intonation. A high-pitched, gentle, mellifluous 'Hello' is often a sign of sexual interest, whereas a clipped, low, matter-of-fact, or perfunctory 'Hi' rarely leads to love."

An astute observer can recognize instantly when a man is speaking to his girlfriend on the phone; his vocal tone, pitch, and quality will soften and become warmer. (His body posture even changes; he becomes relaxed and open.) He will often shift his posture at the same time that he adjusts his pitch, tone, and quality of speech. A softer pitch is innately friendly and suggests a nonaggressive, non-hostile pose. Men and women use higher-pitched voices in greetings and courtship to show they are harmless and to invite physical close-ness.

Gender Prescriptions

Men and women bring different vocal repertoires to the table, each with their own inherent advantages and disadvantages. But as with other nonverbal cues, men and women must monitor their voices to break automatic, habitual styles. Many people are under the impres-sion that they just are born with their voices and there is nothing they can do to change or alter them. Wrong. Ask any voice coach, speech therapist, singer, or actor. We can train our voices to be different than they are by increasing the volume, lowering the pitch, altering inflec-tion (to eliminate those pesky tag questions), and projecting. How-ever, I am not suggesting we swap voices. (I am reminded of a *Saturday Night Live* routine in which the men use little-girl, high-pitched voices while the women speak in the deepest baritones!)

Both men and women need to develop a sensitivity toward the use of their voices. They must ask themselves, Is this the appropriate con-text for these vocal cues? What is my goal? What do I want to ac-complish?

GENDER RX

- Credibility is associated with determined, short speech. Though some women enjoy conveying the whole story, they might be more effective in their interactions with men if they cut to the chase.

- Meaningless chatter undermines credibility. Women are advised to keep this under control in business situations.

- Soft-spoken women are at a disadvantage when negotiating or trying to persuade. In these situations, it's important to speak up and command the floor with other nonverbal cues.

- Tag questions can cause listeners to doubt a speaker's resolve. They are to be avoided unless the speaker invites cooperation and discussion. A lowered pitch at the end of a sentence indicates that a decision is final.

- Silence can make men seem remote, even if they don't want to be. They should notice if their habitual silence undermines their relationships with female co-workers and friends.

- Although vocal cues such as deeper pitch, less inflection, and greater volume convey authority and persuasion, men may need to monitor them when interacting with women.

- If subjected to a man's loud voice, a woman should remain calm but assertive.

- A weeping woman can undermine her credibility at work. It's best to pre-cue, announcing to others that she is upset and may cry.

- Videotaping themselves in action can help women recognize and correct ineffectual paralinguistic cues.

Dress Code

Dress changes the manners.

—VOLTAIRE

Human behaviorist Desmond Morris wrote in *Man Watching: A Field Guide to Human Behavior,* "It is impossible to wear clothes without transmitting social signals. Every costume tells a story, often a very subtle one, about its wearer." Dress is an important element of first impressions; it is a big nonverbal communicator. We do judge books by their covers; it's how we quickly form stereotypes. Whether or not we choose what we wear to intentionally make an impression, apparel *does* communicate. Our clothes convey messages that help other people perceive themes representing much of whom we are.

Physical appearance, particularly dress, sends a message as to how we want to be seen. We have fifty years of research that tells us you can change perceptions of a person by changing his or her clothing. There is no getting around it. Dress has a persuasive value that influences the behavior of others. The consequences for forming that first impression are great! There are no second chances at first impressions, no dress rehearsals, so to speak. Clothing may influence the extent to which another person may consider us credible. It is often read as a sign of character.

In fact, our attire can even influence how we behave. We act out what we have on. As Napoleon is reputed to have said, "A man becomes a creature of his uniform." This was brought home to me recently when I was called in on a sexual harassment case at a dot-com company. As I walked up to the reception counter for my initial interviews with the alleged perpetrator, the victim, and the CEO, my eyes quickly flew beyond the front desk to the cubicle behind it. There sat a barefoot guy in khaki shorts and a Hawaiian shirt. It looked to me as if he thought he was on vacation! I truly believe the lax dress code at this company contributed to the frat house behavior that many of its male employees exhibited. Loose and lively may be a climate ideal for spring break and wild parties, but at this office, it contributed to a sexually charged work atmosphere that set the stage for salacious comments and antics.

The reverse is also true, however. Have you ever noticed how even children will respond to being dressed up? They act more dignified and reserved when clad in their Sunday best. As one pro golfer explained, "If you wear an outfit you really like, it gives you a psychological lift and you play better." Women, in particular, will wear something to help elevate their mood. Apparel can also affect us indirectly through the reactions we get from others. Clothes, it seems, do make the man. Indeed, dress can be a marker for sex, age, occupation, personality traits, and group membership.

The Symbolism of Clothing

If any group is sensitive about clothing, it has to be adolescents. They can spend hours mooning over teen magazines and MTV shows, trying to determine exactly what they need to wear in order to fit in—or not—with the current "in" crowd. Educator Lawrence Gurel conducted a study of adolescent clothing styles in the 1970s. At that time, students categorized classmates according to their dress as:

- *Greasers.* Knit pullovers, loafers, black leather jackets, and greased-down hair for boys and teased hair for girls.

- *Hippies.* Unkempt, old grubby clothes and peace symbols.

- *Mods.* Expensive, fashionable clothes influenced by the early Beatles (of course, those of my generation know that later the Beatles turned hippy in their dress).

When I asked my children and their friends how they would sort today's adolescents by clothes, they responded with their own categories:

- *Gothic.* Black trench coats and boots, dyed black hair, dark glasses, pierced body parts, and tattoos.

- *Preppy.* Name brands, expensive designer outfits, and a clean-cut tailored look.

- *Jocks.* Athletic gear, sweat suits, and running shoes.

- *Gangsta or Hip Hop.* Low-riding (sagging) oversized jeans, baggy sweatshirts, and big jewelry.

- *Grunge.* Tattered, torn, or otherwise worn, mismatched clothes.

Clothing serves as a symbol of our status. If we fail to dress as expected, our occupational ability may be negatively affected since people associate our clothing choices with our socioeconomic level, goals, and satisfactions.

Recently, Katie Couric interviewed Colin Farrell, star of the movie *Phone Booth,* on the *Today* show. At twenty-eight, Farrell was dressed in jeans and cowboy boots. On his head, he sported a knit watch cap. He was an up-and-coming actor, a relatively unknown, yet he dressed for his national TV appearance as if he were ready to do house chores or yard work. Couric called attention to Ferrell's outfit. "What's with this?" she said, motioning toward his get-up.

For her part, Couric wore a saucy plaid kilt with knee socks. Farrell didn't waste a minute. "What's with this?" he retorted, indicating her somewhat flamboyant apparel.

I believe this was a generational gap. Farrell had dressed down, big time, but Couric was also making a fashion statement, being trendy, chic, and so characteristic of New York. It was a self-conscious moment; their dress was at cross-purposes!

Communications professors Loretta A. Malandro and Larry Baker suggest that the symbolic messages inherent in our clothing can be conveyed and received intentionally or unintentionally. There are four possibilities:

- *The wearer intentionally sends a message that is intentionally received.* During the 1960s, sewing an American flag to the back of your jeans was a way to protest the Vietnam War or simply flaunt authority, and going braless was a feminist statement. On the other hand, a prostitute dresses seductively or flashily to communicate her profession to potential clients.

• *The wearer unintentionally sends a message that is intentionally received.* Miranda is interviewing for a job as vice president of operations in a Fortune 50 company. The interview panel is composed of two men and a woman. Miranda deliberately selected her clothing for the meeting, but she paid little attention to her jewelry. She wears a large diamond engagement ring and a diamond-studded gold Rolex watch.

The interviewers are always looking for additional information about her. From her jewelry, they presume she is married and in the 50 percent tax bracket. (Maybe they also think they can offer her a lower salary since she clearly seems quite well off.) Miranda inadvertently communicates a message with her jewelry (perhaps one she doesn't want to send) that the interview panel carefully receives and evaluates.

• *The wearer intentionally sends a message that is unintentionally received.* Dick is a young, hip university professor who is often mistaken for a student. To counteract this impression, he decides to trim his shoulder-length hair, grow a neat goatee, and stop wearing jeans to class. He now dresses in slacks and a blazer to communicate his higher status as professor. His colleagues on the faculty and his students unconsciously know something is different, but they can't put their finger on it.

• *The wearer unintentionally sends a message that is unintentionally received.* My son gets dressed for school in his everyday clothing—jeans and a T-shirt. The other students and teachers unconsciously react to his dress, treating him like everyone else.

No intentional messages have been sent or received, and he doesn't stand out for any particular reason.

Bearing these possibilities in mind, did Colin Farrell intentionally dress down to convey a studied nonchalance about his big movie break? *I'm cool. It's no big deal.* What message did Katie Couric unintentionally send with her ersatz Scottish costume? I'm sure she didn't want to convey that she's a fashion victim, or did she? These are issues we need to consider every morning when we get dressed. In this chapter, I'll help you learn how to think about them.

Power Dressing: The Male Perspective

Ralph Waldo Emerson once wrote, "I have often wondered how long men would retain their ranks if divested of their clothing." Probably not very long! Our attire is often associated with status and prestige—think Louis XIV in his gold-embroidered ermine robes. In *National Geographic Fashion,* Cathy Newman writes, "All cultures tap into the power, real or imagined, of dress." The nineteenth-century Mandan war chiefs of North America wore necklaces of bear claws to testify to courage, Newman points out. The Queen of England's jeweled crown has its counterpoint in the bird-of-paradise feather headdress of Minj tribesmen in New Guinea. Masai kings and Mayan shamans drape themselves in lion and jaguar skins to transmit their super potency. Even Mike Deaver, Ronald Reagan's advisor, put his boss in power ties—the ones that slap you in the face with big bold colors, prints, and broad stripes and not those with little red or blue polka dots.

Gandhi is a political leader who used clothing to make a statement. In fact, his evolution was marked by increasingly radical alterations of dress. He began his career wearing British-made, conservative business suits and ended it in humble, unstitched dhotis fashioned from khadi, the traditional Indian hand-woven cotton cloth of the lower classes.

Of course, when it comes to clothing and political statements, one can move in the opposite direction as well. Several of the Chicago Seven, known for their antiwar activism during the 1968 Democratic Convention, began as students in bell bottoms, long hair and beards, and love beads. Several ended up clean shaven on Wall Street in traditional suits and short hair. It was such a contrast to see them thirty years later in clothes symbolizing that they had joined the establishment they'd once reviled.

Dress can also have an impact on political events. For instance, it has been noted that the clothing the candidates wore might have influenced the outcome of the famous Nixon-Kennedy debate during the 1960 presidential election. According to communications professor Randall P. Harrison, whereas Richard Nixon was dressed in a light suit and tie, Kennedy's dark suit and tie contrasted more sharply with the background, making him stand out. Moreover, Nixon had lost weight so his clothes seemed ill fitting. "The neck of his coat collar gapped. And his stance caused wrinkles to appear across the front of his jacket," Harrison explains. All of these tiny flaws helped the voting public infer that Kennedy seemed the better choice for president that year.

As Valerie Steele, a scholar of costume and the acting director of the museum at the Fashion Institute of Technology in New York explains, "Clothing has been used as part of the invention of tradition." Clan tartans, for example, were largely the product of the nationalist movement in eighteenth-century Scotland, a vivid symbolic rejection of British rule. Also, it is important to note that this is one of the few moments in world history when it was acceptable for men to wear skirts! (During World War II, the Germans called the Scots the "Ladies from Hell" because they were relentless fighters and generally size-able men! There was nothing effeminate about these guys in skirts!)

Women's Wear Daily: The Female Perspective

Fashion is a big nonverbal issue for women. Female clothing is more open to interpretation than men's because women have more choices and more wares to show off than their male counterparts. Besides, just as the quality of the female voice is more open to criticism, so is their physical appearance more carefully watched. As Deborah Tannen explains, "Because we are so much judged by our appearance, women don't take lightly any indication that our weight, our looks, or our clothes are less than perfect." Matters of personal appearance and dress are lightning rods for most women. Culturally, they learn they should care about how they look and care more than men do. In one study of appearance and social acceptance among adolescents, teenage girls said that clothing was the most important first attribute considered in describing the characteristics of the most popular girl in the class. It's not who you are, it's what you wear!

In the 1960s, psychologist Lewis Aiken correlated dress to personality traits in a female population. According to his view, how women dress indicates what kind of person they are:

- *Interest in dress.* Conventional, conscientious, compliant before authority, stereotyped in thinking.

- *Economical in dress.* Alert, efficient, intelligent, controlled.

- *Decoration in dress.* Nonintellectual, sociable, submissive

- *Conformity is dress.* Moral, sociable, traditional, submissive.

- *Comfort in dress.* Socially cooperative, self-controlled, thorough, deferential to authority, controlled extrovert.

Whether or not this theory holds true, we do know that women's clothing is often dictated by social, cultural, and religious norms. And those who run afoul of these standards are often corrected or must fight disciplinary action. Successful businesswomen Kay Ainsley of Detroit traveled to Saudi Arabia to negotiate a major deal. She was to sell the rights for Domino's Pizza to a Saudi concern. Dressed in a conservative business suit, she was asked to change into an "abaya," a long black robe that Saudi women traditionally wear. American servicewomen in Saudi Arabia have confronted the same dilemma. They have been asked to abide by the Saudi code of dress for women, although many have refused.

These norms do not apply only to dealings in foreign lands. An Associated Press story recently described how Carol Grotts arrived for her first day at Brink's Inc. She had completed the company's orientation training to be a relief messenger and was ready to get to work, but she had not counted on one final question, "What size pants do you wear?"

Pants? Grotts didn't wear pants. "They're against my religion," she explained. She was a Pentecostal Christian, a faith that forbids women from wearing slacks.

This response displeased her new manager. "We never would

have hired you if we'd known you did not wear pants," he said. He terminated her employment.

Grotts won a $30,000 settlement against the company on the grounds of religious discrimination, and the company was forced to rehire her at a different office. She got to wear culottes in her new position. Her settlement demonstrates once more that clothing is a factor in defining who we are, including our cultural and religious views. In the United States, how we dress is part of our constitutional right to freedom of speech. Clothing is a symbol of who we are, and we have a right to it.

There is also the famous case of a successful stockbroker—a top producer in her company—who was denied a promotion because her clothes and appearance were not up to the company's standards. A single head of household with two small children who obviously had a lot going on in her life, this woman sued the brokerage company and won! She claimed more emphasis was put on her attire than was placed on the appearance of men in the firm. This case confirms what Betty C. Spence, president of the National Association of Female Executives, has said, "Women are not judged just by performance. They are judged much more harshly on their hair or hemlines."

However, women are still expected to abide by the old rules. A man's credibility isn't at stake the way a woman's is if she dresses improperly. Unfortunately, because of her gender, her credibility in the business world is already down a peg from a man's. I was at a meeting of about twelve managers at a Fortune 500 company. Of the dozen assembled, only one was a woman, and she had a dress on. The men were all attired either in suits or sport coats and slacks. The jacket is the symbol of authority, and a woman can get away with a dress-jacket ensemble. But a dress all by itself? Not good enough.

Although Darla was a colleague and peer, she looked out of place at this meeting, dressed as she was like an administrative assistant. In fact, many administrative assistants wanting to gain more respect and credibility wear jackets to create the illusion of power.

And womenswear is far less comfortable or functional. My dresses and suits seldom have the same number of pockets that menswear does because bulky keys or wallets would jeopardize the line of the garment. Female clothing in our culture is more restricting and only allows for a narrow range of movement. The kick pleat that allows women to walk in straight skirts is torn on all my suit skirts because I'm always running to catch a plane or cab. Panty hose, a requirement with a skirt, is like a man's tie. It feels constricting. It chokes you all day!

Need we look beyond the issue of shoes? In a *Wall Street Journal* article titillatingly titled "Fashion Slaves Get Kicks from Spike Heels," reporter T. Agins comments that stilettos—shoes with pencil-thin, daggerlike heels that are typically five to six inches high—are supposed to represent "high glamour." How fast do you think you could do the fifty-yard dash in such shoes? They do accentuate a sexy, curvaceous leg as Carrie, the lead character of HBO's popular *Sex in the City* series would attest, tottering around as she did in her feather-strewn Jimmy Choo and Manolo Blahnik high-heeled confections. (How she managed that feat on the potholed streets of New York City remains a mystery to me!) But to what end?

Los Angeles–based radio talk show therapist Laura Schlessinger has said, "It never ceases to amaze me how much pain, discomfort and self-destruction women will go through in order to look good." Suzanne Levine, a podiatric surgeon in Manhattan, points out that women have far more frequent and more serious foot problems than men, and that high heels are the culprit! We act as though women have a choice in these matters of dress, but to show up for work in an outfit other than a suit and heels? In many professions, women would not get or keep their jobs if they did so. And to attend a formal wedding in Birkenstocks and jeans? Now that would start people talking.

The current popular term "arm candy," indicating something pretty on a man's arm that boosts his status, reinforces the fact that women are often seen as decorative objects. A woman depends more on appearance. Her clothing is designed to call attention to her body and make it attractive to others. Consider the omnipresence of spandex, formfitting skirts, and knit tops that cling to the body.

Dress for Success Evolves

Remember the outfit of the prototypical 1950s housewife, as epitomized by Lucille Ball and Doris Day in their heyday and more recently Julianne Moore in *Far from Heaven* and *The Hours* or Joan Allen in *Pleasantville*—cinched-in waist, flouncy skirt, Peter Pan collar, pearls. It was the picture of prim and proper, even if other, more primitive emotions were seething just below the surface.

The 1960s brought with it a clothing revolution that paralleled the cultural and social upheavals of the times. Alternative dress—hippie outfits—symbolized the counterculture and helped one determine at a glance on which side of the issues a person stood. The advent of miniskirts—a part of the blatant display of sexuality that accompanied the introduction of birth control pills—seemed part and parcel of the "free love" atmosphere. We were in the midst of a sexual revolution. But then society evolved. Women moved from the kitchen and the streets into the workforce. How were they to dress?

Because work clothes reflect corporate culture, many women began emulating the men with whom they worked. Sometimes the dress code was formally institutionalized. The classic example is the IBM decree in the 1960s and '70s that all company representatives and executives wear white shirts, dark suits, and stiff collars. The men sported power ties, and as women trickled into the business, they were soon obliged to attach little rosettes to their collars. These were formal symbols of status and credibility. JC Penney and Sears implemented similar dress codes.

New to the corporate workforce, women suddenly needed dress guidelines and prescriptions. In the mid-1970s, John Molloy became the king of clothes. In his best-selling *Dress for Success* and *The Woman's Dress for Success Book,* for instance, he warned women against the evils of sweaters, especially if they were tight or made of soft fabric; they were for attracting men. "In the office," he cautioned, "it spells secretary! Any woman at any level who wants to move up should not wear a sweater to work." Because women coveted the power men had, they began sporting power suits with padded shoulders and big lapels. Some even went so far as to wear shirts and ties. Those who were less bold wore silk blouses with large, soft bows at the collar, a feminization of the tie. In fact, the mantra in the 1980s was dress the level or position to which you aspire!

Even Barbie got into the act. In the mid-1980s, Mattel came out with a day-to-night version of the doll. Her business suit skirt reversed to something appropriate for evening wear and she came equipped with an attaché case, a calculator, tiny business and credit cards, all of the accoutrements intended to make her, according to a *Newsweek* article of that time, into a "woman of substance." Barbie and her businesswoman accessories reflected the shift in our culture.

Today, it's hard to believe the outcry that women's pants suits caused in the 1960s and '70s. Pants allow for more freedom of movement, but they were viewed as inappropriate—actually taboo and forbidden—for women in the workplace. In fact, some theaters in New York would not admit women wearing such radical dress! These outfits were considered a crossover to the male side, and many men as well as women could not tolerate it. As Amy Bloom wrote in an *O, The Oprah Magazine* article titled "Why Can't a Woman Be More Like a Man? And Vice Versa," "We are so much better than we were before. . . . I remember freezing my tail off all winter in 1966 because we couldn't wear pants to school even in deep snow." And I remember having to wear pants or heavy leggings under my skirts and dresses in cold weather! It was not so long ago that women were forced to wear clothing that was impractical for function or movement. Let's reverse roles for a moment. Would a man want to wear a skirt? It would benefit him in no way! Pants are functional and practical.

Just as men have their uniform—the suit—a woman in business needs a suit too. The jacket is the symbol of authority. With the jacket off, a working woman wears only a skirt and blouse or a dress, which are inadequate to establish her credibility. Agreed—jackets can be hot and binding. But observe what men do at work. They hang the jacket on the back of their desk chairs. They don't have to wear it when they sit down for lunch with their buddies, but if it's time to go to a meeting, particularly one with the boss or CEO, they put on that jacket.

Sarah Trenholm's advice for women: "A traditional two-piece suit consisting of matching jacket and skirt in a solid color should be worn with a cotton or silk blouse with a simple collar. Shoes should be closed toe. . . . Acceptable suit colors include gray, white, off-white, beige, and navy." Need a credibility boost? Stay away from suits in pastels and bright colors or those with floral patterns and lace. Stick with the power colors, navy, gray, and black.

Yes, women should wear suits, but should they dress like men to make it to the top? Three decades ago, John Malloy cautioned women "to avoid imitating their male counterparts." He certainly would not have approved of the 1980s trend for women to wear power suits with large shoulder pads and lapels, pants, and men's ties. These I believe were an attempt to equalize the power differential between the genders in the workforce. I say temper the suit with a softer pastel blouse or a single unostentatious piece of jewelry.

Since business outfits of working women on television are sexier and more provocative than those who do not work "on camera," women should be careful not to model themselves after their favorite television personality. My friend and colleague Linda Manning was raised in the suburbs of Washington, D.C., so she has an East Coast mind-set when it comes to clothes. She's often shocked by what passes for acceptable fashion choices in our Boulder/Denver area. "I think women and men are well advised to err on the side of too dressed up," she told me. "Dress in a higher status position. The research supports that those who are dressed 'higher status' get more compliance from others."

Today, of course, there is much more flexibility in the bending and breaking of the rules. Am I for pushing some boundaries? You betcha. Am I for women making the rules? Of course. But there are some contexts in which rules hold hard and fast, and a woman had better not break them until she owns the company. The suit is still a symbol of authority. Female work attire must be balanced with the field a woman works in. If she's in a conservative, traditional field, such as banking, accounting, finance, or Wall Street, her clients and boss want her to project a serious look. They do not want to see people dress down or practically undressed!

For God's Sake, Put Some Clothes On!

A friend of mine recently told me the story of her elderly mother dressing after a workout at the gym. "I was putting on my clothes," eighty-year-old Mary explained, "when the young woman next to me pulled on her slip and walked out just like that! I know I'm old, but do people go out in the street in their underwear now?" I thought my friend's story was hilarious and so appropriate to how some young women dress (or don't) today. In fact, a recent article in *Time* magazine documents how today's teens are actually wearing their pajamas out on the street—apparently a new spin on the radical 1970s concept of wearing nightgowns to cocktail parties.

With the exception of the male disco craze of the 1970s (when tight pants, gold chains, and open shirts were de rigueur), it is difficult for a man to dress in a sexy manner. Not so for women, whose clingy, low-cut, or otherwise alluring attire may attract wanted or unwanted sexual attention. Erin Brockovich not withstanding, cleavage—even toe cleavage (as in the wearing of sandals or heels that are cut low on top to show the toes)—is out of place in the business setting. Yet somehow the message hasn't gotten through.

Today there seems to be no dress code in corporate America. I was waiting in the reception area of a major telecommunications company when a thirty-something woman came zooming around the corner with a skirt on the size of a postage stamp! Outside work, on a date, let's say, such an outfit may be okay. But at work? She was not dressing for success; she was dressing for *access!* Women jeopardize a lot, especially their credibility, when they wear sexual clothing at work. And these kinds of scanty fashions contribute to the sexualization of the workplace. Sure, we should all be judged by the quality of our work, not the length of our skirts. But do know that by making the choice to dress provocatively, others may (rightly or wrongly) jump to conclusions about you.

In dating situations, we dress for appeal and sexuality. Carrie's wardrobe in *Sex and the City* is once more a case in point to the degree that her clothes were almost another character in the story—they couldn't be ignored. Female teenage attire emphasizes sexuality. From stiletto heels to flimsy tank tops, bared midriffs, and hip-hugger jeans designed to show the navel (not to mention navel piercing), all of these fashions call attention to an adolescent's burgeoning female anatomy.

Movie and pop icons like Cher, Madonna, Jennifer Lopez, and Britney Spears raise eyebrows with their navel-baring and otherwise skimpy or scandalous attire. Of course, they breathe the rarified air of Hollywood, where dress codes dictate the more outrageous, the better. But that may be changing soon. One of the things that sets scrappy singer Avril Lavigne apart is that she performs fully clad. She recently told a *Newsweek* reporter, "I have moms come up to me all the time and say thank you for wearing clothes." She went on to say that if she let the record label dictate her image, it would be "bleached-blonde hair . . . [and] wearing a bra for a shirt." "I hate sex object music," she declared. How ironic. This young singer is causing a stir because she's *wearing* clothes, not because she performs in a state of relative undress.

Less glamorous women in the public eye have also been criticized for their dress and hairstyles. Marcia Clark, one of the prosecutors at the O. J. Simpson trial, changed her coiffure and wardrobe several times during the trial after she was told to soften her image. And reams have been written about former First Lady Hilary Clinton's evolving hairdo and attire.

My single biggest piece of advice: when in doubt, don't wear it! If you are questioning whether a blouse is too transparent, don't go there! Err on the side of dressing conservatively! This goes for company picnics and outings, too. I was leading a company retreat at a luxury five-star resort in the Caribbean. Much of the time, I worked outdoors with the group, either around the pool or at the beach. One of the female attendees wore a brief, revealing bikini. It seems Melissa forgot she was supposed to be at work; she thought she was on vacation. She was the talk of the retreat and the brunt of snide jokes for months thereafter! A one-piece or modest two-piece bathing suit is in order, not a sexy thong, especially when hanging out (literally) with co-workers.

Other specific female work clothing dos and don'ts include:

• Don't wear anything too short. Men will be too busy looking at your legs and not focusing on your brilliant ideas. Remember, all the research shows that men think about sex an average of twelve times a day.

• Don't wear anything cut too low or too tight.

• Do the bend-over-and-look-at-yourself-in-the-mirror test. Make sure nothing is going to fall out and that the color of your bra is not revealed. Is anything hanging out? Get rid of that slip! Walk in the sunlight. If you can see through your skirt, don't wear it.

Clothes Make the Man

Men's clothes are plainly more functional than women's. Pockets in pants and jackets offer men the practical ability to carry necessities (keys, wallet, PDA, cell phone). The loose fit coupled with flat-heeled, close-toed shoes enables activity and de-emphasizes physical appearance. Changes in menswear are relatively subtle when compared to women's fashions—slightly larger lapels one year, slightly thinner tie the next, a more tapered or boxier suit jacket, perhaps. Maybe a deep blue shirt with matching satin tie will be in vogue, or a T-shirt under a blazer. Men's clothes are generally not as colorful or bright as women's. There are limits. But these more conservative outfits convey a sense of seriousness or power and not the frivolity of lace, flowers, and flounces so prevalent in womenswear.

It's not that men aren't judged for how they appear. They are, when it becomes a question of manliness. In *The Right Words at the Right Time,* Ralph Nader writes in his essay of a painful childhood incident that underscores how males will censure each other if their norms are not observed:

> I remember the teasing started in class early that afternoon. The boys in my fourth-grade class started picking on me for the way I was dressed. . . . Any kind of difference is bound to be bait. And there I was, the only boy in the class still wearing short pants. . . . At the time it was popular for little boys in the first, second, and third grades to wear short pants. By the fourth grade, all boys in school were wearing long pants. . . . Wearing long pants meant you were a big boy. . . . If you continued to wear short pants in the fourth grade you were considered a little boy, a sissy even.

For the boys of Nader's generation, graduating to long pants was a major rite of passage into manhood. If you failed to conform, you were admonished. Males must adhere to their gender's dress norms. In fact, some of our favorite comedic movies over the years, such as *Some Like It Hot, Tootsie,* and *Mrs. Doubtfire,* involved straight men dressing up as women because it helped them out of a tight spot. (Even Tom Hanks's first success on television's *Bosom Buddies* required him to parade around in women's clothes.)

However, in a more general sense, the appropriateness of clothing still falls under the female purview. I know a male accountant, a partner in one of the big public firms, whose only real ding on his annual review was that he wore unmatched socks (two different colors) and that his shirts were often not completely tucked in (the slob look). Imagine a woman coming to work dressed like that! People would whisper that she was depressed or otherwise mentally ill. For Jack, it was not a big deal—he wasn't going to lose out on his promotion because of it—but his superiors mentioned that his wife should look him over before he comes to work because women are "good at that." It's their department!

Navigating Casual Fridays

Casual Friday blossomed in the early 1990s. Until then, the business suit was de rigueur, especially for men, in the workplace. In fact, the wearing of the suit and white shirt and tie was originally influenced by the Industrial Revolution as a way to distinguish the managers and bosses from the blue-collar factory workers. But changes in business attire are always influenced by social shifts and trends. The suit in all its manifestations—three-piece, gray flannel, double-breasted, wide-lapelled, pinstriped, and so on—gave way to casual dress in part as a result of the social movements of the 1970s that said, "Let's question the establishment and how we do things." Indeed, casual Friday flies in the face of traditional business and many members of the old guard, believing it's too casual and inappropriate for the workplace, are appalled and flabbergasted by it.

Recently, this trend was accelerated by the advent of the home office and the Information Age, which allows us to plug into work from anywhere in the world. As business image consultant Sherry Maysonave explains in *Casual Power,* "The push of a button brings worldwide business transactions directly into bedrooms, tanning salons, bathrooms, cars, and gyms—anywhere one chooses to be." These virtual workspaces and the "frenetic, ever-changing pace of the Information Age," Maysonave continues, "demand the flexibility of casual wear."

Dressing down is an attempt to relax people, to redefine the workplace as a spot where employees can also have fun. It is meant to increase morale and productivity. This was particularly true in the dot-com industry during Internet boom of the 1990s. Workdays and workweeks were flexible at these fledgling companies, and employees were encouraged to engage in on-site impromptu basketball games and billiard matches as a way to unwind from the heavy demands of their 24/7 jobs.

My complaint is that in some industries casual Friday has evolved into casual Monday, Tuesday, Wednesday, and Thursday too. No one wears a suit anymore, and khakis and shorts are even acceptable in some companies. We've gotten so casual, employee behavior begins to get out of hand, since there are no precedents for this kind of dress. As Maysonave sees it, "Casual Confusion Syndrome operates in full force at many Fortune 500 companies. . . . Owners and employees at all pay scales are puzzled about how to balance professionalism with casual attire." Soon men will forget how to tie their ties, and women will forget how to wear pantyhose. Am I for having fun at work? Of course. But work doesn't need to turn into a party. That's a dangerous place to go.

How should men dress? Communication professor Sarah Trenholm offers a prescription to men to enhance their credibility: "Men are advised to wear classic, conservative two-piece suits made of wools and wool blends. Trendy styles, unusual fabrics and large patterns are to be avoided. Acceptable suit colors are gray and navy. Jewelry should be limited to one conservative ring, a watch, and a tie bar or tiepin."

To men who would prefer that casual Friday were every day, my advice: remember you're still at work. You're not gardening or playing tennis. If you insist on being more relaxed in your garb, cardigan sweaters or navy blazers worn over khaki pants or relaxed-fit jeans can maintain some of the look of authority that you'll need in order to be effective. But save the tight jeans, luau wear, T-shirts, and shorts for your own leisure activities!

According to Phyllis Mindell, communications consultant for women and author of *A Woman's Guide to the Language of Success,* it was men who brought the idea of dress-down day once a week: "Their idea of theater is that it's okay to change costume in the absence of other changes. Whatever the benefits of dress-down days, they cause women anxiety." Why? It is hard for a man to appear sexy if he's dressed casually. After all, what can he expose? Neither cleavage nor legs are an issue for him. For a woman, on the other hand, casual Friday is a clothing minefield. Women are more at risk because they have so many more choices in clothing. With these greater options, they have more potential to enter the dangerous territory of conveying sexual messages, particularly by wearing suggestive outfits.

The wearing of pants and casual Fridays are attempts to gender neutralize. Blue jeans, khakis, and polo shirts are clothes both genders can wear. Once again, in the business world, it is men dictating the dress code. Women do not institute it, but must follow these "rules." What's the bottom line here? According to Maysonave, to be successful today, "a person must be able to dress casually and still exude as much power, credibility, and authority as when wearing a traditional business suit." Now that's a tall order!

Personal Artifacts

Personal artifacts are items with which we decorate ourselves other than clothing—jewelry, belts, hats, scarves, glasses, gloves, hairstyles and hair ornaments, nails (polished or ragged), purses, briefcases, cell phones, beepers, shoes, makeup, body piercings, tattoos. These too are often gender specific. In fact, we begin our lives with particular artifacts—the blue and pink receiving blankets hospitals use to identify males and females. These are the first items that mark gender! Artifacts contribute a great deal to the perceptions others have of us. In the film *Working Girl,* secretary Melanie Griffith learned to tone down her big hair, dangly earrings, jangling bracelets, and brightly colored eye shadow to look more like the executive she aspired to be. Dazzling jewelry, large purses, open-toed and/or stiletto-heeled shoes are other artifacts that contribute to a less-than-professional look. Credibility markers in jewelry are gold and pearls. Even silver is considered too casual.

Humorist Dorothy Parker's famous line, "Men don't make

passes at girls who wear glasses," has been borne out by the use of contact lenses and more recently corrective eye surgery. Glasses have been perceived as unattractive. However, studies show that people who wear glasses are thought to be more intelligent. Mirrored sunglasses, on the other hand, are impenetrable and masklike. They play a role in the male monotonic face.

Perfumes are also considered artifacts. Strong scents call attention to one's sexuality; all advertising related to fragrances is sexually charged. Scents can be useful in dating situations, but attraction based on smell is inadvisable at work. Perfumes can be offensive to others, and some co-workers may suffer from allergies.

Men are subject to artifact rules as well. In happier times, Arthur Andersen's employees were required to wear fedora hats when visiting clients, no matter what the weather, to convey a sense of fastidiousness. Today, however, baseball caps are far too dressed down for the workplace. Beaten-up briefcases, tired shoes, and flamboyant jewelry send their own messages. And too much aftershave can also be a faux pas. In fact, men will be ridiculed more than women for overdoing the aftershave. I believe it borders on being too feminine. "He is too foofoo," a woman said to me, referring to one of her co-workers.

"What do you mean?" I asked.

"He wears so much aftershave," she answered. "I will not get on the elevator with him."

A woman could more easily enter the realm of cologne than a man. We expect men to be subtler. They should err on the side of the conservative when it comes to the use of perfume or aftershave.

While the quality of the artifacts is important, their condition should also be observed. Scuffed loafers, worn belts, frayed collars or cuffs, wrinkled shirts, and stained ties all send the wrong message.

This is true for women as well as for men. Sherry Maysonave reminds us that the condition of your clothes, shoes, jewelry, hair, and nails are "all visual clues to the level of your success." She points to the scene in *Pretty Woman* in which Julia Roberts, playing a prostitute, claims to earn $100 an hour at her trade. Richard Gere's response, "You make $100 an hour and you have a safety pin holding up your boot?" We give it all away in the details.

Gender Prescriptions

There are always dress codes in schools, businesses, and even religious institutions. Sometimes these rules are written and sometimes they're merely understood. Although many of us think it's unfair to judge a person by their cover (clothes), this is how the world works!

The most important rule for dressing: is this the appropriate attire for this context? As Jo-Ellan Dimitrius, a jury trial consultant, claimed, "An unusually short skirt worn to a conservative job interview would raise eyebrows. The woman's good sense, her understanding of appropriate office behavior, and the reasons why she would choose attire that might sexualize the interview all deserve your attention. But the same skirt worn out to dinner with her boyfriend would not deserve the same scrutiny unless it was so revealing that it was remarkable even for that occasion." Women do not have the freedom to dress that the magazines claim they do. When they own their own companies, then they can do what they want in dress. Until then, like it or not, they still have to play by the rules. As Maysonave puts it, "You can never overdo real quality and excellent grooming. To nonverbally communicate success, make *quality* your middle name."

GENDER RX

- A jacket is a symbol of authority and can convey power (for both men and women) in a business setting.

- Attire must be balanced with the field one works in. Conservative, traditional fields require serious clothes in power colors, such as black, gray, or navy.

- Alluring or skimpy clothes are inappropriate for the workplace. No cleavage allowed, not even toe cleavage. When in doubt, don't wear it!

- Men should wear classic, conservative suits and avoid trendy styles and fabrics.

- For those men who want to dress in a more relaxed way, cardigans or blazers over khakis are acceptable. But no shorts, tight jeans, or luau wear!

- Artifacts are a dead giveaway. Women should avoid large, dangly jewelry; open-toed shoes; and glitzy accessories and makeup and stick to a conservative palette and modest gold or pearl jewelry.

- Men must convey a sense of fastidiousness in their attire—no worn, stained, or frayed clothes or accessories.

- Both genders would be wise to avoid too much perfume or cologne in the workplace.

CHAPTER TEN

Listening with Two Ears

People talking without speaking, people hearing without listening.

—PAUL SIMON, "THE SOUNDS OF SILENCE"

"Of all the life lessons that my mom taught me, I remember the one that shaped my life most: I was around five years old when my mother sat me down, looked me in the eye, and told me how to listen to people. When people talk to you, look them in the eyes and focus on what they're saying. Really listen. Do your best to understand what they're trying to say."

Few parents would train their children to listen, as House Minority Leader Richard Gephardt's mother did. Listening is most critical in communication; when you listen, you communicate to the other person that he or she is important. When you listen, you show respect. And to get respect, you have to give respect.

As important as it is, you'd think we would focus on listening. But it is not taught in school. Many of our university communications departments are still called the "Speech Communications Department," not the "Speech-and-*Listening* Communications Department." Listening is an ignored skill, but it's so central to good communication! No one gets formal guidance in it until adult corporate training or even parenting classes—and that's if they're lucky enough to be involved in these programs! Somehow, we're just supposed to glean these skills or pick them up by osmosis. I did not, and most people I know personally and professionally have not received this kind of explicit instruction.

We don't just listen with our ears. We also listen with our eyes, as they help us discern gestures, eye behavior, or facial expressions that reveal the intensity or authenticity of the verbal message. That's why listening is also about understanding. But let's not confuse "understanding" with "accepting." You can understand a person's feelings and message, but you may not necessarily agree with them! A couple that truly listens to one another stays together and builds a solid foundation to their relationship. As Daniel Goleman explains, "Listening is a skill that keeps couples together." But its import goes far beyond marital relations. A father who listens to his teenage son— really listens—creates trust and rapport with his son. A management team whose members listen to each other is the most effective! Listening is the highest form of respect. When you listen, you say, "I value you, therefore, I listen empathically." This will disarm the hostility inherent in any relationship!

The Split Ear: The Female Advantage

Listening is a part of the female job description and the key component in facilitating interpersonal relationships. In Chapter 6, I described Monty Roberts's observations of an alpha mare meting out discipline to a herd of wild mustangs. He noticed that the mare, when confronting a renegade and abusive young stallion colt, held one ear forward and one backward, as if she'd divided her attention. The ear facing backward was aimed at the rest of the herd and especially at a young foal this colt had just kicked. The forward ear was trained on the "bad boy" colt. I believe this is analogous to the split or double ear we observe among women. Human females have the ability to "listen with two ears." At any one time, they may be paying attention on two or more disparate levels.

A woman hears the verbal message just as a man would, but she is also reading between the lines to intercept feelings. That's her socio-emotional ear. She evaluates facial expressions, voice, gestures, and posture—the whole repertoire of nonverbal behavior—and draws conclusions from these, as well as from the other person's words. "Women's ability to manage the flow interaction, to really listen and hear what people say, and to gather information from others in a non-threatening way is a strength," management consultant Judith Tingley claims. Certainly in the work world, most consider the participation of subordinates as essential to the effective influencing of staff. But we also observe this skill every night at the dinner table, where a woman attempts to regulate the flow of conversation to include her most reticent child and restrain her most precociously verbal child from dominating the conversation!

Perhaps this is why the men and women in my gender communication survey all made the point that women are better listeners than men. Here are how some of the men responded to my question, "What do you feel is the greatest strength in women's communication?"

- "Women have better listening skills. They look at the whole picture."

- "They have the ability to pick up on nonverbals and to listen completely."

- "They're sensitive to the speakers' feelings and mental state."

- "Empathy, inclusiveness, compassion. They have feelings and emotions."

- "Women listen to what is meant beyond the words."

- "Mind reading!"

Why do women listen differently? Part of the answer may be tied to brain structure. For women, emotional responses reside in both hemispheres of the brain, which are connected with the "corpus callosum," which is a thick bundle of nerve fibers that is thicker in women than in men. These fibers facilitate the exchange of information between the two halves of the brain. According to genetics expert and television producer Anne Moir, "this means that more information is being exchanged between the left and right sides of the female brain" than between those in the male brain. The more connections one has, the more fluent one is in understanding emotions.

Predictably, anthropologist Helen Fisher takes a more anthropological outlook on female listening superiority. From her point of view, millions of years ago on the grasslands of Africa, women stayed around the hearth when men left for months at a time to hunt. A woman's acute sensitivity to listening probably developed because of her babies—she had to listen for their cries while defending against predators.

Feminists would argue that since much of female survival and sex role prescription has depended on the ability to encode and decode accurately others' nonverbal cues, women have had to develop their listening skills more effectively. In fact, Gloria Steinem has suggested that women's so-called "intuition" (or "mind reading," as one of my male survey participants put it) is not some extraordinary ability but really a by-product of their better-developed listening skills.

Whatever the reason, unfortunately, many men feel threatened by a woman's ability to glean more from their communication than they do. They don't like it. They'll accuse the woman of reading too much into their verbal statements. "Well that's not how I feel!" they will protest. But women are paying attention to the nonverbals that qualify the verbal. "You said you don't like the furniture I picked out," a woman may say, "but here's what I really think is going on with you."

Moreover, men don't want to listen to all the detail that women feel compelled to share, especially in business situations. "What's the bottom line?" and "Get to the point!" were born out of male culture in response to women going on and on. Men complain to me, "Women over-communicate." and "They have to talk about everything, and they have to beat the topic to death." A male manager told me that his female colleague gave him some excellent insights about their respective boss. "However," he said, "it was way more than I needed or wanted to hear!" Indeed, since women are process (and not goal) oriented, men believe they are too easily distracted. This adds to the credibility gap between the genders.

The solution? Women can strive to keep their communications short and to the point. It's wise to cut back on excessive verbiage. This is truly a case of less is more; the men in their lives may listen better with less! Learning to be more precise in speaking is equivalent to learning to be a good editor of one's own writing. Judith Tingley suggests the only context in which a woman should use "excessive wording" is "when she is talking to women or groups of women, when she wants them to see her as similar to them."

If a woman has been accused of going on too long or if she's been told to "Just get to the bottom line," she should learn to use a pyramid answer style. First reply with only a one-word or one-sentence answer. To the question, "Is the report going to ready on time?," the proper answer is, "No it isn't." She can then build with details in two to four more sentences, using a bullet-point style and short, succinct sentences. "The computers were down. We couldn't get them up for three days . . ." and so on rather than giving a long-winded history of the project's failures and successes before coming to the point— "Well, you won't believe what happened to me last week. . . . The computers crashed, I had two people out with the flu, Janet's baby got sick, and my car broke down."

Are Men Bad Listeners?: The Male Perspective

A man asked his wife, "Honey, what would you like for your fiftieth birthday?"

"I'd love to be six again," she replied.

On the morning of her birthday, he got her up bright and early and off they went to a local theme park. What a day! They went on every ride in the park. Five hours later, she staggered out of the theme park, her head reeling and stomach upside down, right to McDonald's, where her husband ordered her a Big Mac, fries, and a chocolate shake. Then it was off to the movies with popcorn! What fabulous adventures! Finally she wobbled home with her husband and collapsed into bed.

He leaned over and lovingly asked, "Well dear, what was it like being six again?"

One eye opened, then the other. "I meant my dress size," she said in exasperation.

The moral of this story: even when a man is listening, he's still *gonna* get it wrong!

Listening is the most critical communication skill, and "He doesn't listen!" is women's number-one complaint about male inter-actions. (No such complaint from men, however, about women's listening skills. This is an area where there is minimal disagreement between the sexes.) Women tend to be other-oriented during communication, even in their nonverbals; men tend to be more self-oriented. They are good at representing the self—what they think, need, feel, and believe. They think they're being assertive, but some women will say that men are self-centered. Here are some of their complaints as compiled in my gender communication survey:

- "They only hear what *they* have to say."

- "Men don't listen to the whole story before responding."

- "They do not read between the lines."

- "They take things at literal and face value."

- "They zero in on only one aspect, the verbal."

- "Men are not as sensitive, not as intuitive as women."

- "Men have an inability to really empathize with another person's feelings because they're too focused on fixing the problem."

In the context of intimacy, I have observed firsthand how poor listening can contribute to the demise of relationships and the high divorce rate in our country. One man told me he had lived with a woman for five years for whom he cared deeply. But Ken was jealous of the time and attention Barbara lavished on her young son. She kept telling him, "Ken, you're jealous of Chase, but there's enough of me for both of you."

"Barbara told me this again and again," Ken confided, "but I didn't hear her. Finally, she'd had it! She kicked me out. I got it later, but it was too late. If I had listened to her, really heard what she was saying, I believe I would still be in the relationship."

Here's how Daniel Goleman characterizes the problem in *Emotional Intelligence*:

He: You're shouting.

She: "Of course I'm shouting—you haven't heard a word I'm saying. You just don't listen!"

He goes on to explain that couples "headed for divorce" get absorbed by anger and fixated on the specifics of the issues at hand, not managing to hear—let alone return—any peace offering.

Interestingly, men concur that they are poor listeners. They'll often plan their "speech" or "counterattack" while the other person is speaking, which prevents them from fully attending to what's being said. Late-night talk show host Conan O'Brien, in explaining the challenges he faces as an interviewer, has been quoted as saying, "On the show now, I sometimes find myself doing something odd when a guest is speaking: *I shut up and listen.* While once my instinct would have been to mentally race ahead to find a funny place, I instead listen to a guest and find the funny moment there." I don't think we would hear a comment such as this from a female host like Oprah or Rosie O'Donnell.

However, brain differences or not, I want to argue that men are *not* bad listeners; they just don't listen the way women would like them to! Many of the reasons women believe men don't listen are tied to how men send and receive nonverbals. They emit messages that cue women into believing and perceiving they are not listening. How does this disconnect occur? Imagine a scene of close male friends engaged in important conversations. Rather than facing one another, the men sit side by side, looking down or around the room as they talk.

There are several considerations here. Women expect men to employ the nonverbal cues—face-to-face orientation and eye contact—that signal they are listening. But with roaming or downcast eyes, men will not pick up on the other person's critical nonverbals such as facial expression. They get only part of the message—primarily the verbal—but they lose the socio-emotional content of the communication!

Whereas a woman would evaluate and draw conclusions from the other person's nonverbal behavior along with his words, a typical man hears a woman's verbal content, but he is often tuned out to her nonverbals. If you ask him what was just said, he can recall it and even repeat verbatim the key points. He is focused on the content, the verbal transcript, what he hears with his ears. But, as mentioned earlier, a major part of listening does not involve *only* the ears. The eyes are a crucial element. What we see helps us grasp the other person's emotions. How upset is she? How happy?

A woman focuses on this socio-emotional information, which is often not said but conveyed through the nonverbals. One of the women who participated in my gender communication survey referred to this phenomenon as total listening, or lack thereof. "Men do not do total listening," she wrote. "They don't have the ability to penetrate all layers." The layers she is referring to are the depth of feeling that extend beyond what is just simply said. It's what's implied about how the person feels!

Second, what messages do men send when they look down or around? For male-to-male interactions, this may be an acceptable code of conduct. In fact, men have told me they might get uncomfortable if a man sat face to face with them and made continuous eye contact. Additionally, some men find women's touch, eye contact, and face-to-face positioning suffocating and even invasive. I have seen them squirm when women do this. But to a woman, the lack of eye contact while listening may tell her that he is really saying:

- "You're not important."

- "Your message is not important."

- "I don't have time for this."

- "I'm distracted."

There is also a power component to this listening business. Communications experts Deborah Borisoff and Lisa Merrill claim in their book *The Power to Communicate: Gender Differences as Barriers* that men are ineffective listeners because listening can render them vulnerable. "One deficiency in the male stereotype has been the negative association for listening," they explain. "Speaking is active. Listening has often been portrayed inaccurately as passive, weak, or feminine behavior, since it necessitates receptivity to others."

Communications professors Barbara Bate and Judy Bowker give an example of this dynamic:

If Charles contradicts his message of, "Yes, I'm listening!" by burying his face in a newspaper, Carlene is left interpreting cultural differences ("I can listen without making eye contact.") and power dimensions as well ("My newspaper reading—or my way of communicating—is more important than you or your way of communicating.").

To maintain his power and status, Charles must do manly things. If he were to say, "Yes dear, let's talk. I am ready to listen. What's on your mind?" while folding his newspaper putting it aside, orienting his body toward Carlene, and maintaining eye contact with her (she would probably fall off her chair at this point!), he might appear too feminine. With these behaviors, he enters the realm of the touchy feely. In fact, when I used this example in one of my seminars, a woman in the audience shouted out, "Where is this guy? In your dreams? If he is real, let's clone him!" Another yelled out a piggyback remark, "That's why we have women friends!" The bottom line: Charles may feel he is in a one-down position because he believes he risked his social status to incorporate these more stereotypically feminine behaviors.

However, Charles's attitude is misinformed. According to communications professor Sarah Trenholm, although listening may seem to be a passive behavior, it really is not. "While we listen," she explains, "we actively create meaning and construct our own versions of reality. Seen in this light, listening is one of the most important forms of communication."

In keeping with the vulnerability inherent in deep listening, novelist Ben Schrank, in an article titled "When Bad Listeners Happen to Good Women" published in O, The Oprah Magazine, discovered that the art of being attentive is a journey to the seat of oneself.

Sometimes listening is too difficult because it brings up painful emotions that a man may not want to deal with. "A woman I was in love with," Schrank wrote, ". . . told me a story about her father, about how furious he'd been after her mother left him for another man. . . . I believed I was listening. I may have grimaced, because the experience sounded bad."

But what was Schrank doing while his girlfriend shared this painful story? By his report, drinking wine and picking at his appetizer plate of scallops. Miffed at what looked to her like inattention, his girlfriend reacted with, "If you can't listen to me, if you can't hear what I'm saying, then I don't want to be with you." Schrank admitted that she was right. He couldn't really hear what she was saying. He went on to confess that the details of how his girlfriend's father treated her during the divorce were "painful" and "scary."

Some men do not do well with emotions, and they certainly feel challenged on how to respond when someone shares upsetting feelings! In *Fire in the Belly,* Sam Keen assesses men and their roles in relationships. He suggests that the private world of feelings has been repressed in men for years. "Warriors" is how he describes male upbringing; men can't show or even feel their emotions. In keeping with this, Schrank had a difficult time with his emotions when listening to his girlfriend, so he simply tuned her out! It was too much for him. This is common among men. In fact, perhaps because the emotions are hard to bear, some men may seek a quick solution to a woman's problems, cutting off further conversation.

Which leads us to yet another common listening issue. One of my female survey participants complained, "Men try to fix the problem without just listening. Women often just want to be heard." Another wrote, "They listen halfway and then fix . . . rather than listening 100 percent." These grievances relate to the paradigm that men are goal oriented in how they speak as well as in how they listen. If they're focused on solving a problem (what I call the "kill-it-and-drag-it-back-to-the-cave syndrome"), they end communication and fail to concentrate on the interactive process itself. That goes to the heart of their inability to engage in empathic listening.

There is no denying that women have an edge in the listening category. But men can learn these skills. In my seminars, I often say, "Listening is a full-body contact sport!" I purposely employ a sports metaphor so men understand my point. I recommend that when conversing with women, men sit face to face, make continuous eye contact, touch (if appropriate), and employ nonfluencies like "uh huh" and "umm" to indicate they are listening. They should also eliminate any props or barriers to listening, which means putting away the remote, turning off the game, or setting aside the newspaper!

One male participant balked at this advice. "Why do I have to do this touchy-feely stuff?" he wanted to know. "My wife ought to know I care about her and what she is saying!"

My reply: "You have to understand that your wife will perceive you as inattentive and unable to 'understand' or empathize with her if you don't do this. You must attend to her (to get all you can get in nonverbals) or you're going to miss something important and risk being misunderstood! How can you claim you're listening if you are not looking at her? How can you pick up on mixed messages that people (especially women) often send if you're not looking at them while you're hearing their words? In fact, those words are a small and probably the least important part of listening!"

Actress Shirley MacLaine has said, "Women directors are more conversant with emotional landscapes. They don't cut because it says that the scene is over. A woman director would let the camera roll because spontaneous emotion doesn't confuse her where a man would cut." This is a perfect example of how women and men think differently about feelings and that some adaptation is necessary on the part of men.

Consider this scenario: It's football season, and games are now on television four nights a week. Stacy is sick and tired of being ignored because of football and decides to vacuum during an important game. Josh jumps up, annoyed at the noise. "What are you doing?" he demands. "I am trying to watch the game for Pete's sake!"

"Football, football, football!" Stacy exclaims. "I am sick and tired of it." What's her real message? If Josh were able to read between the lines, he'd know she is saying, "Football gets all the attention, and I am getting none!" And if Josh were really smart he would say, "Honey, after the game is over, I want to take you to dinner and spend some time with you!" Bingo. The unspoken message is addressed, and he can watch his game in peace!

On the other hand, while women appear to be the champions in the listening department, they still have some homework to do! They must be sensitive to a man's level of discomfort when they are actively listening! He may dislike all the attentiveness (face-to-face position, eye contact, touch); in fact, it can cause him to shut down. Women must be patient—involved, but not too intense. They can self-disclose, but shouldn't tell too much, too soon. It may overwhelm the man. Remember, he is wrestling with his own feelings, and he's listening even though he may not be maintaining eye contact. If he really appears distracted and tuned out, ask him, "Is this a good time for you? You seem distant." Giving attention is generally not a man's forte!

Empathic Listening

Daniel Goleman explains that the most powerful form of nondefensive listening is empathy—actually "hearing the feelings behind what is being said." Empathy refers to the ability to feel as someone else does, to put yourself in his or her shoes. In fact, we have a saying in my field: Empathy is communication, communication is empathy. I have not truly communicated with you until I have empathized with you. How can I understand how you feel if I don't take into account the entire message, especially the nonverbals? Empathic listening is important in the boardroom as well as in the bedroom. However, I can't imagine an intimate relationship without empathic listening as the glue that sustains and maintains the loving relationship.

Yet many women wish men would show concern when listening through nonverbal cues like nonfluencies ("Oh wow!" "Really?"), eye contact, and facial expressions such as grimacing and knit eyebrows. Men don't orient their bodies toward the speaker. They may not look at a woman or only offer a blank expression. This has a domino effect. A man's lack of ability to express himself nonverbally coupled with a stony demeanor and other nonverbal cues undercut his communication of empathy. Moreover, if a man is strategic and tactical when listening, busy formulating responses, or channel surfing but still claiming to listen to his partner, she will feel emotionally abandoned. In truth, all she wants is empathy and understanding, but his blank face or lack of attentiveness doesn't show compassion. She believes he doesn't care, and he feels hurt that she thinks poorly of him.

We know from research that both men and women choose women more often for self-disclosure. If we have something personal and private to share, we open up to a woman. Why? One of the primary reasons is that women are empathic listeners. They attend and respond with that socio-emotional ear. However, this may not always be an asset. Since women are such good listeners, they also can encounter the problem of listening too much. Many believe it is their job to always be available to listen—whether or not they have the time for it. Indeed, often their time is not respected.

I've seen co-workers barge into a woman's office while she's on the phone and demand her immediate attention by waving and mouthing, "I need to speak with you." They'd likely never do that to a male colleague. It is important for women to establish listening boundaries, to say, "You know, now is not a good time for me to listen to you. Let's set up a time to talk later." This technique could even give a woman power over a man who felt that it was acceptable to force his way into her attention.

Men, of course, have different problems when it comes to lending a compassionate ear. Rather than empathizing, they often try to take women's feeling away from them, especially if opinions differ. ("How can you feel that way? There's nothing to be afraid of!") This validates their perception (and no one should have a different point of view). But feelings are facts. Women get frustrated when men do not empathize with or understand their emotions.

Also, a prerequisite for empathy is being in touch with your own feelings; we cannot empathize with another if we are disconnected from how we feel. As Daniel Goleman explains in *Emotional Intelligence,* "Self-awareness—recognizing a feeling as it happens—is the keystone of emotional intelligence." The ability to monitor our feelings and the feelings of others is critical to psychological insight and self-understanding. If we are not opened to our own feelings, how will we be able to read others'?

Empathic listening is not usually part of a man's social training.

How are men raised? *Feelings make you vulnerable. Feelings are feminine.* As Goleman claims, "The emotional notes and chords that weave through people's words and actions—the telling tone of voice or shift in posture, the eloquent silence or telltale tremble—go by unnoted [in men]." This is applicable to all parts of our lives from parenting to managing people at work and political action! As Goleman explains, "Empathy, it should be no surprise to learn, helps with romantic life!" A man who shows empathy will connect better with the opposite sex!

Author Sam Keen suggests that both men and women need to work to heal and understand the "wounds" with which each gender has had to deal. To that end, men may have to practice their listening and empathy skills. The good news is that these abilities can be learned. We all have felt confusion, disappointment, joy, frustration, excitement, or mistrust. A man can identify how his female colleague feels and express his understanding of her emotion without necessarily sharing it, as in the following scenario:

SARA: I don't trust our new VP of operations.

JOHN: Wow! Greg seems okay with me. But it has to be hard for you to work with someone you don't trust! That's got to be difficult!

John has a different perception than Sara of the new VP. However, he can empathize with her problem even if he doesn't mistrust Greg. Were he to lack empathy, John would say, "Wow! I don't know why you feel that way. I think Greg is a great guy." Now there's a turnoff for a woman!

Let's go back to Ben Schrank's story of his inability to listen to his girlfriend. Fortunately, he learned from his failings with this relationship and moved on from there. "Now I'm involved with another woman," he writes. "And I know she has stories that she must tell for us to grow closer, to trust each other, to be more in love. When she tells me a story . . . I work against physically turning away from her or folding my arms." Schrank now understands the nonverbals he must send to cue his new love that he cares and is listening to her!

Nodding: It Doesn't Mean "Yes!"

Len is intent on his sales pitch. "This car will suit all your driving needs," he tells Chris, the young mother of two, as she stands on the showroom floor, her baby perched on her hip.

She listens to him intently, nodding through his spiel.

This encourages Len to believe he's making headway. "Great!" he thinks. "She's hooked! I've got this sale in the bag!"

When he's done, Chris responds, "Thanks for telling me about your new SUV, but I'm not interested. I don't think it will work for my family. I need something smaller and more fuel efficient."

Len is stunned and stymied! Didn't she want the car?

Was Chris intentionally trying to mislead Len into believing he'd made a sale? No, not at all. Nodding is an excellent example of the same behavior meaning different things to each gender. For women, nodding while listening conveys understanding and consideration. Chris was nodding as a feminine courtesy. To her, the nod didn't mean she was buying Len's product, only that she was paying attention and that she understood him. But confusion arises because for men nodding signifies not just understanding but also *agreeing*. If a woman nods, a man thinks, "Oh good, she's buying everything I'm saying." But at the end of the conversation, she may say, "No, I don't think that's a good idea."

To avoid this muddle, a woman must recognize how men interpret her nods. She can then put her true intentions on record. She might say, for instance, "I understand what you're saying, but I have a different opinion." There is no need for women to stop nodding, since there are too many positive interpersonal values connected to it. And a man must take a woman's nod for what it is in her world—a sign of understanding. Nodding is an empathic gesture that makes others comfortable and encourages openness. All that's called for is a bit of clarification.

The Gatekeepers

When our daughter Alexandra was two, my ex-husband and I consulted an ear, nose, and throat specialist about her frequent ear infections. Typical of most mothers in this situation, I came prepared with clipboard and questions. I began the interview as my husband sat by quietly and listened.

The doctor had a hard time with this arrangement. I was about halfway through my list of questions when he interrupted, oriented his body away from me, discontinued eye contact, faced my ex-husband, and tried to reroute the flow of the conversation to include Adam. "Do you have any input on this?" he asked.

Adam wasn't having any of it. He replied, "I'm a pilot. I'm not at home as much as Audrey is to observe Alexandra and her symptoms firsthand. She researched this, and I am confident to let her run this show!"

Gatekeeping behaviors are those that decide the flow of conversation—who initiates the conversation, who gets to talk and who interrupts, when they get to talk, for how long, and with whom. The specialist purposefully manipulated these elements of conversation to suit his own needs and make himself feel comfortable; he apparently didn't like that I was in charge. Let's look at these nonverbal behaviors more closely:

• *Initiating.* Initiating refers to who begins the conversation. Men initiate conversation as a power move. When I ask questions of an audience, the men in the group will answer 75 percent of the time. Women initiate conversations to bond and connect as part of the social maintenance and taking care of relationships. One man told me, "I share a cubicle with Nan. She would lean over and show me some forms—the very elementary parts of our work—and ask me inane questions like, 'This is how we take care of the shipping, isn't it?' And I'd wonder, 'What, is she stupid or something?' But as I got to know her, I saw that she was exceptionally bright. Those questions were her way of connecting with me."

• *Turn-taking.* At some point in any interaction or meeting, we all have the need to present our ideas and learn that talking does not necessarily mean getting the floor. We must take turns. Turn-taking encompasses several nonverbals. Having one's turn is usually dictated by others' body orientation, eye contact, smiles, and gestures (such as pointing with the inference, "What do you have to say?"). Yet turn-taking in conversation is a communication behavior that varies significantly by gender.

Research shows that at work and even in social interactions outside of work, in general men get more turns talking in a mixed group, and when it's their turn, they talk louder and longer than women. There are obvious career implications here: if John talks sixty minutes and Carrie only holds the floor for ten minutes, who will hold sway? And who will get more attention from the higher-ups? In social situations, male conversational dominance may cause women to congregate among themselves and carry on their own side conversations so that they don't have to deal with the interruptions and can explore topics such as relationship issues that may be less interesting to their male partners.

Women must also become conscious of who is getting more airtime. Even if they are not in a leadership position and see that men are dominating the discussion, they can pull in more acquiescent women with questions such as, "Susan, you have expertise in this area. What do you think?" or "I'd like to hear from others on this. Heather?"

• *Interruption.* Not surprisingly, people of both genders find interruptions a source of irritation. Interruptions are violations of the unwritten rules governing turn-taking. (The right place to change speakers is at the end of an utterance or a possible unit of thought, not while someone is in the middle of talking.) However, just because interruptions are considered rude doesn't mean they don't occur.

Research has found that in same-sex conversations, interruptions are distributed evenly among participants, but in male-female conversations, the pattern is dramatically different. Male speakers make nearly all the interruptions (96 percent!). Men talk more than women do in a mixed group. They hold the floor, in part, by interrupting women or answering questions that are not addressed to them. Men have been found to interrupt women more than women interrupt men. In fact, most women have experienced situations in which a man spoke over them—they started to say something but were overwhelmed by his louder male voice. When that happens, the right moment can pass and good ideas may be left unexpressed. This can be even more frustrating in formal meetings where women strive to make a good impression and want to be heard.

Male speakers make 96 percent of all interruptions.

Such interruptions are associated with power. As Marian K. Woodall explains in *How to Talk So Men Will Listen,* "Allowing interruptions or neglecting to challenge people who interrupt are habits of weak and powerless people." The person who can take the floor away from another controls the conversation. Many women have difficulty getting and keeping the attention of a group, perhaps due to the fact that their voices are softer and because they are more likely to be interrupted than a man is. Also, since women often engage in explaining the background and process, men may interrupt because they want the bottom line. "Get to the point!" they'll shout in exasperation.

When someone takes the floor away from a woman, it requires highly assertive skills on her part to reclaim it. How should she deal with interruptions and keep the floor when it's her turn? She might say, "Excuse me, Tom. I wasn't quite through with my point yet," then break eye contact with him, turn to the group, and continue her discourse.

Consider Andrea's situation. Andrea was one of the few female architects in her firm and was thrilled to be put in charge of the rebuilding of a major hospital—a complicated and demanding project. During one of her weekly meetings with Larry, the VP of her firm, she began to complain about the trouble she was having with an important contractor. Rather than letting her finish, Larry immediately interrupted her, broke eye contact, turned his body away, and began problem-solving the issue with Frank, another senior member of their team who was sitting next to him at the conference table. Because Larry disconnected from the interaction, Andrea never had a chance to tell him how she had already fixed the problem.

"I was so frustrated, I left the room in disgust," Andrea admitted to me. Larry was simply behaving as many men do; when presented with a problem, he had to kill it and drag it off, caveman-style. But his nonverbal behavior was hurtful to Andrea. By interrupting and disconnecting nonverbally, Andrea believed that Larry was demeaning her to the point that she felt like a nonentity. She didn't even tell him about her success with the contractor, which eventually hurt her own credibility.

Andrea's reaction is understandable, since regaining the floor once it has been taken away is one of the most difficult moves any woman can make. Such an attempt requires a great deal of tactful assertiveness, especially if one doesn't wish to appear "ballsy." Nevertheless, Andrea didn't have to abandon this interaction filled with resentment. Although her boss interrupted her, she could still reclaim the floor in a face-saving way and command the attention she deserved.

What might she have done differently? First, she could raise her voice a little; the quality and tone would have to be low in pitch and more assertive than before (no squeaky, high-pitched, little girl's voice is effective here). Then she could say, "Just a minute, Larry, I need to finish," coupled with brief (a millisecond) eye contact with Larry (any longer, and she would appear to be asking permission). She could also lean forward and put her hands on the table for emphasis. If that didn't work, and if appropriate, she could briefly touch her boss's forearm to get his attention and say, "Larry, hold on. I took care of the problem. I need to make my point." Her unspoken message is that she is fully competent to deal with this problem, and she doesn't need to be rescued.

And my advice to Larry and other men who engage in this behavior? Don't interrupt. Hear the other person out before you react. I know you are eager to make your point or solve the problem, but remember women are the recipients of far more interruptions than men! Let her finish! Be empathetic. Don't patronize, condemn, or argue—the usual male reactions to an opposing point. Check in with eye contact and try to listen with all your senses!

• *Overlap.* Whereas an interruption is a vocalization before the last word that could signal the possible end of a sentence, question, or other unit of thought, overlaps are instances in which two people speak at once, talking over each other. A new speaker may begin to speak at or very close to a possible transition or ending point in the present speaker's talk. This allows some margin of error in the change between speakers. However, if a man talks louder, literally shutting down the other person, the overlap can be considered a power move. Like interruptions, men employ far more overlapping than women in mixed gender interactions.

Research has found that in same sex conversations, the overlaps and interruptions were distributed evenly among participants. In cross sex, male-female conversations the pattern is drastically different. Practically all the interruptions and overlaps were by male speakers (96 percent and 100 percent respectively). Interruptions occur dramatically more often in mixed sex groups (with men attempting to control the floor) and far less in same sex groups.

Women who find themselves being overlapped should speak louder than the person trying to out-talk them. If the overlap continues after they've raised their volume, they can go quiet (they won't get anywhere if everyone is talking at once) and let the man finish. When he's done, they can say, "I'd like to complete my point without interruption now," or "Mark we're both talking at the same time. Let's stop and take turns." People are more amenable to listening after they have been heard out.

Gender Prescriptions

During the listening process, it is critical to consider the nonverbal cues as carriers of the real message even if the words tell us something else.

GENDER RX

- When conversing with women, men should sit face to face, make continuous eye contact, touch (if appropriate), and employ nonfluencies like "uh huh" to indicate they are listening. They should also eliminate barriers like newspapers or crossed arms.

- As they listen, men should pay attention to other nonverbal cues in order to detect emotions.

- Men should recognize that women initiate conversations to bond and as part of social maintenance.

- A man can identify how a woman feels and express understanding without agreeing with her—the core of empathic listening.

- A man should not interrupt; he should hear the other person out before reacting.

- Women who tend to be long-winded must learn to cut to the chase. I recommend a pyramid answer style.

- Women can listen too much. They need to establish listening boundaries so their time is respected.

- Nodding means "I agree" to a man but "I understand" to a woman.

- When interrupted, a woman must act assertively to regain the floor. She can raise her voice a little coupling this with brief eye contact. She can also lean forward and put her hands on the table for emphasis or verbally assert, "Just a minute. I need to finish."

- When overlapped, a woman can raise her voice. If this doesn't work, she can go quiet until there is a break in the conversation, at which point she can insert her comments.

CHAPTER ELEVEN

Gender-Flexing

Neither sex, without some fertilization of the complimentary characteristics of the other, is capable of the highest reaches of human endeavor.

—H. L. MENCKEN

M**y significant other, Geoff, is among other things a real estate developer. He often hires Manuel to paint the houses he builds. One day, Manuel showed up at my home, ready to paint the interior and exterior. He began by admiring the colors I'd set out for him to use.

"These are great colors!" he said.

"I wish I could say I chose them myself, but I didn't," I admitted.

"I bet Geoff did!" Manuel replied, with a glint in his eye. "You know Audrey, Geoff is like a woman. He knows a lot about colors and decorating."

Anyone who interacts with Geoff knows he's not effeminate in the least. But like every human being, he has a masculine and feminine side. We all do. Swiss psychiatrist Carl Jung talked of the two parts of our personalities—the anima and the animus. The Chinese have taught us about the masculine and feminine—the yin and yang. As Susan Sontag pointed out, "What is most beautiful in virile men is something feminine; what is most beautiful in feminine women is something masculine."

In an article in O, *The Oprah Magazine* playfully titled "Why Can't a Woman Be More Like a Man? And Vice Versa," author Amy Bloom makes this point quite eloquently. "Our mistake is to think that the wide range of humanity represents an aberration when in fact it represents just what it is: a range. Nature is not two little notes—masculine or feminine—on a child's flute. Nature is more like Aretha Franklin: vast, magnificent, capricious—occasionally hilarious and infinitely varied."

The key to effective communication in all settings is inclusiveness of this wide range. This requires behavioral flexibility from both sexes. In this chapter, we will explore this kind of inclusiveness— what I like to call "gender-flexing" or "androgyny."

What Is Androgyny?

When many of us think of androgyny, we are reminded of the character Pat on *Saturday Night Live*. This gives the term unflattering, asexual connotations and is a more colloquial use of the word than I intend. From my point of view, androgynous people combine a variety of masculine and feminine characteristics, all in one package. They are not asexual, but rather more fully alive because they explore all aspects of themselves.

Contemporary business experts such as Tom Peters and Kenneth Blanchard refer to gender-flexing with the psychological term "androgyny." The word derives from a combination of the Greek words "andros," meaning man, and "gyne," meaning woman (as is the prefix to *gyne*cology). Communication, professors Virginia Richmond, James McCroskey, and Steven Payne define an androgynous person as "One who can associate with both masculine and feminine characteristics. In terms of psychological gender orientation, this type of individual is able to adapt to a variety of roles by engaging in either responsive or assertive behaviors, depending on the situation."

Think of it this way: an androgynous man might be a weightlifter but also a social worker who helps underprivileged children, a gourmet cook, and a rose gardener. An androgynous woman could be a physicist who enjoys watching professional football, hanging wallpaper, reading maps, and doing needlepoint. Typically androgynous people are highly flexible. They don't feel limited in their nonverbal communication with others. They are fully aware of and can adapt to another person's needs to be either affiliative or controlling, and they can adjust their behavior accordingly. They are not defined by stereotypically male or female behaviors. And, it is important to remember that gender-flexing has nothing to do with sexual orientation. Androgynous people are no less masculine or feminine in their sexuality than are those who more rigidly adhere to gender roles.

According to Louise Y. Eberhardt, author of *Bridging the Gender Gap,* current gender role research shows that people who are adept at gender-flexing are actually happier and better adjusted:

- Women and men who strongly identify with and fit into the traditional gender stereotype roles experience more anxiety, lower self-esteem, and neurosis.

• Women with extreme femininity often exhibit dependency and self-denial. They may fear taking the initiative and may be risk-averse.

• Men with extreme masculinity may be arrogant. They may exploit others and even tend toward violence.

• Androgynous people tend to be more creative and flexible and less anxious, and gender-flexing women may be even more nurturing than those who are highly feminine.

• It is possible for men to have more of their strengths on the feminine side and vice versa. This is not negative and often indicates high creativity and intellectual development. Professional women often tend to have many strengths traditionally associated with masculinity.

Besides allowing for more satisfying interactions, gender-flexing has many personal benefits. There is a correlation between androgyny and self-esteem. People who have expanded their behavioral repertoire feel better about themselves. They have a bigger bag of tricks and more options available to them. Their interactions are more successful. In fact, they can appear more familiar to the opposite sex, which increases comfort levels and allows for more fluid communication. A woman engineer of my acquaintance was the envy of some of her female colleagues because she was like "one of the boys." JoAnn grew up with brothers and told me that it was a breeze for her to float into male culture. The other women couldn't believe that she read the sports page cover to cover, played a good game of golf, and placed bets on football games with her male counterparts. And John was the ultimate androgynous teacher. All the women on the faculty claimed they would forget he was a man because he could join in on their conversations about "girl stuff" with no problem.

You might think of gender-flexing as a way to strengthen and tone your nonverbal muscles. After all, nonverbal behaviors are in great part centered in the body. We all have masculine and feminine nonverbal behaviors at our disposal—it's just a matter of using these oft-ignored "muscles." Who doesn't recognize the feeling you get when during a workout you use a muscle you haven't stretched in a long time? You often feel sore and uncomfortable. But the more you work that muscle, the stronger it gets, and the more secure you become in your newfound strength and flexibility. Using the same analogy, think about those steroid-popping muscle-heads at the gym who work exclusively on building their arms and shoulders, but ignore their legs. They almost look like burly lollipops (especially when their overdeveloped shoulders engulf their necks). In the same way, if we rely exclusively on masculine or feminine ways of communicating nonverbally, our nonverbal physique can be way out of balance.

Behavioral flexibility is the key to effective communication strategies in all personal and organizational settings. I have been recommending gender-flexing behaviors throughout the book, especially in the Gender Prescriptions sections of each chapter. Let's consider now how gender-flexing has arisen and evolved at work and at home.

Aren't Gender Roles Set in Stone?

Imagine it is a moonless night and you're out walking the dog. You see a person in dark clothing in the distance. Even under these limited conditions impoverished by distance and lack of light, you can accurately distinguish male from female. Under normal circumstances, it is impossible not to notice another person's gender. Small displays such as stride, the thrust of one's shoulders, or the movement of a hand can give it all away. Men are men and women are women.

Yet, when American society was first organized around agriculture, the differences between masculine and feminine roles were less distinct than they are today. Both women and men assumed responsibility for the family and for economic survival. Since a husband's work was in the same physical location as his wife's or very close to it (in the fields or the barn), the two were very much more interdependent. However, although agrarian societies were more equal in sharing responsibilities, sharing did not translate into social influence for women.

During the Industrial Revolution, when men began to work away from home in factories, distinct gender identities developed and then diverged greatly. Men's working environment and separateness led to an impersonal public façade. Do the job with a utilitarian attitude. Women remained at home and became more directly associated with the personal, private, nurturing, and the emotional. Women also began to be referred to as weak, decorative, inferior, negative, and trivial.

In one way or another, these attitudes continued into the mid-twentieth century (with a break for "Rosie the Riveter," the women who worked in defense industry factories during World War II). According to Diana K. Ivy, professor of communications at Texas A & M University and Phil Backlund at Central Washington University, "For a boy growing up in the 1950's and the early 1960's male gender roles were well defined. Movie and TV role models included John Wayne, Robert Young, Marshall Dillon. Macho images of 'We can do it all!' ruled. Men didn't cry, never showed their feelings, handled everything, were invulnerable and dominated women."

Because our culture has held so fast to these familiar gender roles for the last hundred years or so, we might have come to believe that they simply reflect human nature. However, in the course of my research I have found that these roles are often mediated by one's culture. For instance, Margaret Mead's studies of societies in New Guinea revealed that among the Arapesh people, both women and men conform closely to what we would label feminine behaviors. Both genders are passive, peaceful, and deferential, and both nurture others, especially young children. In contrast, the Mundugumor tribe socializes women and men to be aggressive, competitive, and independent. The mothers wean babies early and do little nurturing. In fact, they spend little time with their newborns.

Julia Wood cites her own awakening to the arbitrariness of American gender definitions when she spent time living with Tamang villagers in the hill country of Nepal. "I discovered that both women and men did what we consider gender-specific tasks," she wrote in *Gendered Lives*. "For instance, men do much of the cooking and childcare, and they seem especially nurturing and gentle with young children. Women also do these things, as well as engaging in heavy manual labor and working as porters carrying 70-plus pounds of trekking gear for Western travelers."

What does all this mean? Simply, the meaning of gender roles varies across cultures. Also it changes across time. I have observed that as people get older, their adherence to strict gender roles becomes blurrier. As expert on aging Betty Polston explains in *Loving Midlife Marriage*, Carl Jung also recognized that at midlife we undergo dramatic changes in our perspective and character: "He perceived life to be divided into halves and the second half begins at about the age of 40. During the first half of their lives, men are intent on developing the 'masculine' characteristics: independence, assertiveness and even aggressiveness, logical focus, and an ability to shut down or ignore their emotions." The second half is devoted to discovering the inner, true, or real self. To become a whole person, a man needs to integrate the neglected, more "feminine" parts of himself, such as introspection, tenderness, affiliation, and interdependence. He becomes more spiritual, more involved in mature, intimate relationships.

By contrast, women at midlife, with family obligations often diminishing, may stretch toward more "masculine" attributes. They may develop more independence, learn new skills, return to school or work, and become more creative, adventurous, and assertive.

Besides, the rigid sex role standards have been evolving. A boy growing up in the 1950s might have looked up to John Wayne as a role model, and a girl might have worshiped Doris Day or Loretta Young, but today both would have many more options. Social change of the 1960s and '70s caused a reexamination of gender roles at the individual and the societal levels, resulting in a broadening of role definitions for all of us. A one-paycheck family could no longer support a middle-class lifestyle. Economic necessity pushed many suburban housewives out of the kitchen and into the workforce and eventually the boardroom.

Crossing Over

When I conduct training in the rural parts of the country, it's clear to me how the farming and ranching environment is highly interdependent in gender-flexing. When it comes time to buck hay, everyone is doing it. A ranch woman can lift forty-pound bales of hay. Men help with the canning when the fruit comes in. Everybody is involved and the roles are more ambiguous. This interdependence creates a sense of shared and relatively equal responsibility for all members of the family.

We might even say that whether one behaves in a more or less gender-defined way can depend on one's situation and circumstances. Take the U.S. Marines' philosophy that combines homophobia and misogyny with the belief that "When you want to create a group of male killers, you kill the woman in them." The military is one of the most notoriously male bastions in existence, and the issue of women in combat is still a hotly debated topic in Congress and at the dinner table.

"Killing the woman in men" is such an evocative image. It renders anything feminine a disease—something that makes you weak. But, then, how do we account for Jessica Lynch, the nineteen-year-old POW from West Virginia who survived two broken legs and other injuries during the 2003 war in Iraq? She was captured, but made it out alive even though most of her cohorts didn't.

This point was brought home to me while I was conducting a seminar in the South. In distinguishing between passive, assertive, and aggressive behavior, I made the point that each of these behaviors has value and is worthy of its own time and place for men as well as women. As I was winding down my discussion, I saw a woman's hand tentatively go up in the back of the room. "Do you have a question?" I asked.

"Well, more of a comment," this participant said softly. "I can't ever imagine being aggressive."

"What if I just attacked one of your children?" I prodded.

"I would kill you!" she responded vehemently.

Sounds aggressive to me. Aggression certainly is not the preferred mode of operation on a day-to-day basis for most women (it has been traditionally associated with male behavior), but given the right set of circumstances, a woman can be more like a man. In fact, a more hyperbolic example of that is a call for women to actualize their masculine side. As feminist author and political activist Gloria Steinem once said, "Some of us are becoming the men we wanted to marry."

The same, of course, is true for men. Today men in the military can also exhibit some behavior we would identify as being relatively feminine. Ellen Goodman, columnist for the *Boston Globe,* wrote an article in 1991 titled "A Shining (Four) Star" about General Norman Schwarzkopf, the commander of Desert Storm I, that captures this evolution: "Schwarzkopf is not John Wayne. . . . Strong but silent doesn't hack it in the 90s. It gets a guy grief and an anniversary copy of *You Just Don't Understand.* Nor is Schwarzkopf another Alan Alda. . . . The right to cry is fine, but sensitivity without self-confidence these days gets the man labeled a wimp."

She described Stormin' Norman as a man who balances feminine characteristics with masculine: "Introspective but decisive, caring yet competent, one of the guys and a leader. Not the stuff that always comes in the same package." Although Goodman doesn't use the terms gender-flexing or androgyny, that is exactly what she means.

Professional sports is another bastion of masculinity; aside from the military, no arena is more macho. Yet I remember Roosevelt Grier, a famous big football player who enjoyed needlepoint. People went nuts over his "unusual" hobby, but he was not ashamed. Rather, he was sure enough of his masculinity to show his feminine side. Men like Rosie have no problem identifying with femininity in their character or development. I have always believed it takes a whole man to identify with his feminine side. (And we're not talking about Dennis

Rodman, who seems to make a mockery of the idea of androgyny by being as outrageous and attention grabbing as he can.)

Rosie is not the only athlete to surprise us with his gender-flexing. Former New York Yankees pitcher David Wells said this after throwing a perfect game: "I dedicate this game to my Mother, Ann. She was a fighter like me. They say, 'Like mother, like daughter.' Well in this case it might be 'Like mother like son.'"

In Lance Armstrong's autobiography *It's Not About the Bike* about his battle with cancer and the road to recovery that led to his wins at Tour de France, he refers to his mother (he was essentially raised in a single head of household) and his wife as being his pillars of strength. Of his wife, he writes, she was "such a stud," using a male metaphor to describe her determination to help him get back to life and riding. She was tough on him when he went through his "I feel sorry for myself and I will never be able ride again" period.

Wells and Armstrong identified with the masculine attributes in their mothers and wives. And perhaps more important, these men were not afraid to say so. They were man enough to admit that they liked and valued their contributions! Still, for an athlete to hold a woman as his role model is counter to our notion of the macho man. Some men may still waver, like John Travolta who said, "If I'm androgynous, I'd say I lean towards macho-androgynous." That's sort of cheating, wouldn't you say?

The flip side to strong men identifying with their mothers is the phenomenon of strong women such as Eleanor Roosevelt identifying with their fathers. Bonnie Angelo, longtime correspondent for *Time* magazine, alludes to this in her book, *First Mothers: The Women Who Shaped the Presidents*. These powerful men were devoted to their mothers (while their relations with their fathers were often more problematic). This devotion had a direct and usually positive effect on their presidencies. But even more striking was the fact that the mothers of many U.S. presidents—from Franklin Roosevelt to Bill Clinton—often had a strong relationship with and/or strongly identified with their fathers. Lillian Gordy Carter, for instance, modeled herself after her father more than her mother in her beliefs and attitudes. There is a real tradition of success for those who actively pursue gender-flexing.

Strategic Flexibility

Strategic flexibility means expanding your nonverbal communication repertoire to use the best skill available for a particular situation. Without using the strengths of both genders, including an awareness of your own nonverbal communication skills and deficits, equal contribution at home or in the workplace is impossible. I have found that strategic flexibility is the primary characteristic of successful people— a vital component of excellent relationships at work and at home. People who possess this ability are happier and more fulfilled.

Conventional wisdom tells us that our greatest strengths can also be our greatest weaknesses. This is particularly true when we fall back on knee-jerk responses, such as, *This is a man's job,* or *That's women's work*. When Abraham Maslow pointed out that everything looks like a nail to a person whose only tool is a hammer, he might well have been talking about one-sided masculinity or overplayed femininity.

The truth is, there is no single way to behave in the world. Three models represent the types of inter-gender communication that each sex can employ:

• *Heightened gender identification.* The man or woman exhibits and intensely defends his or her sex-typed nonverbal patterns.

• *Gender reversal.* The person moves forcefully in the direction of emulating the other gender's communication ideals.

• *Inclusiveness.* The strengths of both genders' traditional styles are respected, and wide variations are allowed when fitting communication behavior to circumstances.

I, for one, argue for the merits of inclusiveness. Learning to understand women's communication styles does not make a man "feminine," just as learning to understand a man's style does not render a woman "masculine." Including some effective communication techniques of the opposite gender is no different than adding to one's technical vocabulary or respecting another country's customs. A woman may develop assertive skills and still be characterized by her sensitivity; a man may develop interpersonal skills and still be characterized by his ability to exercise power. In *Gendered Lives,* Julia Wood shares a journal entry from "Miguel" that illustrates the notion of combining and valuing the full range of human qualities:

> I like to be strong and stand up for myself and what I think, but I would not want to be only that. I am also sensitive to other people and how they feel. There are times to be hard and times to be soft . . .

By urging gender-flexing, I am not implying that men should become women and women become men. Heaven forbid! But they can learn from one another without abandoning successful traits they already possess. Both men and women bring different nonverbal skill sets to the table. The more they can each expand their respective repertoires, the more successful they will be in relationships both at work and home. They have more options and choices!

As Alice Sargent wrote in *The Androgynous Manager,* "Men can learn to be more intuitive, yet remain result oriented. Women need not give up being nurturing in order to learn to be comfortable with power and conflict." I say amen to that. Men can be better empathic listeners and readers of nonverbal cues yet remain credible and assertive in their nonverbal behavior (using a strong, loud voice, for example). And women do not need to give up their abilities to read the nonverbal environment or facilitate dialogue with their nonverbal cues (such as head nodding, engaging in eye contact, standing closer) in order to become more assertive. Your ability to monitor yourself and accurately determine how your behavior impacts others is a key step in successfully changing your behavior.

The Flip-Flop Technique

We all know people who don't have an extensive repertoire of nonverbal behaviors. They have only *one* style. They are the individuals about whom we can say with great predictability, "Yup, there goes Fred, pounding his fist again." We know how he's going to behave because he has only one note—gruffness. Or "There goes Betsy, crying again." Consequently, they use the same worn-out interaction pattern, the only one they know, much to their detriment. These behaviors work if the situation calls for them, but not all situations are alike. Situational adaptability is the key to connecting with others, and especially to those of the opposite sex.

Situational nonverbal communication is critical to an effective outcome. If a woman is not being heard and a crisis mandates that her input be included, she must use a louder voice. She may also need to interrupt the speaker because he missed her point. These are typically "male" behaviors. If a man must glean information from another person's demeanor, he must make eye contact. He may also need to silence his own inner dialogue and instead attend to the speaker's tone of voice or posture. These are typically "female" behaviors.

The ability to demonstrate interpersonal skills associated with both sexes has a wide appeal. People who know how to do this have the nonverbal choices to navigate the demands of daily living. But how do we translate the idea of gender-flexing to nonverbal prescriptions for your life?

The following questions can help you tailor effective communication:

- Does my nonverbal behavior fit the context?

- Will it be the most effective in this situation?

- What are my goals?

- What do I need to achieve in this situation right here and now?

- Can I be flexible and move in and out of various approaches especially if my day presents numerous situations that call upon me to employ different styles?

One afternoon, Jane may be negotiating with her boss for an increase in her budget using strong gestures and serious facial expressions. On her way home she stops at the auto repair shop and with an adamant tone refuses to pay an unauthorized charge on her bill. An hour later, she's consoling her college-age daughter about a D on a paper with a soothing voice, an uninterrupted ear, a look of concern, and a hug. Different contexts require different behaviors.

John may also blend male and female nonverbals simultaneously. His subordinate, Mary, repeatedly turns in late assignments. She is also going through a difficult divorce. With a caring look and slight touch on the arm, John leans closer to her and says, "I know this is a demanding time for you. It must be awful to get divorced after so many years of marriage. However," he continues sitting back in his chair and using a firm tone and serious facial expression, "I need you to step up to the plate on your assignments. Your lateness is jeopardizing the team's performance and our ability to secure this contract." He reverts to his caring facial expression and asks, "How can we help you manage your workload more efficiently?"

A Double Standard?

Research and common wisdom suggest that women have made more progress toward an androgynous style than men. In the 1980s, for example, the trend was toward assertiveness training for women. I recall designing such a program for one of the largest seminar companies in the United States. Its title: Taking Charge! It identified strengths and skills (such as risk-taking, independence, and the ability to stand alone without the approval of others) that contributed to male success in the business world and taught these skills to women.

However, there is some danger in going overboard. While we rarely see men acting like women due to homophobia, women have been known to act like men. I observed this with the original female partners in one of the Big Six accounting firms in the 1990s. Only 10 percent of the 950 partners nationwide were female. Unfortunately, the pioneering women in this company behaved just like men; they looked, talked, and walked like them! They had relinquished their femininity for the masculine role model. They believed they had to in order to survive. It was the price they had to pay to fit into the good-old-boy network.

All that is accomplished in such attempts is to exchange one half of a person for the other. In other words, these women threw the baby out with the bath water. The goal is for women to keep their feminine characteristics and skills (such as their ability to be sensitive and read nonverbal cues) while they also incorporate and add to their communication repertoire some male characteristics (such as assertiveness).

On the other hand, there has been much less support for men at home and on the job to encourage incorporation of feminine skills. The reward system, especially at work, simply was not there! However, recently there has been a movement in the corporate world, especially influenced by gurus Tom Peters and Kenneth Blanchard, to move toward a more feminine work model incorporating quality circles, community, and team building.

We know that androgynous people demonstrate more crossover nonverbal behaviors. We also know that men and women may suffer different fates for doing so. Adopting male nonverbal communication behaviors (without abandoning their own) can make women more effective. Those who do incorporate masculine modes into their communication style are often more likely to effectuate and realize their goals than more traditional women. At worst, a woman is told to tone it down, she's called a bitch, or others ask her if it is her time of the month. This epithet, while distasteful, does not challenge her sexual orientation. But men can pay a higher price due to homophobia. Maleness is more entrenched than femaleness in our culture. Femalelike behavior can call into question a man's sexual orientation! (Being called a "sissy" or being told "You run like a girl" are among the highest insults for young boys!)

We need to break this double standard and create a new paradigm that allows men and women to live outside the box, able to experience and employ the full range of nonverbal behaviors available to all of us. Androgynous communication is really a way of saying that we want to use and value both masculine and feminine nonverbal abilities. Gender role transcendence is the key to successful communication. There is no guarantee that all gender-flexing, androgynous people will be successful in all situations. But they do have a wider range and bigger bag of tricks. Why not enjoy the advantages?

Does Nonverbal Literacy Make a Difference?

In today's world where face time is a rarity even in our own families and we all increasingly rely on email and voicemail to communicate, certainly every encounter in which we engage becomes crucial. Yet opening the lines of communication between men and women begins with asymmetry. How can we meet each other on the bumpy road of communication?

There is a fundamental problem. Men and women are different. Not better or worse, just different. Anthropologists, psychologist, sociologists, and other scientists have recognized this fact for centuries. But these differences contribute to the potholes in which we often find ourselves when dealing with the opposite sex. Despite these distinctions, however, relationships between men and women can work. They only become rocky when both genders fail to recognize the differences and have certain rigid expectations of how they and the opposite sex should communicate.

There are questions that we need to ask: Can gender-flexing be learned? Can people develop an awareness of subtle nonverbal cues? Our natural tendency is to believe that the opposite sex is the one that needs to change and get "fixed." But we must start with ourselves. We each have a responsibility in the communication process. We may not be able to control the other person's communication style, but we can manage our own. Blaming the opposite sex gets us nowhere. Taking responsibility for our own nonverbal communication may not prevent communication misunderstandings completely, but it can help us prevent breakdowns and minimize out-of-control situations.

Nonverbal self-awareness, yours and that of the opposite sex, is the first step toward enhancing effective communication. Understanding that nonverbal cues are the shortest route to revealing emotions is another necessary shift toward awareness. Yet, nonverbal communication operates at a "stealth" level of existence; we leave an interaction feeling something happened, but we're not sure what. One of the reasons we are so poor at this critical skill is simply because most of us do not know that these behaviors exist and how they operate. To narrow the chasm between the sexes, we need to turn our attention to this decisive part of the communication process.

I have referred to gender nonverbal communication as "the elephant in the middle of the room." It is often unconscious and needs to be made more conscious. That was the goal of this book. I want us to be more self-aware, more self-conscious, if you will, of the nonverbal messages men and women send and to identify and make more concrete the component parts of a successful face-to-face encounter. We need to pay more attention to those subtle nonverbal messages that we send and receive. Why? Because on the home front and in the workplace as well as during the countless errands that consume our day, we continually experience nonverbal minidisasters, often unintended. Our divorce rate holds steady at more failures than successes. At work, subtle micro-behaviors that support the macro-structure are enacted daily between men and women maintaining the glass ceiling or sticky floor and ultimately resulting in less earning potential for women.

In my work, I see smart, hardworking, well-intentioned people self-destruct interpersonally because they are just plain unaware of what they and others are communicating. Although we may not always get the results we want in an encounter, knowledge of how nonverbal communication works will increase our effectiveness and enhance all our interactions between men and women.

Gender-flexing implies movement and action, and *You Don't Say* is about change. This book has brought up unsettling questions that go to the core of how we define ourselves as male or female. It was meant to stimulate you to question your behavior, examine yourself, and at times even feel a little uncomfortable. We must consider new ideas of what it means to be male and female. Once we embrace the journey by observing nonverbal cues and questioning the traditional conventions that our culture and society have accepted, we will be better able to reach out to, respect, and understand each other.

BIBLIOGRAPHY

Adler, Ronald, and Neil Towne. *Looking Out, Looking In.* San Francisco: Reinhart Press, 1975.

Agins, T. "Fashion Slaves Get Kicks from Spike Heels." *Wall Street Journal.* Jan 20, 1995, p. B1.

Aiken, L. R. "The Relationship of Dress to Selected Measures of Personality in Undergraduate Women." *Journal of Social Psychology.* 59: 119–128, 1963.

Ali, Lorraine. "Anarchy on MTV?" *Newsweek.* Jan 6, 2003, p. 79.

Anderson, Janis F., Peter A. Anderson, and Myron W. Lustig. "Opposite Sex Touch: A National Replication and Extension." *Journal of Nonverbal Behavior.* 11: 89–109, Summer 1987.

Angier, Natalie. *Woman: An Intimate Geography.* New York: Houghton Mifflin, 1999.

Armstrong, Lance. *It's Not About the Bike: My Journey Back to Life.* New York: Putnam, 2000.

Bibliography

Axtell, Roger. *Gestures: The Do's and Taboos of Body Language Around the World*. New York: John Wiley & Sons, 1998.

"Bad Break: Airplane Bathroom User Arrested Under New Law." ABC News.com, February 12, 2002.

Bate, Barbara, and Judy Bowker. *Communication and the Sexes*, Second Edition. Waveland Press, 1997.

Bavelas, Janet Beavin, Linda Coates, and Trudy Johnson. "Listener Responses as a Collaborative Process: The Role of Gaze." *Journal of Communication*. Sep 2002, p. 566–580.

Birdwhistell, Ray L. *Kinesics and Context*. New York: Ballantine Books, 1970.

Bloom, Amy. "Why Can't a Woman Be More Like a Man? And Vice Versa." *O, The Oprah Magazine*, Oct 2002.

Blunt, Judy. *Breaking Clean*. New York: Alfred A. Knopf, 2002.

Borisoff, Deborah, and Lisa Merrill. *The Power to Communicate: Gender Differences as Barriers*, Second Edition. Prospect Heights, IL: Waveland Press, 1985.

Bouton-Jones, Ng. "Nonverbal Communication in Children." *Nonverbal Communication*. Edited by R. A. Hinde. Cambridge: Cambridge University Press, 1972.

Brod, Harry. "Who Benefits from Male Involvement in the Wife's Pregnancy?" *Marriage and Divorce Today*. 12: 3, 1997.

Buchanan, D. R., M. Goldman, and R. Juhnke. "Eye Contact, Sex, and the Violation of Personal Space." *Journal of Social Psychology*, 103: 19–25, 1977.

Burgoon, J. K., and J. L. Hale. "Nonverbal Expectancy Violations: Model Elaboration and Application to Immediacy Behaviors." *Communication Monographs*. 55: 58–79, 1988.

Burgoon, Judee, and Thomas Saine. *The Unspoken Dialogue: An Introduction to Nonverbal Communication*. New York: Houghton Mifflin, 1978.

Burns, Alyson, L. G. Mitchell, and Stephanie Obradovich. "Of Sex Roles and Strollers: Male Attention to Toddlers at the Zoo." *Sex Roles*. 20: 309–315, 1989.

"Busting the Bhagwan." *Newsweek*. November 11, 1985, p. 26.

Carton, John S., Emily A. Kessler, and Christina A. Pape. "Nonverbal Decoding Skills in Relationship Well-Being in Adults." *Journal of Nonverbal Behavior,* 31: 91–100, 1999.

Condry, J., and S. Condry. "Sex Differences: A Study of the Eye of the Beholder." *Child Development.* 47: 812–819, 1976.

Coopersmith, S. *The Antecedents of Self-Esteem.* San Francisco: Freeman, 1967.

Crusko, A. H., and C. G. Wetzel. "The Midas Touch: The Effects of Interpersonal Touching on Restaurant Tipping." *Personality and Social Psychology Bulletin.* 10: 512–517, 1994.

Dally, Michelle. "Stunted Growth." *Health,* Jan/Feb 2003, p. 52–56.

Davis, F. "Skin Hunger: An American Disease." *Women's Day,* Sep 27, 1978, p. 48–50.

"Dear Abby" column, Universal Press Syndicate, January 10, 1982.

de Jong, Peter J. "Communicators and Remedial Effects of Social Blushing." *Journal of Nonverbal Behavior.* 23: 197–217, Fall 1999.

Devor, H. "Becoming Members of Society: Learning the Social Meanings of Gender." *Gender Images: Reading for Composition.* Edited by M. Schaum and C. Flanangan. Boston: Houghton Mifflin, 1992.

Dimitrius, Jo-Ellan, and Mark Mazzarella. *Reading People: How to Understand People and Predict Their Behavior Anytime, Anyplace.* New York: Ballantine Books, 1998.

Dobosz, A. M. "Thicker Thighs By Thanksgiving." *Media Journal.* Nov–Dec 1997, p. 89–91.

Donaldson-Evans, L. "Love's Fatal Glance: A Study of Eye Imagery in the Poets of the Ecole Lyonnaise," *Romance Monographs.* 1980, p. 21, cited in Grummet, Jerald W. "Eye Contact: The Core of Interpersonal Relatedness." *Journal of Psychiatry.* 28: 172–180, 1983.

Dovido, J. F., S. L. Keating, K. Heltman, and C. Brown. "The Relationship of Social Power to Visual Displays of Dominance Between Men and Women." *Journal of Personality and Social Psychology.* 54: 233–242, 1988.

Dowd, Maureen. "Times Thieving Progress." *Rocky Mountain News.* Feb 16, 2002.

Dutton, Jane E., Peter J. Frost, Monica C. Worline, et al. "Leading in Times of Trauma." *Harvard Business Review.* Jan 2002, p. 55.

Eakins, Barbara W., and R. Gene Eakins. *Sex Differences in Human Communication.* Boston: Houghton Mifflin, 1978.

Eberhardt, Louise Yolton. *Bridging the Gender Gap.* Duluth, MN: Whole Person Associates, 1995.

Efron, David. *Gesture and Environment.* New York: King's Crown, 1941.

Eibel-Eibesfeldt, I. "Similarities and Differences Between Cultures in Expressive Movements." *Nonverbal Communication.* Edited by R. A. Hinde. Cambridge: Cambridge University Press, 1972.

Ekman, Paul, and W. V. Friesen. "Hand Movements." *Journal of Communication.* 22: 353–374, 1972.

Ekman, Paul, and W. V. Friesen. *Unmasking the Face.* Englewood Cliffs, NJ: Prentice Hall, 1975.

Eller, Daryn. "Life: The Sculptor." *O, The Oprah Magazine.* April 2002, p. 140.

Ellyson, Steve L., John F. Dovidio, and B. J. Fehr, "Visual Behavior and Dominance in Women and Men." *Gender and Nonverbal Behavior.* Edited by Clara Mayo and Nancy M. Henley. Springer Series in Social Psychology, NY: Springer-Verlag, 1981.

Etcoff, Nancy L. *Survival of the Prettiest: The Science of Beauty.* New York: Doubleday, 1999.

Exline, R.V. "Visual Interaction: The Glances of Power and Preference." *Nebraska Symposium on Motivation.* Edited by J. Cole. Lincoln, NE: University of Nebraska Press, 1971.

Fast, Julius. *Body Language.* New York: M. Evans and Co., 1970.

Field, Tiffany. "Individual Differences in the Expressivity of Neonates and Young Infants." *Development of Nonverbal Behavior in Children.* Edited by Robert S. Feldman. New York: Springer-Verlag, 1982.

Firestone, Shulamith. *The Dialectic of Sex.* New York: Bantam Books, 1970.

Fisher, Helen. *The Anatomy of Love: A Natural History of Mating, Marriage, and Why We Stray.* New York: Fawcett-Columbine, 1992.

Frammolino, Ralph, and Jeff Leeds. "Anderson's Reputation in Shreds." *Los Angeles Times,* Jan 30, 2002, p. A1.

Fromme, Donald K., William E. Jaymes, Deborah K. Taylor, et al. "Nonverbal Behavior and Attitudes Toward Touch." *Journal of Nonverbal Behavior.* 13: 3–14, 1989.

Gass, Robert H., John S. Seiter. *Persuasion, Social Influence, and Compliance Gaining.* Boston: Allyn and Bacon, 1999.

Bibliography

Geller, Adam. "Religion Increasingly a Source of Tension in U.S. Workplace." *Daily Camera.* Jan 18, 2003, Section D.

Golant, Mitch, and Susan Golant. *Finding Time for Fathering.* New York: Ballantine Books, 1992.

Golant, Mitch, and Susan Golant. *Disciplining Your Preschooler and Feeling Good About It,* Third Edition. Los Angeles: Lowell House, 1997.

Goleman, Daniel. *Emotional Intelligence.* New York: Bantam 1995.

Goodman, Ellen. "A Shining (Four) Star." *Boston Globe* City Edition. Mar 14, 1991.

Gould, K. H., "Old Wine in New Bottles: A Feminist Perspective on Gilligan's Theory." *Social Work.* 411–415, Sep–Oct 1988.

Grumet, Gerald W. "Eye Contact: The Core of Interpersonal Relatedness." *Nonverbal Communication Reader: Classic and Contemporary Readings,* Second Edition. Edited by Laura K. Guerrero, Joseph A. De Vito, and Michael L. Hecht. Prospect Heights, IL: Waveland Press, 1999.

Gurel, L.M., J. C. Wilbur, and L. Gurel. "Personality Correlate of Adolescent Clothing Styles." *Journal of Home Economics.* 64: 42–47, 1972.

Guthrie, R. D., *Body Hot Spots: The Anatomy of Human Social Organs and Behavior.* New York: Van Nostrand Reinhold, 1976.

"Guys 'n' Dolls." *Daily Times Call,* Sunday, February 9, 2003, Section E, p. 1.

Hall, Edward T. *The Silent Language.* New York: Fawcett, 1959.

Hall, Edward T. *The Hidden Dimension.* New York: Doubleday, 1966.

Hall, Judith A. *Nonverbal Sex Differences: Communication Accuracy and Expressive Style.* Baltimore: Johns Hopkins University Press, 1984.

Harrison, Randall P. *Beyond Words: An Introduction to Nonverbal Communication.* Englewood Cliffs, NJ: Prentice Hall, 1974.

Henley, Nancy M. *Body Politics: Power, Sex, and Nonverbal Communication.* Englewood Cliffs, NJ: Prentice Hall, 1977.

Henley, Nancy M., and Freeman, Jo. "Sexual Politics of Interpersonal Behavior." *Women: A Feminist Perspective.* Edited by Nancy Henley and Jo Freeman. Palo Alto, CA: Mayfield Publishing, 1975.

Heslin, R. *Steps Toward a Taxonomy of Touching.* Paper presented to the Mid-Western Psychological Association. Chicago, IL, 1974.

Hess, E. H. "Attitude and Pupil Size." *Scientific American.* 46–54, 1965.

Hinde, R. A., ed. *Nonverbal Communication.* Cambridge: Cambridge University Press, 1972.

Hocking, John E., and Dale G. Leathers. "Nonverbal Indicators of Deception: A New Theoretical Perspective." *Communication Monographs.* 47: 119–131, June 1980.

Houle, Rene, and Robert S. Feldman. "Emotional Displays in Children's Television Programming." *Journal of Nonverbal Behavior.* 15: 261–271, Winter 1991.

Hoult, R. "Experimental Measurement of Clothing as a Factor in Some Social Ratings of Selected American Men." *American Sociological Review.* 19: 324–328, 1954.

Hwang, Suein. "Dressing for Success with a Shot of Botox." Accessed from the *Wall Street Journal* online, Sep 11, 2002.

Ivy, Diana K., and Phil Backlund. *Exploring Genderspeak: Personal Effectiveness in Gender Communication,* Second Edition. New York: McGraw-Hill, 2000.

Janik, Stephen A., Rodney A. Wellens, Myron L. Goldberg, and Louis F. Dell'Osso. "Eyes as the Focus in the Visual Examination of Human Faces." *Perceptual and Motor Skills.* 47: 857–858, Dec 1978.

Jourard, Sidney. *The Transparent Self.* New York: Van Nostram-Reinhold, 1964.

Jourard, Sidney. "An Exploratory Study of Body-Accessibility." *British Journal of Social and Clinical Psychology.* 5: 221–231, 1966.

Kaleina, G. "More Than Other Folks, Pets Get Loving Strokes." *Arizona Republic,* Mar 3, 1979, p. 2.

Keeley-Dyreson, Maureen, Judee K. Burgoon, and William Bailey. "The Effects of Stress and Gender on Non-Verbal Decoding Accuracy in Kinesic and Vocalic Channels." *Human Communication Research.* 17: 584–605, Jun 1991.

Keen, Sam. *Fire in the Belly: On Being a Man.* New York: Bantam Books, 1991.

Key, May Ritchie. *Paralanguage and Kinesics.* Metuchens, NJ: Scarecrow Press, 1975.

Kimble, Charles E., and Steven D. Seidel. "Vocal Signs of Confidence." *Journal of Nonverbal Behavior.* 1599, 1991.

Knapp, Mark L., *Essentials of Nonverbal Communication.* New York: Holt, Reinhart and Winston, 1980.

Bibliography

Knapp, Mark L., and Judith A. Hall. *Nonverbal Communication in Human Interaction*, Fifth Edition. Belmont, CA: Wadsworth, 2002.

Kneidinger, Linda M., Perry L. Maple, and Ann A. Stewart-Tross. "Touching Behavior in Sport: Functional Components: Analysis of Sex Differences and Ethological Considerations." *Journal of Nonverbal Behavior.* 25: 43–62, Spring 2001.

LaFrance, Marianne, and Clara Mayo. *Moving Bodies: Nonverbal Communication in Social Relationships*. Monterey, CA: Brooks/Cole Publishing, 1978.

LaRusso, Dominic. *The Shadows of Communication*. Dubuque, IA: Kendall/Hunt Publishing, 1977.

Leathers, Dale G. *Nonverbal Communication Systems*. Boston: Allyn and Bacon, 1976.

Leathers, Dale G. *Successful Nonverbal Communication: Principles and Applications,* Third Edition. Boston: Allyn and Bacon, 1997.

Legman, Gershon. *Rationale of the Dirty Joke: An Analysis of Sexual Humor*. New York: Castle Books, 1968.

Lerner, Harriet. *The Dance of Anger: A Woman's Guide to Changing the Patterns of Intimate Relationships*. New York: HarperCollins, 1997.

Lewis, M., and R. Freedle. "Mother-Infant Dyad: The Cradle of Meaning." *Communication and Affect, Language, and Thought*. Edited by P. Pliner, L. Krames, and T. Alloyway. New York: Academic Press, 1973.

Ludington, Susan. "Effects of Extra Tactile Stimulation on Growth and Development of Vaginally and Cesarean Born Infants." *Communicating Nursing Research*. 50–58, Spring 1977.

Ludington-Hoe, Susan, and Susan K. Golant. *How to Have a Smarter Baby*. New York: Bantam, 1987.

Maccoby, Eleanor E. "Gender and Relationships: A Developmental Account." *American Psychologist*. 45: 513–520, 1990.

Maccoby, Eleanor E., and Carol Nagy Jacklin. "Gender Segregation in Childhood." *Advances in Child Development and Behavior,* Volume 20. Edited by H. W. Reese. New York: Academic Press, 1987.

Malandro, Loretta. *Your Every Move Talks*. Dubuque, IA: Gorsuch Scarisbrick Publishers, 1977.

Malandro, Loretta A., and Larry Baker. *Nonverbal Communication*. Readings, MA: Addison-Wesley, 1983.

Bibliography

Maltz, D. N., and R. A. Borker. "A Cultural Approach to Male-Female Mis-communication." *Language and Social Identity.* Edited by J. J. Gumperz. Cambridge: Cambridge University Press, 1982.

Marosi, Richard. "South Gate Councilwoman's Silence Disturbs Critics." *Los Angeles Times.* California Section, Jan 29, 2002.

Mayle, Peter. "Return to Provence." *GQ.* May 1998, p. 256.

Mayo, Clara, and Nancy M. Henley. "Nonverbal Behavior: Barrier Agent for Sex Role Change?" *Gender and Nonverbal Behavior.* Edited by Clara Mayo and Nancy M. Henley. Springer Series in Social Psychology. New York: Springer-Verlag, 1981.

Maysonave, Sherry. *Casual Power: How to Power Up Your Nonverbal Communication & Dress Down for Success.* Austin, TX: Bright Books, 1999.

Mead, Margaret. *Sex and Temperament in Three Primitive Societies.* New York: Dell, 1968.

Mehrabian, Albert. *Silent Messages: Implicit Communication of Emotions and Attitudes,* Second Edition. Belmont, CA: Wadsworth Publishing, 1981.

Michael, G., and F. N. Willis. "The Development of Gestures as a Function of Social Class, Education, and Sex." *Psychological Record.* 18: 515–519, 1968.

Mindell, Phyllis. *A Woman's Guide to the Language of Success: Communicating with Confidence and Power.* New York: Prentice Hall, 1995.

Minielli, Maureen C. "The Nonverbal Communication of President Bill Clinton." *New Jersey Journal of Communication.* 7: 190–205, Fall 1999.

Moir, Anne, and David Jessel. *Brain Sex: The Real Differences Between Men and Women.* New York: Dell, 1991.

Molloy, John. *Dress for Success.* New York: Warner Books, 1975.

Molloy, John. *The Woman's Dress for Success Book.* Chicago: Follet Publishing, 1977.

Morris, Desmond. *Man Watching: A Field Guide to Human Behavior.* New York: Harry N. Abrams, 1977.

Morris, Desmond. *The Naked Ape: A Zoologist's Study of the Human Animal.* London: Jonathan Cape, 1967.

Morris, Desmond. *The Human Zoo: A Zoologist's Classic Study of the Urban Animal.* New York: Random House, 1969.

Bibliography

Morris, Desmond. *Intimate Behavior: A Zoologist's Classic Study of Human Intimacy.* Tokyo: Kodansha International, 1997.

Morris, Desmond, Peter Collett, et al. *Gestures.* New York: Stein and Day, 1979.

Nelson, Audrey. "Women's Nonverbal Behavior: The Paradox of Skill and Acquiescence." *Women's Studies in Communication.* 4: 18–31, 1981.

Newman, Cathy. *National Geographic Fashion.* New York: Simon and Schuster, 2001.

Noonan, P. "Why the Speech Will Live in Infamy." *Time.* August 31, 1998, p. 36.

Nowicki, Stephen Jr., and Marshall Duke. *Will I Ever Fit In?* New York: Free Press, 2002.

Pathier, Dick. "Who Can Resist Smiling at a Baby?" *The Nonverbal Communication Reader,* Second Edition. Edited by Laura K. Guerrero, Joseph DeVito, and Michael Hetch. Prospect Heights, IL: Waveland Press, 1999.

Pearson, Judy. *Gender and Communication.* Dubuque, IA: W C Brown, 1985.

Pickler, Nedra. "Gender Income Gap Widens." *Los Angeles Times,* January 29, 2002, p. A1.

Piercy, Marge. *Small Changes.* New York: Doubleday, 1973, p. 438, cited in Eakins, Barbara W., and R. Gene Eakins. *Sex Differences in Human Communication.* Boston: Houghton Mifflin, 1978.

Polston, Betty, and Susan K. Golant. *Loving Midlife Marriage.* New York: John Wiley & Sons, 1999.

Richmond, Virginia P., James C. McCroskey, and Steven K. Payne. *Nonverbal Behavior in Interpersonal Relations.* Englewood Cliffs, NJ: Prentice Hall, 1991.

Robbins, Anthony. *Unlimited Power.* New York: Fawcett Books, 1991.

Roberts, Monty. *The Man Who Listens to Horses.* New York: Random House, 1997.

Roggman, Lori A., and J. Craig Peery. "Parent-Infant Social Play in Brief Encounters: Early Gender Differences." *Child Study Journal.* 19: 65–79, 1989.

Rosenfeld, Lawrence, and Gene Savickly. *With Words Unspoken: The Nonverbal Experience.* New York: Holt, Reinhart and Winston, 1976.

Rosenthal, Robert, Diane Archer, et al. "Measuring Sensitivity to Nonverbal Behavior: The PONS Test." Address given at the first International Conference on Nonverbal Behavior, The Institute for Studies in Education, Toronto, Ontario, May 11, 1976.

Sadker, Myra, and David Sadker. "Sexism in the Schoolrooms of the '80s." *Psychology Today.* 19: 54–57, 1985.

Sadker, Myra, and David Sadker. *Failing at Fairness: How America's Schools Cheat Girls.* New York: Macmillan, 1993.

Salter, Michael V., H. Nicholson, M. Williams, and P. Burgess. "The Communication of Inferior and Superior Attitudes by Verbal and Nonverbal Signals." *British Journal of Social and Clinical Psychology.* 9: 222–231, 1970.

Sargent, Alice. *The Androgynous Manager.* New York: AMACON, 1983.

Savelle, Jan. "Sleepwear for the Day." Letter to the Editor. *Time.* March 24, 2003, p. 15.

Schrank, Ben, "When Bad Listeners Happen to Good Women." *O, The Oprah Magazine.* June 2002, p. 64.

Seligman, Martin. *Authentic Happiness.* New York: Free Press, 2002.

Shemnum, William A., and Daphne B. Bugental. "The Development of Control over Affective Expression in Nonverbal Behavior." *Development of Nonverbal Behavior in Children.* Edited by Robert S. Feldman. New York: Springer-Verlag, 1982.

Smith, Alma I. *Nonverbal Communication Through Touch,* Doctoral dissertation. Georgia State University, 1970.

Spence, Betty C. "Ten Dos and Don'ts of Media Visibility." *Executive Female.* June 2002.

Spitz, R. A., and K. M. Wolf. "The Smiling Response: A Contribution to Ontogenesis of Social Relations." *Genetic Psychology Monographs.* 34: 57–125, 1946.

Steinem, Gloria. *Outrageous Acts and Everyday Rebellions.* New York: Holt, Rinehart and Winston, 1983.

Stewart, Lea P., Pamela J. Cooper, and Sheryl A. Friedley. *Communication Between the Sexes: Sex Differences and Sex-Role Stereotypes.* Scottsdale, AZ: Gorsuch Scarisbrick, 1986.

Stewart, Lea P., and Stella Ting-Toomey, Eds. *Communication, Gender, and Sex Roles in Diverse Interaction Contexts.* Norwood, NJ: Ablex Publishing, 1987.

Bibliography

Strainchamps, Ethel, Ed. *Room with No View: A Woman's Guide to the Man's World of the Media.* New York: Harper and Row, 1974.

Swenson, Joy, and Fred L. Kasmir. "The Impact of Culture-Sameness: Gender, Foreign Travel, and Academic Background on the Ability to Interpret Facial Expression of Emotion in Others." *Communication Quarterly.* Spring 1998, p. 214–230.

Tannen, Deborah. *Gender and Discourse.* New York: Oxford University Press, 1994.

Tannen, Deborah. *Talking from 9 to 5: Women and Men at Work.* New York: Quill, 2001.

Thomas, Marlo. *The Right Words at the Right Time.* New York: Atria Books, 2002.

Thorne, B., and Nancy Henley. "Womanspeak and Manspeak: Sex Differences and Sexism in Communication, Verbal and Nonverbal." *Language and Sex: Differences and Dominance.* Rowley, MA: Newberry House, 1975.

Thunberg, Monika, Monika Ulfdinberg. "Gender Differences in Facial Reactions to Fear: Relevant Stimuli" *Journal of Nonverbal Behavior.* 24: 45–51, 2000.

Tingley, Judith C. *Genderflex: Men & Women Speaking Each Other's Language at Work.* New York: AMACON, 1994.

Trebay, Guy. "Conducting Diplomacy with a Cape." *New York Times.* Jan 31, 2002.

Trenholm, Sarah. *Thinking Through Communication.* Boston: Allyn and Bacon, 2001.

Umiker-Sebeok, Jean. "The Seven Ages of Women: A View from American Magazine Advertisements." *Gender and Nonverbal Behavior.* Edited by Clara Mayo and Nancy M. Henley. Springer Series in Social Psychology, New York: Springer-Verlag, 1981.

Valian, Virginia. *Why So Slow? The Advancement of Women.* Boston: MIT Press, 1998.

Vaughan, Susan C. "Keeping Your Sunny Side Up: Five Ways to Buck Up and Stay Bucked." *O, The Oprah Magazine,* Feb 2002, p. 60.

Wallis, David. "Negotiator at Large." *New York Times Magazine.* Jan 26, 2003, p. 13.

Webbink, Patricia. *The Power of the Eyes.* New York: Springer Publishing Company, 1986.

Bibliography

White, S. E. "A Content Analytic Technique for Measuring the Sexiness of Women's Business Attire in Media Presentations." *Communication Research Reports,* 12: 178–185, 1995.

White, Theodore H. *The Making of the President,* 1960. New York: Atheneum, 1961.

Williams, M. C., and J. B. Eicher. "Teenagers, Appearance and Social Acceptance." *Journal of Home Economics.* 58: 457–461, 1966.

Wilson, D. C. *Bright Eyes.* New York: McGraw-Hill, 1974.

Wood, Barbara. *Children and Communication: Verbal and Nonverbal Development,* Second Edition. Englewood Cliffs, NJ: Prentice-Hall, 1981.

Wood, Julia T. *Gendered Lives: Communication, Gender, Culture,* Fourth Edition. Belmont, CA: Wadsworth, 2001.

Woodall, Marian K. *How to Talk So Men Will Listen.* Chicago: Contemporary Books, 1990.

Woodward, Bob. *The Choice.* New York: Simon & Schuster, 1996.

"Your Eyes Are Talking." *Family Health.* 10: 22–25, 1978.

INDEX

Index

Index

Enthusiasm, female tendency toward, 25–27, 68, 192
Etcoff, Nancy, 72
Executive Female, 194
Exline, R. V., 105–6
Eye contact
 authority and, 102–4, 108
 bold, 98–99
 continuous, 97, 107–10
 cultural differences in, 93, 98–99
 defined, 94
 downcast, 98–99
 female advantage of, 104–6
 functions of, 100–101
 gazing v., 94–95
 gender differences in, 109, 110–12
 gender prescriptions for, 116–18
 infant-mother, 94
 listening with, 101
 male advantage of, 107–10
 meanings of, 91–92
 minimal, 97
 politics of, 101–4
 power of, 92–93, 102–4
 reasons for, 95–96, 104–6
 romantic, 113–16
 rules of, 95
 sophistication of, 43
 statistics on, 90, 94–95, 110–11
 types of, 91
 winking and, 112–13
 workplace, 111–12

"Face time," 4
Face-lifts, 71–73, 77–78
Face-to-face conversation, 164–65, 166
Facial expressions. *See also* Smiling
 acquiring, 58–59
 actor's, 63
 attractiveness determined by, 65
 blushing as, 73–75
 Botox effects on, 71–73, 77–78
 contagious, 65–66
 cultural differences in, 66
 de-emphasizing, 77
 drug-induced, 61
 family similarities in, 58
 gender prescriptions for, 86–89
 infant, 38–41
 masking, 75–80, 87

 mirroring, 80–82
 neutralizing, 77
 perplexity of, 57–58
 reading, 24–25, 31–32, 84–86
 resting, 60–63
 rules for, 59
 stress fractures of, 79–80
 substituting, 77
 words conflicting with, 14–15
Failing at Fairness: How America's Schools Cheat Girls (Sadker & Sadker), 50
Families
 facial expressions among, 58
 social unit of, 44
Far from Heaven, 237
Farrell, Colin, 229, 231
"Fashion Slaves Get Kicks from Spike Heels," 236
Fast, Julius, 36, 114
Females. *See also* Girls
 androgynous, 282, 294–95
 brain structure of, 255
 communication styles of, 14, 22–23, 164–65, 166
 conversation adjustments for, 167–69
 crying perceived by, 219–22
 decoding ability of, 24–25, 84–85
 dress code for, 233–37
 enthusiastic tendencies of, 25–27, 68, 192
 expressiveness of, 57, 63–65, 85–86
 eye contact advantages for, 104–6
 fathers appreciated by, 289–90
 female opinions of, 22–23
 hand gesture advantages for, 191–93
 hand gestures used by, 188–89, 194–96
 listening advantages for, 65, 253–57
 male communication viewed by, 21–22
 male opinions of, 22–23
 paralinguistic cues of, 208–13, 217–19
 posture of, 172
 resting face of, 62–63
 self-disclosure to, 131–32, 266–67
 self-monitoring behavior of, 105–6
 size of, 169–71
 soft-spoken, 209–10
 territories of, 156–57, 173–75
 touch advantages for, 131–32
 in workforce, 8, 18–19, 25–26, 111–12
Fiorina, Carly, 194
Fire in the Belly (Keen), 263

Index

Index

Index

MacLaine, Shirley, 264–65
The Making of the President, 1960, 157
Malandro, Loretta A., 229
Males. *See also* Boys
  androgynous, 282–83, 295–96
  Botox application for, 77–78
  communication style of, 14, 21–22,
    164–65, 166–67
  crying perceived by, 219–22
  decoding inability of, 31–32, 85–86
  dress code for, 231–33, 244–45, 249
  eye contact advantages for, 107–10
  female opinions of, 21–22, 258
  females viewed by, 22–23
  hand gestures of, 188–91
  listening perspectives of, 21–22, 257–
    65
  male opinions of, 20–21
  masked emotions of, 75–80, 87
  mothers appreciated by, 289–90
  paralinguistic advantages for, 213–16
  paralinguistic confusion for, 217–19
  posture of, 172
  power role of, 29–32
  size of, 170–71
  social inattentiveness of, 30–32
  territories of, 175–77
  touch advantages for, 134–37
  touch rules for, 132–34
  in workforce, 18–19
Maloney, Carolyn, 19
Man Watching: A Field Guide to Human Be-
  havior (Morris), 119, 226
Manipulation
  eye contact for, 102
  female expressiveness as, 64
Manning, Linda, 98–99, 157, 161–62, 212,
  240
The Man Who Listens to Horses (Roberts),
  102–3, 176–77
Maple, Perry L., 133
"Marasmus" disease, 125
Masking, 75–80, 87
Maslow, Abraham, 290
Mayle, Peter, 140
Mayo, Clara, 49
Maysonave, Sherry, 246–47, 248, 250
McCartney, Paul, 140
McCroskey, James, 187, 281
Mead, Margaret, 285

Media
  gender roles portrayed in, 48–49
  paralinguistic cues used in, 205
  touch used by, 121
Mencken, H. L., 279
Merrill, Lisa, 209, 261
Micro-behaviors, 19–20. *See also* Facial ex-
  pressions
Mindell, Phyllis, 211, 247
Minielli, Maureen C., 159–60, 215
Mirroring, 80–82
Moir, Anne, 255
Molloy, John, 238, 240
Monotonic faces, 75–80, 87
Moore, Julianne, 237
"More Than Other Folks, Pets Get Loving
  Strokes," 121
Morris, Desmond
  dress code studies by, 226
  paralinguistic cues studies by, 222
  staring studies by, 107
  touch studies by, 119, 122–23, 124, 130,
    141, 142
Moss, Kate, 170
My Fair Lady, 205

Nader, Ralph, 244
The Naked Ape (Morris), 107, 122–23
Napoleon, 227
National Geographic Fashion, 231
Nature *v.* nurture, 37
Negotiating, 82–83, 139
New York Times, 72
Newman, Cathy, 231
Newsweek, 238, 242
Nixon, Richard, 97, 186, 200, 232
Nodding, 269–70
Nonfluencies, 202–3, 264
Nonverbal expressions
  awareness for, 4–5
  children's ability to read, 4
  conflicting, 14–15
  cultural differences in, 7, 16
  decoding, 24–25, 31–32, 84–86
  defined, 3
  gender differences in, 6–8, 16
  identifying, 5–6
  infant, 38–43
  misinterpreting, 31–32
  number of, 2–3

Index

Winking, 112–13
"Wipe That Smirk off Your Face. It's Bad for Business," 77
Wolf, K. M., 94
A Woman's Guide to the Language of Success (Mindell), 211, 247
The Woman's Dress for Success Book (Molloy), 238
Wood, Julia T., 3, 70, 285, 291
Woodall, Mary K., 273
Words
  facial expressions conflicting with, 14–15
  number of English, 2
Words Unspoken: The Non-verbal Experience (Rosenfeld & Savickly), 153

Workforce/place. *See also* Credibility
  crying in, 220–22
  dress code in, 227, 230, 234–41, 243, 245–48, 249–50
  eye contact in, 111–12
  females in, 8, 18–19, 25–26, 111–12
  hand gestures in, 191–92
  listening in, 267, 268, 274–75
  males in, 18–19
  paralinguistic cues in, 214, 215–16
  survival in, 76, 77–78
  touching in, 132, 144–45, 146
Working Girl, 248

A Year in Provence (Mayle), 140